Advances in African Economic, Social and Political Development

Series Editors
Diery Seck, CREPOL - Center for Research on Political Economy, Dakar, Senegal

Juliet U. Elu, Morehouse College, Atlanta, GA, USA

Yaw Nyarko, New York University, NY, USA

Africa is emerging as a rapidly growing region, still facing major challenges, but with a potential for significant progress – a transformation that necessitates vigorous efforts in research and policy thinking. This book series focuses on three intricately related key aspects of modern-day Africa: economic, social and political development. Making use of recent theoretical and empirical advances, the series aims to provide fresh answers to Africa's development challenges. All the socio-political dimensions of today's Africa are incorporated as they unfold and new policy options are presented. The series aims to provide a broad and interactive forum of science at work for policymaking and to bring together African and international researchers and experts. The series welcomes monographs and contributed volumes for an academic and professional audience, as well as tightly edited conference proceedings. Relevant topics include, but are not limited to, economic policy and trade, regional integration, labor market policies, demographic development, social issues, political economy and political systems, and environmental and energy issues.

More information about this series at http://www.springer.com/series/11885

Adeoye O. Akinola • Henry Wissink
Editors

Trajectory of Land Reform in Post-Colonial African States

The Quest for Sustainable Development and Utilization

 Springer

Editors
Adeoye O. Akinola
Department of Public Administration
University of Zululand
KwaDlangezwa, South Africa

Henry Wissink
University of KwaZulu-Natal
Westville, South Africa

ISSN 2198-7262   ISSN 2198-7270   (electronic)
Advances in African Economic, Social and Political Development
ISBN 978-3-319-78700-8   ISBN 978-3-319-78701-5   (eBook)
https://doi.org/10.1007/978-3-319-78701-5

Library of Congress Control Number: 2018942020

Printed on acid-free paper

This Springer imprint is published by the registered company Springer International Publishing AG part of Springer Nature.
The registered company address is: Gewerbestrasse 11, 6330 Cham, Switzerland

Introduction

One of the decisive contradictions of colonialism in Africa was the distortion of use, access and ownership of land. Land related issues and the need for land reform have consistently occupied unique positions in public discourse in many developmental states, and particularly in Africa. The post-colonial African states have had to embark on concerted efforts at redressing historically grounded land policies and addressing the growing needs of land by the poor, and previously disadvantaged persons who lost access to land during the colonial eras. However, agitations for land continue, while evidence of policy gaps abound. Consequently, land has assumed a major driver of structural violence and impediments to human and rural development in Africa. Thus, the need for holistic assessment of land reforms in post-colonial African states will be imperative in order to alleviate growing needs for access to land and in particular to ensure that while post-colonial states evolve, a more equitable dispensation can be created for farmers who come from previously disenfranchised and disadvantaged contexts can be provided with access to enough land to farm and compete commercially.

The realities of land reforms across Africa have been wrought in mass agitations and socio-political crises; from Rwanda to Ghana, and from South Africa to Zimbabwe, cases of land hunger and conflict persist. Land policies have failed to meet public expectations and governments' targets. Many of the hitherto agrarian economies, like that of South Africa, that had relied on land as the most important factor of production have become industrial; hence, diversification of African economies, and its attendant rural-urban surge has dwindled the importance of land to human livelihood. However, in Africa, access to land, is fundamental to most households, and remains the means of livelihood, 'centre of gravity' to communities, as well as sources of natural capital, social sustainability and spiritual fulfilment. Despite the importance of land resource, women continued to be denied land rights and exempted from access and use of land. In general, land stands at the foundation of countries' productivity. Therefore, land is germane to individuals and societal survival and prosperity.

The central objective of this book is to identify post-independence and current trends in land reform and address the grievances in relation to land use, ownership, distribution and tenure system in Africa. The book presents a critical perspective to the reform agenda of African states and queries the adoption of liberalism to resolving the land conflict and inequality created by the promoters of liberalism. Chapter contributors were carefully selected based on their expertise and active involvements in land research and land-related community development.[1] The book draws strength and uniqueness from its adoption of country-specific case studies, and utilization of qualitative and quantitative research methods, which generates 'new' knowledge on the Africa's land reform schemes. Finally, the text proposes practicable policy options towards addressing the land hunger and conflict that pervades many African states, which could derail the 'moderate' socio-economic achievements and political stability recorded by post-colonial African nation-states.

Aside from the introductory section, the book is divided into several chapters. Chapter 1, *Africa and the Land Reform Question*, presented by Akinola locates the Africa's land schemes in context. It presents the argument that colonialism engenders the distortion of land arrangements, which places huge responsibilities on post-colonial African states to immediately initiate land reform schemes and effect changes in the inherited land tenure system. Land reforms, as implemented by many African states, became the instruments to redress the skewed land patterns and effect socio-economic transformation on the continent. The chapter draws on historical experiences as well as contemporary realities and explores how state policies on land reform affect African states, economies and societies.

In Chap. 2, *Land Reform and the Calculus for Power in Zimbabwe's Democratic Transition*, Chitanga locates the Zimbabwean land reform within the broad spectrum of sustainable development. The chapter examines the intersection of land reform and domestic struggles for democratic transition, and evaluates the motivations and interests of stakeholders within the broader socio-economic and political debates over land reform. The chapter argues that the colonial legacy of land reform and the inescapable logic for addressing such injustices has shielded authoritarian politics that sought to stump democratization in Zimbabwe. Based on unstructured interviews, this chapter examines the convergence of land reform and democratic transition in the country. He concludes that the survival of electoral hegemony rests on a strategic manipulation of land resource and hegemonic coercion to attain political goals.

Chapter 3 focuses on *Food and National Security in Nigeria: A Study of the Interconnections*. Yagboyaju draws the interconnections between land, land use, food production and national security in Nigeria. He maintains that land is the primary source of food, and food is a basic necessity for human existence, thus its access impacts on Africa's peace and security. Despite Nigeria's huge arable land area; one of the biggest in Africa, and the country's enormous human population coupled with favourable climatic conditions, the country evidently suffers food insufficiency which, by extension, threatens national security and even the corporate existence of the country. He concludes by emphasizing the fact that sustainable food production and national security depend on the emergence of a transformational

---

[1] This book was subject to a rigorous peer-review processes from the editors, and publisher.

leadership and effective public institutions, which would drive the developmental agenda of the country.

In Chap. 4 – *Transforming the Bodi from Pastoralists to Outgrowers: Land and State Capitalism in South Omo, Southwest Ethiopia* – Gebresenbet engages on the broad land question in Ethiopia, presents how sugar industrialization has accelerated the pace at which villagized Bodi households are incorporated into a monetized, capitalist system by making them out-growers and by advancing a more exclusive land tenure system. The chapter examines the prevalent state projects, sugar industrialization and villagization, and the resultant policy changes the agropastoral conceptions of land, land governance and economic life. It finally presents the implications of the policy changes on land tenure, property rights and production relations.

Chapter 5 – *The Struggle of Land Restitution and Reform in Post-Apartheid South Africa* – by Wissink, employs a historical approach to presenting the process through which the colonial powers took dominance of land in Africa in the 19th and 20th centuries. The necessity to redistribute land in post-colonial Africa explains the adoption of land reform. Thus, this chapter provides an overview of the existing policy framework that proposes to deal with the vexing problem facing South Africa. The chapter particularly found that land reform has become complex and difficult in the continent and particularly in South Africa. The complexity does not only have to accommodate the land hunger problem, and agitation for land ownership, but the drafting and implementation of land tenure, restitution and redistribution policies to address the diverse challenges confronting land reform in South Africa. Furthermore, it is required in the context of a democratic constitution that was moulded to transition peacefully into a democratic state or much desired "rainbow nation", and to prevent post-apartheid conflict and in particular "land-grabbing" actions that would have the potential not only to destabilise the state, but also that of the very buoyant agricultural economy.

In Chap. 6 – *Land Policies in Africa: A Case Study of Nigeria and Zambia* – Mowoe evaluates how land policies are directed at re-adjusting the structural landscapes of rural and urban areas that were distorted by colonial powers, and offers a comparative analysis of the realities of land reform in the two countries. The chapter recognizes the importance of land as veritable political and economic resources, explores how the countries' initiated the conversion of customary lands into leasehold lands, in order to increase the existing land markets under the ideological dispensation of industrial capitalism. The chapter emphasizes the need to use land reform as an instrument to redress inequalities and denials of land resource to the poor and advocates for a more flexible approach to land policies in Nigeria and Zambia.

Chapter 7 – *Land Governance in the Context of Legal Pluralism: Comparative Cases of Kenya and Ghana* – by Fayth Ruffin examines African indigenous modes of land governance and opposing scholarly arguments in terms of ontological and epistemological standpoints on land governance and ownership, and assesses comparative land governance in environments of post-colonial legal pluralism in the two countries. Furthermore, it explores the convergence of African Indigenous

Knowledge Systems (AIKS) and contemporary epistemological approaches to land governance, and highlights its implications for gender construction. The chapter identifies how concurrent legal system impedes land governance and concludes by recommending how such legal tensions could be approached to benefit all the stakeholders in the land schemes in Kenya and Ghana.

Eniola and Akinola present their thoughts on *Cultural Practices and Women's Land Rights in Africa: South Africa and Nigeria in Comparison* in Chap. 8. The chapter reiterates the prevalent poverty, gender inequalities and socio-economic underdevelopment that characterised Africa and explores how gender inequality in land policy has aggravated Africa's socio-economic crisis. This chapter examines the reality of women's land rights in two major powers in Africa - Nigeria and South Africa. It reveals the traditional practises that acts as impediments to gender inequalities in terms of land ownership and rights and argues that denials of women's land rights explain land-related problems. In conclusion, the chapter calls attention to the urgent need to enhance gender parity in the land sector of the economy.

In Chap. 9 – *The Chasm Between Sexes in Accessing Land and its Produce: The Case of Rural Women in Mwenezi District, Masvingo Province, Zimbabwe* – Yingi draws attention to the patriarchy nature of Africa's society and the resultant discrimination against women in respect of land ownership and use. The author decries women's denials of decision-making power and of property rights over the produce of their own toil; thus access to land in Zimbabwe is highly gendered. Based on data generated from field study, the Chapter reinforces the contradictions between land reform and gender equality in Zimbabwe, and attributes this to the continual denials of the womenfolk's access to the means of production. He submits that to evade structural violence and underdevelopment in Zimbabwe, land rights should be extended to the female gender.

In Chap. 10 – *Land Conflicts in Southern Ghana: A Reflection of Multiple Ownership of Land and Usufruct Rights to Land Use* – Adu-Bempah examines the land disputes that have bedeviled southern Ghana, and in particular, Accra for ages. It engages the disconnection between pervasive commodification, monetization and commercialization of land and their implications for multiple ownerships of land and the usufruct rights to land use in Ghana. Based on primary data, he reveals the linkages between the aforementioned variables and multiple ownerships of land. The chapter recommends the establishment of 'Land Bank' and 'Land Banking' as policy option to deregulate the land resource as part of the measures to curtail land conflict that continue to threaten peace, stability and development of Southern Ghana.

Chapter 11 – *Land Tenure and Family Conflict in Rwanda: Case of Musanze District* – by Rukema and Khan delves on how colonialism, which distorted traditional land arrangement in Africa, impacted negatively on traditional structures that sustained land ownership and its use in Rwanda. It advocates for a return to customary prescriptions for achieving land security amidst rising land hunger precipitated by urbanization and commercial agriculture. As part of its post-conflict peacebuilding processes, land tenure in Rwanda is now perceived to be a gateway towards peace building and social stability. Founded on focus group study, the chapter explores the extent of family conflict over land ownership, the causes of land-related family conflicts and the nature of community and government mechanisms for settling family disputes over land, especially in the Musanze District. Rwanda, noted for family conflicts over land, land relations threaten social cohesion and sustainable peace in the country.

The last, Chap. 12 – *Land Reform in Africa: Towards Resource Utilization and Sustainability* – Akinola and Wissink- intellectually confront the policy implication of land reforms in Africa, and reconciles the trends in land reform to the developmental realities of the modern states in Africa. Although African states has seen the land reform as veritable means to redress post-colonial land grab and dispossessions; it is important to consider the social-economic implications of demands to 'give us back our land', amidst the widespread concerns of the lack of productivity of vast tracks of land, food insecurity and other land-related human rights violation and underdevelopment issues that has confronted the African states and societies.

Adeoye O. Akinola

Henry Wissink

Contents

Contributors

Adeoye O. Akinola Department of Public Administration, University of Zululand, KwaDlangezwa, South Africa

Collins Adu-Bempah Brobbey Department of Social Studies, Ghana Institute of Journalism, University of Ghana, Accra, Ghana

Bolanle Eniola Faculty of Law, Ekiti State University, Ado Ekiti, Nigeria

Fana Gebresenbet Institute for Peace & Security Studies, Addis Ababa University, Addis Ababa, Ethiopia

Chitanga Gideon Centre for Democratic Studies, Rhodes University, Grahamstown, South Africa

Sultan Khan University of KwaZulu-Natal, Durban, South Africa

Robo Mowoe Nelson Mandela Metropolitan University, Port Elizabeth, South Africa

Fayth Ruffin Public Governance, University of KwaZulu-Natal, Durban, South Africa

Joseph R. Rukema University of KwaZulu-Natal, Durban, South Africa

Dhikru A. Yagboyaju Political Science, University of Ibadan, Ibadan, Nigeria

Listen Yingi Department of Sociology, University of Limpopo, Polokwane, South Africa

Henry Wissink University of KwaZulu-Natal, Durban, South Africa

About the Editors

Dr. Adeoye O. Akinola obtained a Doctoral Degree in Political Science from the University of KwaZulu-Natal, South Africa. He completed Masters and Bachelor Degree in Political Science from the Obafemi Awolowo University, Nigeria. He has more than 10 years of teaching and research experience in three Universities in Africa. Upon completion of Post-Doctoral fellowship in Public Governance, University of KwaZulu-Natal, Akinola is presently a Post-Doctoral Research Fellow in the Department of Public Administration, University of Zululand, South Africa. He has widely published, and recipients of the 2013 UPEACE/IDRC Doctoral Award, Africa Programme for Rethinking Development Economics (APORDE) 2015, and South African National Research Foundation, KIC Individual Travel Grants in 2016. He is the author of 2 books published in 2018 respectively: *Globalization, Democracy and Oil Sector Reform in Nigeria*, New York: Palgrave Macmillan; and (eds.) *The Political Economy of Xenophobia in Africa*, Cham: Springer International Publishing AG. He specializes in Globalization, African Political Economy, Governance, Qualitative Research Methodology, Peace and Conflict Studies.

Prof Henry Wissink obtained PhD, Masters and Honours Degree in Public Administration (University of Stellenbosch), and Bachelor Degree in Parks and Recreation Administration (4-year professional degree). He became employed in the University of Stellenbosch, the PE Technikon, that later became the Nelson Mandela Metropolitan University in 2005. He served in academic management capacities since 1991, firstly as a Head of Department of Public Administration and Law, and later Dean of the Faculty of Commerce and Governmental Studies. He moved to the University of KwaZulu-Natal, where he held the position of the Dean and Head, School of Management, Information Technology and Governance, University of KwaZulu-Natal, Westville Campus, South Africa. During his career, he produced 90+ academic and scholarly outputs, which include 28 peer reviewed papers at national and international conferences, published 6 academic textbooks as author/co-author; published 39 articles and chapters in peer reviewed journals and textbooks as well as 19 popular and unpublished research publications. His research interests are Public management and governance, Public policy analysis and management, Development management, E-Learning and E-Governance systems in the public sector.

Chapter 1
Africa and the Land Reform Question

Adeoye O. Akinola

Introduction

From the North to South, East to the West, land had been a thorny issue during colonial and has become a vexed issue in post-colonial Africa. Although this fact has not received the attention it deserves: land and land-related issues had been one of the factors responsible for colonialism in Africa. Even in the post-colonial dispensation, land "has always been at the centre of shaping the interaction, events, and transactions unfolding between the global north and the global south" (Chasukwa 2013). To further the hegemony of global capital on African land, African states have been influenced by externalities to adopt the liberalization policy in the land sector, which have deepened land hunger and land-related conflicts in the continent. The global powers have also succeeded in imposing liberal approach to land reform on African states. Aside the African story, land-related question has dominated global discourse. According to Encyclopedia,

> The issue of land reform not only encompasses Zimbabwe and the Native Americans in the United States; it also includes the Zapatista movement in Chiapas Mexico, the Indians of Ecuador and Peru, the rubber tappers in the Brazilian rain forest, and the Maori of New Zealand. The specific circumstances may differ, but the consequences of an unequal distribution of land in the developing world are very similar (Encyclopedia 2016).

Literature records history of resistance against imperialism and colonialism because of land security for African indigenous population. Thus, land policies in the contemporary age have taken the centre-stage in the quest to redress historical distortion of land, achieve sustainable peace, development and combat structural violence. In the last decades, Africa has witnessed diverse escalation of land-related

A. O. Akinola (✉)
Department of Public Administration, University of Zululand,
KwaDlangezwa 3886, South Africa
e-mail: AkinolaA@unizulu.ac.za

© Springer International Publishing AG, part of Springer Nature 2019
A. O. Akinola, H. Wissink (eds.), *Trajectory of Land Reform in Post-Colonial African States*, Advances in African Economic, Social and Political Development, https://doi.org/10.1007/978-3-319-78701-5_1

conflicts in countries like Nigeria, Ethiopia, Rwanda, Zimbabwe, Côte d'Ivoire, and Cameroun. This exposes the inability of African states to facilitate sustainable development through land and agrarian reforms. States continue to record failures due to the adoption of neo-liberal approach to land reform.[1] This is based on the monetization of land resource and subjection of land to market forces, which contradicted popular demands for redistributive reforms (Moyo 2009). This further puts strain on the land schemes and deepens the pressures on implementing effective land policies. Therefore, post-colonial African states see changes in land tenure system and land relations as part of the broader process of state-building and agrarian development. Implementation of land reform programmes was therefore conceived as a matter of necessity and urgency. The inequality engendered by colonialism and minority rule was more evident in the lopsided land use, access and ownership in the continent; thus the need for land reform schemes in post-colonial Africa.

Land reform in Africa have been based on one or combination of the following – economic consideration, political settlement, equity, justice and regime populism. Land reform is conceived as the altering of the subsisting legal framework or customs regarding land use, ownership and access. Land reform means "the redistribution of property or rights in the land for the benefit of those who do not own land: the tenants and farm labourers" (Peters 2016). Constructively, land reform goes beyond the popular rhetoric, 'give us back our land'. Thus, land agitation should be viewed from two perspectives: demand for land use, land ownership, and access to land on the one hand; and calls for significant support (capital, structural and organizational) for the utilization of land by new beneficiaries on the other.

Despite the decades of reforming land relations, the prevalent land arrangements are still engrossed in contradictions and complexities that downplayed the moderate development of land policies, and explains the calls for rethinking the present land schemes in the continent. The continental land questions are germane in determining subsisting social transformation and in driving Africa's development programmes. Furthermore, land hunger and limitations to access constitutes the major source of persistent food insecurity, rural poverty, underdevelopment, and protracted land-related conflicts in the continent. As affirmed by scholars, studies on land reform initially focused on customary land tenure and issues on livelihood without paying particular attention on the larger land questions underlying agrarian, mineral resources and industrial transformation.

Through a focus group study, drawn from stakeholders in the Africa's land reform programmes, held in Pietermaritzburg (October 2017), the chapter takes a political economy approach to understanding Africa's land relations and explore how the liberalization of land resource has engendered contradictions in the continent. The chapter is made up of different sections, starting with the introduction, and followed by an overview of the subsisting land arrangement in the continent. The third section deals with the political economy of land policy and the last section presents the conclusion.

---

[1] Land reform is generally conceived as the redistribution of property or rights in the land for the benefit of the landless under the broad category of tenants and farm laborers (Peters 2016).

Rethinking the Prevalent Land Policy

In Africa, despite the implementation of policies towards land redistribution, agricultural productivity has dwindled. Many African countries have experienced food insecurity and crisis, while few - like Somalia and South Sudan - are at the point of mass starvations. It would be erroneous to underestimate the importance of agriculture to regional development and survival. For instance, in Ethiopia, the sector records for 47% of Gross Domestic Products (GDP), generates 85% of employment and accounts for 90% of foreign currency earning (Flintan 2011). Nigeria was noted for cocoa production and palm oil, while Cote D'Ivoire also flourished in cocoa production. Distortion and restriction of the application of African indigenous knowledge system to farming practises have led to the decline of agricultural development at the grass-root levels. In post-colonial Africa, the foremost losers in the land question are the traditional authorities, who were disposed of societal land by the colonial powers, thereby losing authority and interests in land-related issues. Traditional rulers are the custodians of local knowledge, but their limited roles in liberal framework, translates to redundant roles in the land reform projects of many African states.

The liberalization of African economies, and influence of global capital on land reform is one of the contradictions of globalization in Africa. African 'economic miracle' is a product of globalization, which has catered to the needs of the affluent few, whilst ordinary Africans, particularly South Africans, are still trapped in shacks, shanty towns, poverty and uncertainty, struggling with black African immigrants for survival (Hussein and Kosaka 2015: 11). This is not only peculiar to Africa, but other developing countries, which was reinforced thus,

> The issue of land reform not only encompasses Zimbabwe and the Native Americans in the United States; it also includes the Zapatista movement in Chiapas Mexico, the Indians of Ecuador and Peru, the rubber tappers in the Brazilian rain forest, and the Maori of New Zealand. The specific circumstances may differ, but the consequences of an unequal distribution of land in the developing world are very similar (Encyclopedia 2016).

Global finance capital, which has penetrated Africa, has become one of the drivers of land-related conflicts, as the exploitation of natural resources like oil and minerals expands into new African enclaves. This highlights the foreign dimension of underdevelopment of the continent. Most conflicts in Africa revolves around the issues of land and/or resources over land. As noted by Akinola and Uzodike (2017: 2),

> "certain groups' desire to control power and resources at the expense of others explains the racism, ethnic conflict, genocide, xenophobia, civil wars, and armed insurrections experienced by many African states, particularly those like South Africa that experienced prolonged foreign domination."

Thus, these realities reinforce the significance of land in the political economy of Africa. The contradictions of the integration of African economy to that of the advanced capitalist world, which started with imperialism and consolidated by colonialism, became evident in Africa. African resources were explored and exploited, leading to land dispossession in some countries like South Africa, and nationalization of land resource in countries like Nigeria. Moyo advanced this assertion thus,

Land property relations are increasingly distorted by growing land concentration and exclusion, the expansion of private landed property and the deepening of extroverted (export) capitalist relations of agrarian production, alongside increased food insecurity and food imports (aid dependence), the continued decline of the value of growing agrarian exports and the collapse of Africa's nascent agro-industrial base (Moyo 2009).

Land accessibility did not constitute a major problem in most African countries in the immediate post-colonial dispensations, the bane of the challenge in the land sector was land utilization, especially in the agro-allied sector, and management. In the last decades, land availability has become a great challenge and source of conflict in Africa. At the period, landlessness or near-landlessness seems to be on the rise all over the world, in the urban as well as in the rural areas. Farm conflict became escalated because the landless agricultural workers do not have access to this productive resource. According to Leonard (cited in Ratten n.d.: 73), near-landlessness has been described as "...access to plots of land too small to provide a minimal livelihood under existing land use patterns and technical capabilities". The recurrent escalation of the land conflict in South Africa, the unresolved land questions in Zimbabwe and the unannounced land-related crisis in other African states like Ethiopia has ignited renewed interests on land reform in Africa. As noted by Moyo,

The land question and persistent rural poverty in Africa highlight the neglect of social justice and equity issues which underlie the unequal control and use of land and natural resources proscribe neoliberal development policy agendas and which represent external dominance of African governance reforms (Moyo 2003: 1).

Land reform in Africa have often been driven by neoliberal thoughts at the domestic and external spheres (Kouame and Fofana n.d.). Liberalization of the reform processes has deepened the marginalization that the land schemes were poised to resolve. Thus,

The economic changes have shifted African land tenure systems away from indigenous customary land tenure systems which are often communal to private property tenure systems. This shift is motivated to a large extent by the fact that customary tenure systems are viewed as constraints to long term investments in land, while individual and private ownership of land are supposed to provide greater security of access and control over land: and therefore increase farmers' incentives to invest. Yet, the benefits from the shift towards private property tenure systems may not be enjoyed by certain groups of the population (Kouame and Fofana n.d.: 8).

Indeed, the liberalization of the land market came with a change in the economic and social perceived value of land, from a source of food to an economic capital. Land is no longer conceived as an abundant resource as a means to provide agricultural produce but rather as a scarce commodity that has monetary value, and subjected to the logic of the market. Thus, the globalization of Africa's land reform schemes and its limitations has led to questions being raised about "the capacity of neo-liberal market and political regimes to deliver land and economic reforms which can address both inequity and poverty" (Moyo 2003: 1). Based on the contradictions inherent in the adoption of globalist-imposed neoliberal policies, in the form of Structural Adjustments Programmes and other policies on the liberalization of Africa's economy, it seems surprising that post-colonial states like South

Africa built its land reform agenda on liberal approach to land reform (willing buyer - willing seller).

Presently, African entrepreneurs, stakeholders in land affairs and their foreign counterparts conceive land as a veritable factor or means of production, in the same manner as labour and capital (Osiany 2015). Land is thus subjected to market forces under the control of the so-called 'invincible hands', and has been integrated to the liberal market economy, driven by a 'willing buyer – willing seller' model. The monetization of land allocation greatly disenfranchises Africa's small farmers, especially the women who have had a long history of denials of economic endeavours and property rights. The liberalization of the land policies favour the farming elites, who has access to enormous capital (both local and foreign), but diminishes land productivity and deepens the skewed land arrangements between the few elites and the majority of the people, who are adjudged 'landless' (Moyo 2003). This further energizes massive resistance to the prevailing land tenure system in many African states. Although the local population cherishes the radicalization or nationalization of the land reform projects; however, many African governments have chosen the market approach to resolving the land conflict.

Ratten (n.d.) reveals that the three major approaches to land arrangements were evident in the continent in the end of 1980s and early 1990s. According to Ratten (n.d.), in some countries, there was a shift towards the socialization of land by way of co-operatives and state farms (Mozambique), in others, the privatization and individualization of land was either continued or begun (Kenya and Malawi), while others implemented land reform to address the relations between the traditional and states' authorities (Gambia). However, by the mid-1990s, countries like South Africa embarked on land reform to redress historical injustices of colonialism and Apartheid. In most societies at the global level, land reform is targeted at resolving the agrarian question. Thus, conventional agrarian demand, concerned with the transition from agrarian society to industrial society, has become a great challenge to African states, which has had to accept the liberal framework for resolving the land question.

Reality of Land Reform in Africa

The major feature of political economy analysis is its insistence in responding to the questions of how politics influences economic outcomes and how power and authority impacts the distribution of economic goods and services (Chasukwa 2013). Ricardo noted that the major challenge of political economy remains the relations and allocation of resources among three classes, namely "the proprietor of the land, the owner of the stock or capital necessary for its cultivation, and the labourers by whose industry it is cultivated" (cited in Hall 2004: 213). According to the perspectives of political economy theorists, processes of policy choice are both technical and political. Thus policy enacted might not be technically perfect other than being politically perfect. Therefore, adopted policies are a matter of trade-offs between technical and political correctness, which explains why state and non-state actors are prevailed upon to grasp the dynamics of the political side if they are to influence the economic outcomes that are of interest. As advanced by O'Malley (cited in Chasukwa 2013: 5), political economy focuses on the interaction between political and economic processes, examining how power and resources are distributed and contested in different social environment and contexts, investigating the allocation of power and wealth between diverse groups and individuals, and the processes that create, sustain and transform the political and economic relationships over a period of time. The importance of land, as an important asset and resource, explains the complexity involved in a change in land tenure system.

Land reform is a complex construct (Bonfiglioli 2004), and very difficult at the best of times and one of the biggest challenges that can confront a country (Peters 2016). The complexity involved in the drafting and implementation of land policies explain the diverse challenges confronting land reform in Africa. Despite the growing prowess of global forces and non-state actors, the nation-state has strategically assumed a domineering position as the major and most powerful actor in land-related matters and occupied the role of the custodianship of land (Flintan 2011). This is based on the conception that the state, somehow seen as neutral but which is noted for serving the interest of the elite, is the most appropriate actor to protect cultural and national heritage or resource like land. More so, the state possesses the legitimate instrument of coercion required to enforce decisions over land. The state has thus become the most visible actor in the land reform agenda of the continent. Due to this, failures of land reform initiatives are always laid at the 'doorstep' of states. African states, noted for its institutional weaknesses and crisis of capacity, have performed poorly in the management of land resource. This has portrayed the state in bad light and set many of them up against the landless (which constitute the majority) in one hand, and land owners (minority) whose land is been re-allocated to new users.

As much as governments has claimed to be impartial, objective and pragmatic in its reform agenda, political consideration, rather than the quest for economic logic, justice, equity or development, should be the driving force behind land policy. Bonfiglioli (2004: 22) holds that "land tenure has increasingly become the point of convergence for two principal objectives: the economic goal of making land profitable, and the political goal of gaining control over social groups". As Moyo (2001: 9) asserts, "land question exists distinctively throughout post-colonial Africa because of the historical evolution of the contests and struggles over land access, use and systems of tenure, founded upon class, gender, race, ethnicity, class and, regional inequities, discrimination and regulation". Flintan (2011: 7) maintains, "land is a highly politicised phenomenon: a melting pot of often conflicting interests of diverse stakeholders. As a result, land and land issues are often extremely contentious and have formed the basis of many power struggle". Some land that has been purchased by the state for redistribution is often been given primarily to loyal supporters of the ruling party, relatives and government officials. Land has therefore become politicized and an instrument of patronage. Zimbabwe used the land reform as a political tool for regime consolidation, while the South African government see the land reform as a machinery to draw support from the black population, especially during election.

Therefore, issues on land has become a campaign tool for mass mobilization. Large parcels of land that has been bought by the state for redistribution have been transferred primarily to loyal supporters and government officials as patronage. A respondent gave instances when, through the 1978 nationalization policy in the land sector in Nigeria, government officials used the opportunity presented by the land reform to amass extensive land for commercial agriculture, entertainment and sports, and other personal endeavours. Land was confiscated from individuals and shared among the political class. This was evident in places like Ogun State, where former political and military officials got large hectares of land. In South Africa, there have been indices of 'land capture', where few emergency black elites have manipulated the redistribution and land restitution to further their interests and those of close associates and families. Members of the same family benefited in the government's land/housing scheme.

The politicization of land reforms has the tendency to plunge the society into socio-economic dismay due to the jettisoning of economic determinants of land reform and its social consequences. Land thus became a commodity to be subjected to market forces like any other goods, or coveted and exploited as natural resources like gold or crude oil. This has put much pressures on the land resource, which reflects the reality in South Africa, where land inequality and conflict continue to be highlighted amidst more than two decades of implementation of land reforms. South Africa presents a country been torn apart by historically skewed land ownership, land hunger and often conflict between landowners and land seekers. This is evident in the incidences of land invasions, illegal land occupations, widespread land agitations, and, land-related farm violence, murders, and worker evictions on farms where many lives have been taken and valuable properties have been destroyed. In Sudan, land hunger and competition for access and ownership of land has heightened. Land conflict in Cameroon commenced during the country's experience of colonialism, which dated back to 1896. The colonial power, Germany, using the Crown Act, appropriated all uninhabited land and claimed it for the state in pursuance of their economic benefits. Despite the enactment of the '1974 Land Ordinance' in Cameroun, land-related conflict persists due to the ambiguity of the land policy and its incapacity to effectively manage the land resource.

The radicalization of the Zimbabwean land reform programme did not also serve the interest of the mass of the people. For instance, aside from denying women their land rights, about 71,000 families that were enjoyed resettlement on some 3.5 million hectares between 1980 and 1996, did not receive the required institutional support for land productivity (Peters 2016). White settler populations maintained access to the best land in the colony, where land holdings were based on colour and ethnicity (Peters Beverly 2016). For instance, Southern Rhodesia's (now Zimbabwe) Land Apportionment Act of 1930 reserved 50% of the land in the country for white settlers, 30% for Africans, and 20% for commercial companies and the colonial government. Many continue to hold President Mugabe responsible for the contradiction that the radicalization of the land reform has engendered, while Mugabe blamed the slow pace of land reform on Britain, which cancelled its promised funding of the program in the face of high levels of corruption.

In Nigeria, the 1978 land acts that transferred land ownership to the government has generated contradictions leading to diverse outbreak of land-driven communal violence that resulted in monumental loss of lives and properties. In Namibia, land reform targeted three separate categories of people, namely landless formerly disadvantaged Namibians, landless livestock owners, or people with income who were landless (Peters 2016). The land reform programme have been stunted by poor planning and inadequate funding from the state. Malawi was not spared of land distortion during colonial rule and resulting land conflict in its post-independence experience. The socio-economic and political liberalization, imposed by foreign donor, has curtailed the sovereignty of the state to control its land resource. Therefore, one of the major concern in democratic Malawi is that the economic liberalization empowered foreign actors, especially multinational corporations, to grab land from vulnerable farmers (Chasukwa 2013).

Across Africa, land redistribution to the emerging farmers in countries like South Africa have faced land-unproductivity. Inability of the governments to provide support for land beneficiaries resulted land-waste. Some of the challenges responsible for land under-utilization are: pressures from globalization and population swell, changes in climatic conditions like global warming, poor land tenure systems, protracted communal or political conflicts that impeded stable settlement required for agricultural development, withdrawal of agricultural subsidies, rural-urban migration, lack of institutional supports and policy weaknesses like low or absence of agricultural subsidy that negatively impact on sustainable agricultural output (Osiany 2015). According to the Department of Environmental Affairs (2008), South Africa have up to 12.76 million hectares of cultivated areas, about 80% of the land surface area utilized for commercial and peasant farming, only 11% are fertile land for agriculture possibilities and the remaining 69% is utilized for foraging purposes. Out of this, about 10.45 million hectares (82%) are commercial farms, while about 0.79 million ha (only 6.19%) are permanently under tilling and farming.

Although, Asia have cases of under-utilized land, Africa have been identified as a continent associated with unproductivity of land. This has become more evident in Zimbabwe and South Africa. In South Africa, farm owners that occupies less arable land and few on barren land continue to struggle in the bid to convert the land resource to agriculturally productive land. The lack of institutional and financial supports has forced many of the beneficiaries to seek alternative forms of livelihood to agriculture, which has aggravated land unproductivity, food insecurity and land conflict in South Africa.

The South African land reform was founded on three components: restitution, redistribution, and tenure policy. Restitution deals with returning land or providing compensation to individuals and groups' who were dispossessed of land after the infamous 1913 Land Act. Redistribution of land was designed to increase black ownership of land in the rural areas through government grants allocated to the landless to acquire land through the market, while land tenure reform advances the security of tenure of rural-dwellers and those on semi-urban land. A strong point for the

South African land reform programme was the settling of about 73% of the 80,000 claims by 2005, although as at 2017, many claims still remained unresolved. Also, these settlements were not directed to enhance agrarian development (Department of Environmental Affairs 2007). Out of these claims, only 854,444 hectares (representing less than 1% of commercial cultivated land) had been transferred by March 2005. As at 2007, about 17,866 claims were yet to be processed, out of this, up to 10,063 were urban and 7803 rural; thus, 72% of claims lodged were urban and 28% rural, indicating the urban bias of the restitution programme. According to a respondent, the costs of land redistribution has put a financial strain on the government leading to depletion of infrastructures and aggravates poor service delivery. The Ministry of Finance, as reflected in the 2017 budget, allocated R32.1 billion for the acceleration of the land reform, while the Department of Rural Development and Land Reform earmarked R10.3 billion for settling land claims (Mkentane 2017).

In Africa, land constituted an important instrument for social cohesion, and at the same time it breeds tension, where the womenfolk have been denied of land access, use and ownership. Between. In the recent past, many African states has extended property rights to the women groups through the establishment of laws that abolishes gender based discrimination in the land sector. Furthermore, evidence from literature (Kouame and Fofana n.d.), and the focus group study supports the huge disparity between the enactment of laws, public knowledge of the laws, and adherence to the rules and regulations, especially in the rural areas. They reveal the ineffectiveness of modern legal framework that abrogates gender inequality in term of access and use of land in Africa. The authors maintain that, "although many of the changes in policy and law appear to be legal and technical, access to and control over land is in practice related to socio-economic characteristics and governed by cultural practices and power relations at the family, community and country levels" (Kouame and Fofana n.d.: 1).

The continued attachment to traditional belief system that reinforces patrimony and gender-based discrimination have deepened impoverishment among the rural dwellers, and the womenfolk in particular. Countries like Kenya, Zambia, Nigeria and South Africa that have tackled the denials of the land rights of women through the legal system, continue to display institutional inefficiency in respect of implementing the laws in the rural areas. Findings from the focus group study reinforces the jettisoning of women's land rights in the rural areas where traditional belief system still reign supreme, but in major cities, women land rights have been respected and enforced. Respondents provides many instances whereby women continued to be denied access and use of land. For instance, despite the establishment of women land rights in Nigeria, many societies in the northern Nigeria continue to deny women land rights. Also in a community in KwaZulu-Natal Province of South Africa, a respondent recalled during the focus group discussion,

> I needed a parcel of land to construct a tuck-shop and approached the land entrepreneurs who directed me to the community leader. I was surprised to be told that 'I am a woman and have no right to own land'. I was asked to wait until I am married and ask my husband for the allocation of the required land. I asked if my mother should buy it on my behalf, but the answer was an emphatic 'no'. You see? What we have in South Africa is enactment of law, in terms of enforcement, the government is deficient.

Indeed, land is not only a source of economic production; it also carries significant historical and cultural importance and gives social prestige and access to socio-political power within the community, and to a larger extent the country as a whole. Therefore, those who control access and rights to land have some degrees of power over the landless, especially in agrarian-based economies.

Conclusion

Post-colonial African states have been confronted with diverse national struggles over land, which reflects their failures to address historical injustice, structural violence and, human rights violation in the land land sector. States' officials seem to approach the land reform initiatives emotionally without paying much attention to the social-economic and political implications of the change in land relations. Thus, land reform in Africa should serve the interests of the people, and not fulfil the emotional outbursts of the population, neither should land become an instrument of mass mobilization during election or determinants of patronage. The state continues to assume a central position in the land reform schemes, focusing on restitution of land rights and land redistribution from large landowners to smallholders. The broader driving force behind the reform programmes hinged on reforming land regulation and land use among smallholders, and also on redirecting the local and customary tenure systems towards redressing the structural violence in African societies. Land agitation and other associated issues have put tremendous weight on the state to become more responsible in performing the core functions of the state, which wealth or resource redistribution. As much as African governments claimed to have redistributed the land resources, there are compelling evidences of land inequality in Africa, and this have deepened poverty and widened the gap between the rich and poor.

Despite the optimism that trails Africa's economic growth and resurgence, the spate of poverty in the continent have generated a recourse to pessimism. The poverty rate in Africa, especially among the rural population could be linked to ineffective land and agrarian reform. In Southern Africa, the indigenous population have been confronted by persistent struggles over access and control of land. In countries that has large parcels of land, the basis for land agitation for agricultural uses was based on the limited availability of developed arable and irrigable land. The lack of financial and institutional supports for new entrants into the farming system and emerging land owners has complicated the land reform initiatives and aggravated land hunger in some African states like Zimbabwe and South Africa. In countries like Nigeria, implementation of a more favourable policy towards the development of large scale commercial agriculture that serves the interests of foreign powers in place of peasant or small scale farming constitutes one of the limitations of states' reform initiatives in Africa. This has further created imbalance in terms of land allocation and use.

It is blatantly erroneous to limit land reform to the enactment of effective property laws by the state. Land should not be seen as a property or resource like every other, it is a social and or communal property, governed by different organic laws, which are deeply rooted in traditional structures and local authorities like the king, chief, communal or family heads. These were the custodian of lands in the pre-colonial Africa, and the jettisoning of their influence over land and replacement of their positions (by the colonial powers) with the modern states' system has constituted one of the bane of land reform in Africa. Stakeholders in the land reform scheme tend to exaggerate the significant of land reform in the development agenda of Africa. Definitely, land reform is very important, but does not constitute the most decisive factor required for the development of the continent. Thus, implementation of pragmatic land reform that addresses the concerns of all stakeholders remain a solid foundation upon which the development goals of African states are constructed.

References

Akinola AO, Uzodike UO (2017) Ubuntu and the Quest for Conflict Resolution in Africa, Journal of Black Studies, pp. 1–23. DOI:10.1177/0021934717736186

Bonfiglioli A (2004) Lands of the Poor: Local Environmental Governance and the Decentralized Management of Natural Resources. New York: UNCDF

Chasukwa M (2013) An investigation of the political economy of land grabs in Malawi: the case of Kasinthula Cane Growers Limited (KCGL). LDPI Working Paper 30. http://www.plaas.org.za/sites/default/files/publications-pdf/LDPI30%20Chasukwa.pdf

Department of Environmental Affairs (2007) State of the environment: land reform. http://soer.deat.gov.za/197.html

Department of Environmental Affairs (2008) State of the environment: land use and productivity. http://soer.deat.gov.za/45.html

Encyclopedia (2016) Zimbabwe's land reform: race and history. History behind the headlines: the origins of conflicts worldwide. http://www.encyclopedia.com/history/energy-government-and-defense-magazines/zimbabwes-land-reform-race-and-history

Flintan F (2011) The Political Economy of Land Reform in Pastoral Areas: Lessons from Africa, Implications for Ethiopia, A paper presented at the Conference: Future of Pastoralism. 21–23 March, Addis Ababa. http://www.celep.info/wpcontent/uploads/downloads/2011/04/Political-economy-of-Land.pdf

Hall R (2004) A political economy of land reform in South Africa. Rev Afr Polit Econ 31(100):213–227

Hussein S, Kosaka H (2015) Xenophobia in South Africa: reflections, narratives and recommendations. Southern African Peace and Security Studies 2(2):5–20

Kouamé EBH, Fofana NB (n.d.) Gender and the political economy of land in Africa. https://www.afdb.org/uploads/tx_llafdbpapers/Gender_and_the_political_economy_of_land_in_Africa.pdf

Mkentane L (2017) #Budget 2017: land reform money 'a drop in the ocean. .IOL News, 23 February. https://www.iol.co.za/news/politics/budget2017-land-reform-money-a-drop-in-the-ocean-7890459

Moyo S (2003) The land question in Africa: research perspectives and questions. Draft paper presented at CODESRIA conferences on land reform, the agrarian question and nationalism in Gaborone, Botswana (18–19 October 2003) and Dakar, Senegal (8–11 December)

Moyo S (2009) Land in the political economy of African development: alternative strategies for reform. http://www.cetri.be/Land-in-the-Political-Economy-of?lang=fr

Osiany A (2015) 'Land utilization' in Africa: a misunderstood concept? https://www.linkedin. com/pulse/land-utilization-africa-misunderstood-concept-andrew-osiany/

Peters Beverly L. (2016) The 40-year failure to fix Zimbabwe's land reform and prevent rural hunger, American University, 18 December. https://qz.com/865978/the-40-year-failure-to-fix-zimbabwes-land-reform-and-prevent-rural-hunger/

Ratten M (n.d.) Land reform in Africa: lessons from Kenya. https://openaccess.leidenuniv.nl/bit-stream/handle/1887/9138/ASC_1268319_017.pdf?sequence=1

Chapter 2
Land Reform and the Calculus for Power in Zimbabwe's Democratic Transition

Chitanga Gideon

Introduction

Although land reform is not a new phenomenon in world history, the Fast Track Land Reform (FTLR) agenda of the Mugabe-led Zimbabwean government has dominated debate within and outside the country because of its character and context. As focus shifts to issues of productivity and rationalisation of land ownership, this chapter revisits the discussion, locating politics at the centre of the land reform. Indeed, land is a political resource which generated political capital for those controlling or seeking state power. At independence, the land reform process was governed by the Lancaster House Settlement.[1] The constitution protected property rights for 10 years, ensuring that land could be acquired on a willing seller willing buyer agreement, based on free market principles.[2]

The expropriation of land from Africans, their subjection to a process of 'peasantization' and 'proletarianization' as cheap labour without any form of compensation sowed the seeds for the struggle for independence.[3] Government, through its posture of nationalism had promised the return of the land as a historical right of a dispossessed people, the government's land policy regulated land as a productive space, thus failing to resolve historical societal grievances over land until 2000.[4] The Government of Zimbabwe (GoZ) inherited a racially highly skewed pattern of

---

[1] The Lancaster House Settlement is a negotiated pact signed amongst the liberation war conflict protagonists to end the war and facilitate majority elections in 1980

[2] Jocelyn Alexander, The Unsettled Land: State-Making and the Politics of Land Reform in Zimbabwe 1893–2003, Weaver Press, Harare, 2006

[3] David Martin and Phylis Johnson, The Struggle for Zimbabwe, Ravan Press, Johannesburg, 1981

[4] Ibid.

C. Gideon (✉)
Centre for Democratic Studies, Rhodes University, Grahamstown, South Africa

© Springer International Publishing AG, part of Springer Nature 2019
A. O. Akinola, H. Wissink (eds.), *Trajectory of Land Reform in Post-Colonial African States*, Advances in African Economic, Social and Political Development, https://doi.org/10.1007/978-3-319-78701-5_2

land ownership, with 42% of the country, constituting most of the fertile and agri-culturally productive land owned by 7500 large scale white commercial farmers.[5] The market based approach to land reform made for limited and insignificant gains for both historical redress and poverty alleviation.[6] From 1980 to 1990, the GoZ resettled a miserly 50,000 families on 2 million hectares of land, and between 1990 and the 2000s it redistributed less than 1 million hectares to about 20,000 families.[7] The global liberal market based economic approaches, and the Economic Structural Adjustment Programme (ESAP) further aggravated conditions for land reform, it was not politically in the interest of the GoZ to facilitate quick radical land reforms in the 1980s. The pressure for land reform had to be a domestic political threat of unavoidable and irrepressible magnitude. The GoZ abruptly plunged the country into extensively intensified process of land redistribution in 2000.[8]

Political Resources, Political Power and Political Legitimacy

Land is an important political resource, which could be exploited by unpopular authoritarian regimes and demagogic leaders to capture the state undermining democracy. The FTLR was conditioned by political interests given that, for the first time in its history, ZANU PF faced the real threat of losing political power. The rul-ing party had lost its social base and legitimacy at the time it was confronted by emerging robust political opposition crystallized around urban civil society.[9] Political resources are the fulcrum around which the political agenda, its program and the various means through which political goals and interests could be advanced. Electoral hegemonic authoritarian regimes possess and exercise political power because of, and through their control of general political resources which are manip-ulated to control political constituencies, processes and outcomes. Political power refers to the capacity to affect, control and shape the political behaviour, preferences and choices of others. Such regimes deploy a variety of political resources to influ-ence and align political preferences in favour of the ruling establishment.

A regime could therefore use political resources to influence, control or modify the political behaviour of key constituencies and individual actors. In seizing land and facilitating its discretionary distribution amongst its constituencies, ZANU PF exercised its power to modify the political behaviour of both opponents and sup-

[5] Robin Palmer, Land Reform in Zimbabwe, 1980–1990, African Affairs, Vol 89, No. 335:163–81, 1990.

[6] Kirk Heliker, et al., Introduction, Contested Terrain: Land Reform and Civil Society in Contemporary Zimbabwe, Sand S Publishing, Pietermaritzburg, 2008

[7] J Alexander, Op cit

[8] Sam Moyo, et al., Fast Track Land Reform: Trends and Tendencies, A Report of the Baseline District Studies, African Institute of Agrarian Studies, Harare, 2007

[9] Brian Raftopoulos," Reflections on Opposition Politics in Zimbabwe: The Politics of the Opposition Movement for Democratic Change(MDC)" in B. Raftopoulos and K. Alexander, (eds) Reflections on Democratic Politics in Zimbabwe, Institute for Justice and Reconciliation, Cape town, 2006a

porters. The control of political resources and the discretionary distribution of rewards or penalties to individuals and constituencies could be utilised to create or capture a power base. Large scale redistributive land reforms tend implemented by authoritarian regimes faced by political insecurity or real threat to their hold on state power.[10] Such regimes use widespread extensive land reforms to secure their hold on state power by expropriating land from landed elites, diluting their influence, emasculating them, distributing the land to the masses and key constituencies.[11]

Given its historical salience across the Southern African region and the African continent, land is a source of continental solidarity. ZANU PF postured to be contesting Western colonial hegemony and monopoly over land to quote continental solidarity. The ZANU PF regime invoked socio-political and economic salience of land and the powerful political symbolism of inequality to align its political goals with the interests of the masses. The vociferous populist calls for repossession of stolen land followed by redistribution had immediate symbolic and practical impact; it was a grand political act with assured immediate political returns.

The interest for political power in hegemonic electoral authoritarian regimes hinges on manipulative exploitation of political resources by dominant electoral regimes to retain political power and legitimize its rule. Such regimes assert exclusive monopoly over political resources, which are the sources and basis of their political power. Political resources are used to acquire, exercise and retain political power, political authority and political influence. Land constitutes a prime source of political power because of its historical societal role and value within the family as well as society in general; hence it is a politically necessary and very important political resource. Land redistribution is therefore not necessarily distributed to improve the living conditions of the poor, but in maintain and enhance diminishing political power.[12] The context of the launch of the FTLR ZANU PF manipulated its monopoly over land to recapture the state and consolidate its power. Current analytical frameworks of land reform neglect the fact that land is a critical political resource which has socio-historical and political salience making it the most important political resource in any African society. Therefore, the FTLR provided a critical political resource whose effective political manipulation and exploitation turned the odds for ZANU PF in the face of domestic threat to its hold on state power.

The ZANU PF regime is a characteristic edifice of an electoral hegemonic authoritarian regime sustaining its hold on state power and legitimacy by holding regular controlled farcical elections which it does not lose.[13] The hegemonic electoral regime

[10] Peter Dorner, Latin American Land Reforms in Theory and Practice: A Retrospective Analysis, Wisconsin University Press, Madison, 1992

[11] Micheal Albertus, Sowing the Land and Harvesting the Votes: The Distributive Politics of Land Reform in Venezuela, Stanford University, California, 2010
Peter Dorner, Latin American Land Reforms in Theory and Practice: A Retrospective Analysis, Wisconsin University Press, Madison, 1992
John Montgomery, International Dimensions of Land Reforms, Boulder, CO: Westview, 1984

[12] Alain de Janvry and Elisabeth Sadoulet, The Three Puzzles of Land Reform, Policy Brief, University of California and Berkeley and FERDI, 2011

[13] Andreas Schedler," The Logic of Electoral Authoritarianism", In A. Schedler (ed) Electoral Authoritarianism, Lynne Rienner Publishers, 2006

strives to project itself as broad based and popular by winning coercive elections, however faulty. A key element of such manipulated elections is the effective use of political resources (material or otherwise) and coercive violence to ensure that citizens channel their votes in favour of the establishment in semi-competitive, illiberal electoral process and outcome.[14] Since 2000 the FTLR became the fulcrum around which coercive mobilization, undemocratic illiberal elections denominated by extensive land seizures couched in exclusive nationalist ideology became the basis for ZANU PF legitimacy and power.[15] ZANU PF used its control of such valued political resource as land to shape and control political constituencies, actors, processes and electoral outcomes. The party used the FTLR to galvanise political support, recapturing its constituencies and social base, seizing and controlling the national agenda and discourse.

The FTLR: Progressive Land Reform or Democratic Reversal

The dual struggles with democratization and land reforms in Southern Africa remain one of the teething historical legacies of the sub-continent requiring rigorous scholarly attention. The dense literature on the FTLR downplays its role in Zimbabwean domestic politics by overlooking the context within which it took place. Contemporary academic reactions dramatize the broad binary of attitudes and reactions in the framing of the FTLR. The radical nationalist perspective rooted in a structural approach forged around a critique of the colonial legacy embraces the FTLR as a progressive expression of bottom up mass struggles. The state legitimately backed the process to advance national goals in the interest of national cohesion and development.[16]

This school of thoughts stressed ZANU PF's redistributive policies focussing on indigenous ownership of natural resources and national sovereignty.[17] Its discourse contends that the FTLR marked a progressive moment of land redistribution to resolve the national question.[18] Its proponents argue that the FTLR was fundamentally pro-

---

Merete Bech Seeberg, The Dynamics of Authoritarian Elections: A Review, A Paper Presented at the Annual Meeting of the Danish Political Science Association, Vejle, 2002

[14] ibid.

[15] Sabelo Ndlovhu-Gatsheni, "The Nativist Revolution and Development Conundrums in Zimbabwe", Occasional Paper Series, Vol 1, Number 4,2006

[16] Ibid

[17] Zvakanyorwa Wilbert Sadomba, War Veterans in Zimbabwe's Revolution: Challenging Neo Colonialism and Settler and International Capital, Weaver Press, Harare,2011

[18] Sam Moyo and Paris Yeros, The Radicalized State: Zimbabwe's Interrupted Revolution, Review of African Political Economy No.111:103–121, 2007

Sam Moyo, and Paris Yeros) Land Occupations and Land Reform in Zimbabwe: Towards the National Democratic Revolution" in S. Moyo and P. Yeros(eds) Reclaiming the Land: The Resurgence of Rural Movements in Africa, Asia and Latin America, ZED Books, London

ZANU PF 2000 Election Manifesto, The Land is the Economy and the Economy is the Land, Harare, Jongwe Printers

gressive, the most important challenge to the neo-colonial state under neoliberalism.[19] The FTLR was therefore seen as progressive character of a radicalising state and a revolutionary moment.[20] Land reform is a necessity whose implementation revolutionized the structure of access, ownership and utilization of land. The role of politics in the FTLR is dismissed, although intensified political competition was a major trigger to the FTLR process.[21]

No academic contribution on the causes, implications and efforts at resolving the Zimbabwe crisis dramatizes the polarization and controversy that characterized the debate than Mamdani's Lessons of Zimbabwe.[22] Mamdani argued that the Zimbabwe crisis was triggered by the punitive reaction to the FTLR and the failure by Western countries and international institutions to support progressive land reform since 1980. Other proponents of the FTLR averred that political explanations to land reform are common sense views held by ZANU PF opponents who saw land reform as political gimmickry and peasants occupying farms as agents of agrarian and environmental destruction at the service of the ZANU PF coercive agenda.[23] They saw political violence as either exaggerated or simply incremental given the high stakes, magnitude and the emotive nature of the issue.[24] Although there is convergence on the necessity of land reform, there are many contradictions on the process and motivation behind the FTLR.

Critics of the FTLR applied the liberal democratic analysis to land reform.[25] They zeroed in on issues of human rights and governance, critical of the state's exhausted exclusionary nationalism and the consequent descent into authoritarianism.[26] These academics argue that the FTLR amounted to the tyrannical reconfiguration of state politics towards authoritarianism.[27] They further posited

[19] Sam Moyo and Paris Yeros, Op cit

[20] Sam Moyo, The Radicalized State: Zimbabwe's Interrupted Revolution, Op cit

[21] Godfrey Mukodzongi, Zimbabwe's Land Reform is Common Sense, in Pambazuka News, 11 March 2010

[22] Mam Mamdani, Lessons of Zimbabwe, London Review of Books, V30, No 23. 4. pp. 17–21, December 2004

[23] Ibid

[24] Fast Track Land Reform in Zimbabwe, Human Rights Watch, www.hrw.org-Zimland0203-02, 03 March 2016

[25] Timothy Scarnecchia and Wendy Urban-Mead, Special Issue on Zimbabwe(11) ACAS Bulletin No. 80,ACAS Bulletin No 82: Reflections on Mahmood Mamdani's 'Lessons of Zimbabwe', winter 2008

[26] David Moore, "Zimbabwe's Triple Crisis: Primitive Accumulation, Nation State Formation and Democratization in the Age of Neo-liberal Globalization" in African Studies Quarterly, 7: 2&3.,2003

Hammah,A, et al. (eds) Zimbabwe's Unfinished Business-Rethinking Land, State and Nation in the Context of Crisis, Weaver Press, Harare,2003

Raftopoulis, B and Phimister,I," Zimbabwe Now: The Political Economy of Crisis and Coercion" in Historical Materialism.12:4.,2004

Patrick Bond and Simba Manyanya S(2003) Zimbabwe's Plunge: Exhausted Nationalism, Neo-liberalism and the Search for Social Justice, Weaver Press, Harare,2003

[27] Ibid

that the FTLR resulted in massive violation rule of law, property and human rights. They criticise the violation of the international and domestic liberal normative order citing socio-economic and political consequences of the FTLR. To use Paul Tiyambe Zeleza's view of "scholarship by epithets" the pro-democracy scholars' characterization of the FTLR fell into description of African politics as "cronyist", "kleptocratic", "parasitic", "patrimonial", "neo-patrimonial", "prebendal", and like a "vampire."[28] Indeed the FTLR could be any or all of these superlatives, in addition to its violation of governance and democratic norms. Critics further noted that the FTLR process and its consequences had adverse consequences on politics, civil society and the economy. They posited that the conflict in Zimbabwe was triggered by ZANU PF misrule, brutal closure of democratic space and state violence mediated through the FTLR.[29]

Critics of the FTLR rejected its violent radicalism and what they saw as exclusive nationalistic historical discourse championed by ZANU PF,[30] and critics of the dominant nationalist position rejected the premise that issues related to democratization and human rights were peripheral to demands for socio-economic redistribution.[31] They posit that Zimbabwe is a blocked transition.[32] The epistemic polarities gloss over the course, context and significance of domestic contemporary political dynamics actualised through paradoxical overlapping dual contestation over the state. A thorough investigation into the political motivations and the dynamics of the FTLR shows that there was an agenda beyond issues of access to land, and improving rural livelihoods.

Intra-Political Party Decline, Capture and Co-Optation of the Land Movement

The FTLR should be understood in the context of internal, intraparty and external contradictions. Paradoxical contradictory political dynamics, within and outside ZANU PF exerted intense pressure on the ruling party and its leadership requiring urgent and radical measures to reverse its internal fragmentation and external

---

[28] P.T. Zeleza, "Imagining and Inventing the Post- Colonial State in Africa" Contours: A Journal of African Diaspora, http://www.press.uillinois.edu/journals/contours/1.1/zeleza.html, 20 March 2016

See also Zeleza, Manufacturing African Studies and Crisis

[29] Brian Raftopoulos, Response to Mamdani Mamdani's Lessons of Zimbabwe, ACAS, Bulletin 82, March 2008

[30] Sabelo Ndlovu-Gatsheni, The Nativist Revolution and Development Conundrums in Zimbabwe, Occasional Paper Series: V1, Number 4,2006

[31] B Raftopoulos, The Zimbabwean Crisis and the Challenges for the Left, Journal of Southern African Studies, Volume 32, Number 2, June 2006

[32] Sabelo Ndlovu-Gatsheni, Dynamics of the Zimbabwe Crisis in the twentieth Century, Op cit

decline.[33] The FTLR drew national focus back to ZANU PF.[34] The FTLR crystallized multiple intersectional factors which snowballed around the "Third Chimurenga", making it a compelling potent political resource whose implementation shook the country to its core.[35] Through the FTLR, ZANU PF galvanized political mobilization and convergence of its constituencies behind its leadership, uniting in confronting the MDC through peaceful and violent political means.[36] The political-security elite alliance inspired the radicalization of the state on realising that ZANU PF's hold on state power was at risky. By allowing impoverished peasants to seize land ZANU PF ensured political support from a huge constituency of rural people who depended on subsistence agriculture for their livelihoods.[37]

Internally, the incipient intra-party decline since the 1990s climaxed into imminent disintegration of ZANU PF's social base as war veterans, war collaborators, youths and peasants embarked on widespread mass demonstration, confronting party and government elites to protest against exclusion and marginalization, demanding pensions and gratuities for their role during the liberation struggle.[38] They also demanded final resolution to the land question, by giving land to war veterans and peasants. These demonstrations threatened to split ZANU PF between its bureaucrats, security and political elites on one end and peasants, youths and war veterans. ZANU PF lost control over key constituencies, as it faced increasing political insecurity and extensive unpopularity. The dire socio-economic situation compounded a political crisis feeding into a shift in the balance of forces. In a dramatic turn of events since 1999, ZANU PF's lost the constitutional referendum to the opposition-civil society alliance. Following the formation of the MDC in 2000, with impending Parliamentary and Presidential elections, the ZANU PF leadership needed urgent means to rally its supporters, galvanise its structures and social base towards a radical pushback.[39]

History, Memory and Hegemonic Domination

ZANU PF invoked the liberation revolutionary tradition forged around a partisan narrative of patriotic history as counter ideology to Western democratic universalism in a bid to claim continuity as the only bearer of liberation and freedom to entrench itself in power.[40] ZANU PF seized the political initiative and momentum to

---

[33] Interview Rejoice Ngwenya, Civil Society KAS Offices, Harare 7 August 2014

[34] Interview Takura Zhangazha, Director, Voluntary Media Council of Zimbabwe, VMCZ Offices, Harare, 18 August 2014

[35] ibid.

[36] Ibid

[37] Interview Rejoice Ngwenya, Civil Scoiety, KAS Offices, Harare, 7 August 2014

[38] Interview Rugare Gumbo, ZANU PF Spokesperson and MP, ZANU PF HQ,Harare, 6 July 2014

[39] Interview Rejoice Ngwenya, Civil Society, KAS Offices, Harare, 7 August 2014

[40] Terence.O.Ranger, Nationalist Histriography, Patriotic History and the History of the Nation:

dominate all forms and platforms of domestic social and political interaction, setting the national discourse. The party located the FTLR as the sole national question over democratic contestation. The regime sought to seal its legitimacy and support in the face of strident institutional and economic failure through a strident authoritarian discourse that depicted itself as true patriots, sole past and future custodian of the independence and sovereignty of the country.[41] The land reform became critical to violent political mobilization not only by peasants seizing land which belonged to them, but also in defence of the liberation legacy.[42]

ZANU PF usurped national history and memory to invent an exclusive nationalistic monologue based on the "Third Chimurenga" to legitimize its wholesale nationalisation of land and its coercive hegemonic electoralism based on disputed controversial electoral mandates. A strident national historiography was robustly peddled to effectively redefine national consciousness against perceived liberal democracy. ZANU PF presented not only itself as a party, but its current leaders and particularly war veterans and President Mugabe as the beginning and the sole custodians of the legacy of liberation from colonialism, with the FTLR as the ultimate realisation and the arrival of national emancipation. In political terms this narrative mythologised Mugabe by venerating him to be the founder and end of the struggle for liberation. The ruling party combined total control and use of traditional media, music and song to sustain a nationalist monologue.[43] Human rights and democracy were subjected at the base of land occupation and mobilization for political domination.

The land question, as historical and political grievances became a source of political power, a political resource and front upon which a broad section of political factions within the ruling party could be mobilised. It also became an appealing frontline for ZANU PF's political pushback against the civil society –opposition alliance. The FTLR was the fulcrum around which a programme of political pushback was forged under the discretionary direction of the ZANU PF Politburo and national coordination of the Joint Operation Command (JOC).[44] Once the ruling party captured the FTLR from war veterans and peasants, it totally controlled the

---

The struggle over the Past in Zimbabwe in Journal of Southern African Studies, V30, Number 2, 2004

[41] Blessing Miles Tendi, How Intellectuals Made History in Zimbabwe, Africa Research Institute, 2013

[42] Norma Kriger," From Patriotic Memories to "Patriotic Memories" in Zimbabwe, 1990–2005", Third World Quarterly, Vol. 27, No.6, pp1151–1169, 2006

Land, Retribution and Elections: Post Election Violence on Zimbabwe's Remaining Farms, Report Prepared by the Justice for Agriculture Trust(JAG) and the Research and Advocacy Unit, May 2008

[43] Jonathan Moyo, The ZANU PF propagandist since 2000 composed a campaign album dedicated to the FTLR and ZANU PF elections campaign since 2000. Mararike, Mupepereki, Makoso and Chivaura hosted weekly television programmes Zimbabwe Television defending ZANU PF and the FTLR.

[44] JOC was officially a government security sector think tank involving heads of military, police, the intelligence and the Presidency. Although it was supposed to be a policy think- tank for the state, it was turned into a source of partisan policy, strategy and tactics for the ZANU PF party state.

process from the top, creating structures which cascaded from the national level to villages.[45] A mutation of actors drawn from partisan youths, traditional leadership, civil servants and security structures were deployed to run the FTLR at national, provincial, district and local community level.

ZANU PF structures mutated with land committees and local community leadership at every level turning what should have been a non-partisan national initiative into an exclusive partisan programme. ZANU PF used the FTLR to retain a range of constituencies from war veterans, former war collaborators, peasants, youths, chiefs and headman as they all worked to move peasants from rural areas to white owned commercial farms. The state allowed so much power to these lately emasculated groups of communities as they forcefully occupied land, constructing new settlements and moving their animals into new farms without interference from law enforcement agents.[46] Externally, political threats to the establishment emerged from a coalition of civil society, the student movement, NGOs and white farmers who rallied behind the trade union federation, the Zimbabwe Congress of Trade Unions, eventually coalescing to form the Movement for Democratic Change (MDC) to drive a political campaign against President Mugabe and ZANU PF's rule, worsening socio-economic conditions, poor governance.[47]

In 2000, ZANU PF lost the referendum to the opposition alliance, for the first time experiencing electoral defeat since its formation in 1963. Between 2000 and 2008, ZANU PF lost its hegemonic domination as the opposition made huge gains in parliament and local government elections displacing the ruling party from all urban constituencies, before penetrating rural constituencies. These internal and external pressures threatened a convergence of social forces with all the signs of a chaotic over throw of the ZANU PF regime from office.[48]

ZANU PF invoked and monopolised the FTLR and coercive mobilization as the anchor of its political agenda and means to assert its power.[49] It demonstrated force of political power by backing, abetting and allocating white owned farms to local land occupiers, blowing off all institutional constraints, ignoring courts of law, domestic and international criticism.[50] ZANU PF used the FTLR to assert influence and control internally and externally. The party applied a twin strategy of co-optation or coercion to deal with the contradictory social and political constituencies, grounded on internal consent and externally directed coercion.[51] ZANU PF co-opted the peasant movement and war veterans by absorbing and extensively driving the FTLR, making it its rallying campaign in the process of deflating political oppositions.

---

[45] Interview: Douglas Mwonzora, MDC Secretary General, Harvest House, Harare, 16 September 2014

[46] Interview Noel Shumba, Peasant Farmer, Mwenezi, 13 July 2014

[47] Brian Raftopoulos, Op cit

[48] Interview Takura Zhangazha, Director, Voluntary Media Council of Zimbabwe, VMCZ Offices,Harare, 18 August 2014

[49] Interview Rejoice Ngwenya, Civil Society, KAS Offices,Harare, 7 August 2014

[50] Ibid

[51] Ibid

Participation in the FTLR became a definer of insiders and outsiders given the definite zones of consent and coercion. Massive coercive mobilization targeted the civil society and opposition alliance while the party internally focussed on reasserting consent amongst its aligned factions and coalition of constituencies.[52] The boundaries of consent and coercion were polarised along partisan lines, with consent and access to land limited to constituencies of alliances constituting the ZANU PF social base and coercive domination preserved for those ranged against it, particularly civil society and the opposition MDC.[53] The ruling party targeted white commercial farmers as a political constituency to bust their economic and political influence.[54] The small community of white commercial were a powerful domestic and international lobby, a contiguous political constituency voting as a block and channelling their material resources, political network and skills towards the MDC.[55] Some of key stakeholders were retired members of former Rhodesian army who were well trained in military, intelligence and sophisticated organizational skills which they were willing to deploy to assist the emerging opposition movement.[56] They equally used their domestic and international network to provide various political resources needed in forging a powerful opposition movement.[57]

The participation of constituencies of white commercial farmers in opposition and politiking within the civil society irked the establishment, particularly Mugabe who felt betrayed.[58] Since independence, constituencies of white commercial farmers and business had defected from former whites only political formations to quietly join ZANU PF or leave politics to focus on business and farming.[59] The establishment felt that local constituencies of commercial farmers owed them loyalty for protecting their farming interests; hence their support for the MDC was seen as total betrayal of the regime.[60] The FLTR decimated and emasculated the former powerful community of white constituencies neutralising their power, direct and indirect multi-faceted support for the opposition.[61] The MDC arguably immensely benefited from the capacity and network of white commercial farmers in terms of resources, political capacity, political organization and mobilization.[62] Some of the strategic actors from this community who had previously served in the former colonial regime deployed their technical skills and resources in support of the MDC.[63]

---

[52] Ibid

[53] Interview Douglas Mwonzora, Op cit

[54] Interview Eddie Cross, MDC-Secretary for Policy, Harvest House, Harare, 19 September 2014

[55] Interview Paul Mangwana, ZANU PF MP and Minister of Indigenisation and Empowerment, Mangwana Law Firm Offices,Harare, 15 July 2014

[56] Interview Rugare Gumbo, ZANU PF Spokesperson and MP, ZANU PF HQ, Harare, 6 July 2014

[57] Ibid

[58] Interview Douglas Mwonzora, Op cit

[59] ibid.

[60] Interview Eddie Cross, Op cit

[61] Interview Rugare Gumbo, Op cit

[62] Interview Rugare Gumbo, Op cit

[63] Interview Paul Mangwana, Op cit

White commercial farmers were viewed as a major threat to ZANU PF because of their material and organizational resources which they provided to the opposition.[64] White people firmly rendered their strong leverage behind the opposition, particularly their material and technical resources.[65] The FTLR also punitively decimated the opposition constituency of more than 300,000 commercial farm workers whose political views and behaviour tended to be influenced by their employers. Campaigns for the occupation overlapped with coercive mobilization for ZANU PF support. Many supporters of the opposition MDC were attacked in waves of associated political violence, displaced, dislocated from their communities, lost property, livestock or simply disenfranchised from voting, denied their freedom of association and assembly in terms of engaging in their preferred political activities and activism.[66]

Political Mobilization Through the Land Movement

Political mobilization during the FTLR was not just a consequence but part of a broader strategy. The sequence and manner of events characterising the FTLR generated a breath-taking unprecedented wave of political excitement leaving admirers spellbound and critics shocked beyond belief. As a historical political event, the FTLR captured the national mood, consciousness and attention of both its supporters and opponents.[67] It was a rousing moment, becoming the mainstay of daily broadsheets, television and radio news, polarised communities and household discussions. Its associated violence left communities totally cowed, griped with absolute fear as they were intimidated into supporting and voting the ruling party.[68]

The FTLR was a nucleus of a well thought out coercive political strategy at the heart of a violent ZANU PF political campaign to shock the nation into submitting to the coercive re-establishment of its political hegemony.[69] Although the trail of political violence reports tended to follow acts of violence perpetrated on white landowners, the majority of victims were by far the black activists and supporters of opposition political parties and farm workers.[70] Acts of open violence, intimidation, beatings particularly in isolated places called "bases" where all night vigils were held, and the messaging of the rhetoric evidently targeted the ordinary black majority accused of supporting the opposition MDC. Prominent activists and leaders of the MDC became direct targets of the state and its informal agents of as many of them were abducted, disappeared, had their homes and property destroyed.

---

[64] Interview Rugare Gumbo, Op cit

[65] Ibid

[66] Interview Douglas Mwonzora, Op cit

[67] Interview Takura Zhangazha, Op cit

[68] Phillain Zamchiya, Pre-election Detectors-ZANU PF Attempts to Reclaim Electoral Hegemony, Crisis in Zimbabwe Coalition, Harare, 2008

[69] Interview Rejoice Ngwenya, Op cit.

[70] Interview Douglas Mwonzora, Op cit

This harassment of opposition supporters with impunity had nothing to do with land redistribution than a process of cowing ZANU PF opponents into submission.

The modus operand of the FTLR invoked excruciating memories of the war of liberation, characterised by extensive pervasive brutal violence, intimidation, fear and murders. ZANU PF activists attacked opponents with impunity as supporters of the opposition faced abductions and unexplained disappearance.[71] Ordinary people including opposition supporters were forced to attend all night vigils for political education typical in character with "comrades" chanting fiery intimidating slogans and radical ZANU PF rhetoric castigating political opponents as traitors emphasizing imminent consequences.[72]

Elections and Domination

The FTLR did not start in February 2000 by coincidence. Political events since 1997 pointed to shifting political grounds as manifested by the increasing convergence of civil society leading to the formation of the biggest opposition party, the MDC, which also rallied the biggest opposition alliance since independence.[73] The constitutional referendum in 2000 proved that ZANU PF had lost political momentum, even the belated insertion of a close to legalise compulsory acquisition of land in the constitutional draft failed to save it from defeat. Given the impending parliamentary and presidential elections, the ruling needed to launch a radical campaign to reverse what seemed to be imminent defeat.

The FTLR sought to legitimize ZANU PF hegemonic rule. ZANU PF successfully presented itself as a victim of Western punitive action for daring to distribute land to poor black people, thus generating more sympathy amongst pro-land reform constituencies who could not wait to access land.[74] The scale of population movement during the FTLR created opaque conditions feeding into shady electoral processes abated by deliberate gerrymandering by skewed partisan delimitation of constituencies to ensure political victory.[75] The FTLR has been at the heart of new delimitation processes, voter registration and management since 2000 as the ruling party pressed its partisan bureaucrats into electoral institutions to subvert electoral rules and the politically controlled electoral field in its favour. Since 2000, the ZANU PF regime used politically and bureaucratically controlled elections and the land reform process to undemocratically retain and consolidate its hold on state power with some semblance of domestic political legitimacy.[76] The FTLR thus

---

[71] Ibid

[72] Interview Rejoice Ngwenya, Op cit

[73] Interview Rejoice Ngwenya, ibid.

[74] Interview Takura Zhangazha, Op cit

[75] Interview Douglas Mwonzora, Op cit

[76] Norma Kriger, Op cit

became the blanket through which ZANU PF operationalised its political tactics to reverse the gains of the opposition under a blanket of the popularity of land reform to retain some semblance of legitimacy, however minimal.

The character, manner, pace and sequence of the FTLR since 1999 indicates that land redistribution was motivated by strategic political goals to gain and re-impose waning authoritarian electoral hegemony.[77] After a swell of socio-economic challenges and widespread demonstrations, the single party electoral hegemony was clearly facing its decline. The FTLR was a political gamble by the ZANU PF authoritarian regime to regain and consolidate its hold on state power.[78] For the first time since its formation, ZANU PF was defeated by any opposition when it lost the 2000 constitutional referendum to the opposition alliance. Since 1980, ZANU PF was facing a huge parliamentary representation in parliament, pushing its majority to less than two thirds majorities against the background of political violence, intimidation and extensive random seizure of white commercial farms by rural peasants largely supportive of Mugabe and the ruling party. The winner take all political contestation characterised Zimbabwean national politics between 2000 and 2016, with the ruling party seeking to reassert its dominance.[79]

The socio-historical and political salience of land within the Zimbabwean context made it the only political resource at the disposal of the state.[80] ZANU PF had held back land reform since 1980; however the balance of social forces against it and the range of domestic and international opponents pushed the regime into the only available option to legitimise itself in the process of maintaining its hold on power, at list amongst the domestic political constituencies.[81] Land as a natural resource appealed to a cross section of fragmenting social forces, some of which were in the process of defecting from the ruling party. Rural communities and veterans of the liberation struggle had land at the top of their demands against the ruling elites whom they accused of marginalization and neglect.[82]

Civil society and the ZCTU led a popular campaign based on the slogan, "Land to the people and not to the politicians". This campaign called for the continuation with the market based land reform process. Supportive actors argued that such an approach had failed because of kleptocracy leading to land based primitive accumulation which. Land intended for resettlement was looted by ruling party elites. By allowing ordinary people to seize farms, ZANU PF moved to co-opt and recapture diverse constituencies whose main grievance was land. ZANU PF determined that its continued stay in power depended on its popularity amongst the domestic constituencies, particularly its rural peasant voters, war veterans and collaborators.

---

[77] Interview Douglas Mwonzora, Op cit

[78] Interview Takura Zhangazha, Op cit

[79] Interview Douglas Mwonzora, Op cit

[80] Interview Sydney Mufamadi, Facilitator of the SADC Negotiations, Emoyeni Hotel, Johannesburg 20 August 2014

[81] Ibid.

[82] Interview Rugare Gumbo, Op cit

ZANU PF faced imminent domestic and international consequences for violation of human and property rights. However the implications of the FTLR for mobilization of political support and capturing the ruling party's social base far
outweighed any possible repercussions.[83] Land seizures, state driven partisan violence, violation of human and property rights attracted external sanctions which
battered the economy, plunging the country into socio-economic crisis.[84] The combined political costs of the economic crisis and sanctions on ZANU PF's short term
political interests were not as negative as believed.[85] The ruling party exploited
Western sanctions to generate domestic and continental solidarity. It further manipulated the FTLR to reorganise political contestation, making the struggle over land
the main issue of contention over the struggle for democratic transformation.[86]

The alarming defeat at the constitutional referendum in 2000 demonstrated that
ZANU PF's electoral hegemony was fading. There was real fear within the party of
losing power in subsequent elections.[87] Accordingly ZANU PF invoked the FTLR as a
pushback strategy during the parliamentary and later presidential elections in 2000 and
2002 simultaneously, generating widespread support in rural and farming areas.[88] The
parcelling of land to supporters, who literally walked into farms of their choice, gave
these formerly emasculated villagers unprecedented power, which they were willing to
brutally flaunt, mainly against the supporters of the opposition, farm workers and white
commercial farmers whom they had since the 1980s coexisted side by side with.[89]

The haphazard extensive redistribution of land in a manner that radically transformed the national distribution of population, impacted on the delimitation of new
constituencies. The sudden massive wave of movement by rural and poor urban
people into farms shifted the spatial demographic distribution of political constituencies.[90] ZANU PF used the process of delimitation of electoral boundaries to
neutralize the urban voter social base controlled by the opposition by reducing the
number of urban constituencies, while increasing rural constituencies.[91] Although
the delimitation process should be representative, implemented by an independent
impartial boundary authority, transparent and non-discriminatory, these principles
were compromised as the government controlled process heavily reduced urban

---

[83] Ibid

[84] Interview Eddie Cross, Op cit

[85] Interview Takura Zhangazha, Op cit

[86] Ibid

[87] Interview Rugare Gumbo, Op cit

[88] Interview Douglas Mwonzora, Op cit

[89] Interview Rejoice Ngwenya, Op cit

[90] Susan Booysen, and Toulou, (2009) "Chapter 15: Zimbabwe" In Kadima, D and Booysen, S(eds)
Compendium of Elections in Southern Africa 1989–2009: 20 Years of Multi-Party Democracy,
EISA, Johannesburg, 644–645
    Zimbabwe Electoral Support Network 2005, Report of the Zimbabwe' s 2005 Elections, 2009.

[91] Interview Douglas Mwonzora, Op cit

constituencies.[92] Urban constituencies were progressively reduced since the 2000s while rural constituencies were increased.[93] The pattern of constituency boundaries equally tended to favour newly resettled farming areas, where new farmers voted almost 100 percent for the ruling party.[94] ZANU PF used its control of the Delimitation Commission to effectively operationalize a strategy of gerrymandering justified by the need to provide equal opportunity for resettled farmers to vote.[95]

In consideration of the previous ZANU PF land policies since 1980, the argument that the ruling party woke up to the need for compelling urgency to fast track the land reform on February 2000 is unsustainable. The sudden radicalization of the state to openly back and drive extensive, sudden and haphazard land reform was premeditated in the context of a socio-economic and political crisis threating ZANU PF. By backing the FTLR, ZANU PF seized and recast the national question, the national political agenda and discourse from the question of democratization insulating its quest for electoral hegemonic dominance in the FTLR.

---

[92] Interview Elias Mudzuri, Secretary for Organizing, MDC-T. Harvest House, Harare, 24 September 2014

[93] Interview Tabitha Khumalo, MP, MDC-T, Holiday Inn, Harare, 27 September 2014

[94] Ibid

Interview Douglas Mwonzora, Op cit

[95] Interview: Tabitha Khumalo, Op cit

Chapter 3
Food and National Security in Nigeria: A Study of the Interconnections

Dhikru A. Yagboyaju

Introduction

Hunger has serious implications and consequences on national security. Adamu (2015:24), quoted former President of Brazil, Lula da Silva, thus:

> When I became the president of the country, half of the people could not sleep because of hunger and the other half could not sleep because of the fear of the hungry.

These remarks should signify a wake-up call for researchers, scholars and policy makers that the focus on security and other related strategic matters may need to be redirected from the military and other "hard" options, to non-military dimensions of security, which include food production, its availability in the right quantity and quality.

Bearing in mind that many chapters in this book are devoted to aspects of land-ownership, utilization, possession, dispossession and the political economy surrounding all of these, it should be noted that the whole gamut of these issues is important to this chapter because land is central to food production and food security. Take for example, apart from the issue of possession or dispossession of land, the fertility or infertility of land also has a role to play in the quantity and quality of available food products and, by extension, in human security as a whole.

In Nigeria, this partly accounts for the perennial restiveness in the country's Nigeria Delta region where, as a result of environmental pollution, land is generally infertile and unproductive, while food production is quite low in most of its communities and non-existence in some others (Amuwo 1998). Similarly, in the arid and semi-desert parts of the country, especially in the North Eastern zone, where global warning and climate change have over the years adversely affected Lake Chad and such other sources of water for irrigation farming (Adamolekun 2016),

D. A. Yagboyaju (✉)
Political Science, University of Ibadan, Ibadan, Nigeria

© Springer International Publishing AG, part of Springer Nature 2019
A. O. Akinola, H. Wissink (eds.), *Trajectory of Land Reform in Post-Colonial African States*, Advances in African Economic, Social and Political Development, https://doi.org/10.1007/978-3-319-78701-5_3

insufficient food production partly accounts for poverty, despondency and insecurity. Obviously, the availability of food, in terms of greener pasture, in different parts of Southern Nigeria almost all year round, also accounts for the perennial restiveness between the local farmers and the itinerant herdsmen from numerous parts of Northern Nigeria.

Conceptual and Definitional Issues

In view of the centrality of the concepts of food and national security to the focus of this chapter, it should be appropriate to offer some elementary explanations. As noted earlier, food is a vital necessity. At the household level, it is a basic means of sustenance and its adequacy a key requirement for healthy and productive life. Evidence abound in the extant literature to prove that the "provision of adequate and balanced food is necessary for the survival of the society in the sense that it is essential for the maintenance of good health", and by extension the successful implementation of development plans and policies in general (Bankole and Fatai 2016:69).

The Food and Agriculture Organization (FAO), in a 2001 report defined food security as "people's physical, social and economic access to sufficient, safe and nutritious food to meet their dietary needs and food preferences for active and healthy life" (FAO 2001). By implication, it means that people will be food-secured not only when sufficient food is available and people have accessed and fully utilized it, but also when food availability, access and adequate utilization are free from the risk of not meeting these three criteria namely: sufficiency, accessibility and utilization.

The prominent outcomes of food shortage include hunger and starvation, malnutrition and several serious conditions of ill-health. While hunger and starvation may first lead to despondency, anger, frustration and, thereafter, security threats, sustained hunger and malnutrition as well as associated conditions of ill-health and diseases are serious causes of death. In other words, hunger and malnutrition among several other conditions that are associated with food insufficiency or lack of the correct intakes constitute security threats. In Statistics show that about "10.9million children, under the age of five, die in developing countries like Nigeria each year", and survey indicates that malnutrition and "other hunger-related diseases cause 60 per cent of the said deaths" (Nwaozor 2015:28). Besides, it is estimated that "684,000 child deaths worldwide could be prevented by increasing access to vitamin A and zinc, which can be obtained from vegetables" (Nwaozor 2015: 28). Therefore, it is no mere accident that hunger has caused so much death and general insecurity, if lack of access to vegetables alone account for so much deaths every year.

Security is simply explained to mean protection or safety from harm and danger. This is expanded by Nwolise (2009:258), to connote the "condition of feeling happy and safe from danger and harm". Apparently, this somewhat elementary conception of security makes it not only a sacred and strategic value, but indeed the utmost value. This is because survival or self-preservation is the first law of nature, and unless one is assured of his physical security or safety, everything else is meaningless (see Tzu 1988; Whynes 1979). Drawing from this explanations, national security can be explained to mean the defence or protection of a nation or country. However, focus has significantly shifted from this state-centric idea of national security to the security of the individuals or human security (Aning 2016). As a modern English terminology, which is traceable to the twentieth Century, "national security" was introduced in the United States after the Second World War, and it became a guiding principle of USA's foreign policy from July 1947, when President Harry Truman signed the National Security Act of 1947.

Throughout the cold war era, security was perceived and defined in the large body of literature on the subject as a state-centric value with emphasis on the amassment of awesome military weapons and large size of military personnel (see Yagboyaju 2015). It is in this light that Morgenthau (1972), like many of his peers, defined the concept in terms of the integrity of the national territory and its institutions, while Lippman (see Nwolise 2014) asserted that security rises and falls with the ability of a nation to deter an attack or defeat it.

Most definitions, formulations and propositions on the subject matter of security and, in particular, national security that emphasize military capabilities as well as the procurement of all forms of weapons often down play what McNamara (1968:129–130) had to say about non-military dimensions of security, especially in respect of the interconnectedness between the latter and human development. According to him:

Security is not military hardware, though it may include it. Security is not a military force, though it may involve it. Security is not traditional military activity, though it may encompass it. Security is development and without development there can be no security. A developing nation that does not in fact develop simply cannot remain secure for the intractable reason that its own citizenry cannot shed its human nature... (McNamara 1968:129–130).

Furthermore, he noted that any society:

... that seeks to achieve adequate military security against the background of acute food shortages, population explosion, low level of productivity and per capita income, low technological development, inadequate and insufficient public utilities and chronic problem of unemployment has a false sense of security (McNamara 1968: 128-130).

Similarly, on the need to re-focus attention on what is supposed to constitute security, whether at the personal, group or national level, Mijah (2008:3) reiterated the idea, which Kofi Annan, former Secretary General of United Nations, advocated for so long. He had this to say:

Today, we know that security means far more than the absence of conflict. We know that lasting peace requires a broader vision encompassing areas such as education, health, democracy and human rights, protection against environmental degradation and the proliferation of deadly weapons. We know that we cannot be secure amidst starvation; that we cannot build peace without alleviating poverty and that we cannot build freedom on the foundations of injustice... (Mijah 2008:3).

For a better understanding of these postulations, some deductions and illustrations that readily fit in should be drawn. Take for example, the 1991 collapse of the Soviet Union as a military super power did not necessarily occur because of superior weapons from some enemies but essentially as a result of the grievances from the generality of the citizenry. Secondly, the 2001 horrendous invasion of the United States of America and the destruction of the twin towers of the World Trade Centre (WTC) that led to the killing of an estimated 5000 people and other serious aftermath were carried out by a handful of angry unarmed Arab youths who hijacked and used fully loaded passenger aircrafts as missiles against the world's acclaimed super power. Although these two instances of the former Soviet Union and USA may not directly be connected to food insecurity, they point to the postulation that military force alone is insufficient to guarantee security.

Similarly, the social fires that eventually transformed into what became popularly known as the 'Arab spring' or 'Arab revolution', which began in Tunisia in 2010 and later spread to Egypt, Libya and Syria; with very devastating effects on the then regimes in Tunisia, Egypt and Libya, were sparked by socio-economic hardships that were, in particular characterized by hunger, relatively high levels of unemployment and general deprivation as well as official corruption. Syria under the Bashar Al-Assad led regime also encountered such uprising with the resultant devastating effects, in terms of large scale destruction and loss of lives. Also, against security agents, hungry and angry youths, adults as well as pensioners protested on the streets of Brazil and Turkey in the year 2014 (Nwolise 2014).

In effect, no matter the sophistication and size of military or "hard" power possessed by a country, the role and impact of the "soft" power (socio-economic and psychological factors), in terms of the general feelings, especially of the ordinary citizens, cannot be underestimated. Indeed, experiences from across the world have at different points in time confirmed that hard power amounts to nothing in an environment that is characterized by hunger, ignorance, unemployment, alienated and suffering masses as well as disempowerment and disillusionment, among several other indications of poor and ineffective governance (Aning 2016).

It is also by no means accidental that the United Nations' Millennium Development Goals (MDGs) and its successor, Sustainable Development Goals (SDGs), like several other similar programmes by other prominent international agencies, emphasize the eradication of hunger and the significant reduction of poverty as key factors to global peace and the attainment of all-round development.

Having done so much in conceptualizing food and national security, I herewith briefly analyze agricultural policies and programmes by successive governmental administrations in Nigeria, especially in the country's post-independence period.

Nigeria's Agricultural Policies, Programmes and Reforms Agenda

In line with the importance of the agricultural sector in the Nigerian economy as well as the central role of food production and its availability, pronouncements by successive administrations as to the improvement of the sector have increased over time. Consequently, policies, programmes and strategies to actualize aspirations and plans have equally changed. However, these have largely been a combination of two or more strategies for the implementation of agricultural policies and programmes at different times (see Ugwu and Kanu 2012). For ease of reference, the more prominent ones among these policies and programmes are classified into four different periods.

These are namely, period of minimum government intervention (1960–1969); period of maximum government intervention (1970–1985); the Structural Adjustment Programme (SAP) era (1985–1990); and the post-SAP era. For this latter part, the emphasis is on the performance of the successive administrations in Nigeria's on-going Fourth Republic (1999–2015).

Period of Minimum Government Intervention (1960–1969)

At this time, government intervention in agriculture was quite minimal. Then, there were strong regional governments in the three regions of the North, East and West. According to Olayemi (1995), government efforts took the form of setting policies and establishing institutions for agricultural research, extension services, export crop marketing and pricing. Thus, government established "farm settlements, research institutes and agricultural development corporations", as well as marketing boards (see Olayemi 1995). There was a lot of emphasis on the mopping and withdrawal of surplus agricultural products and labour for transfer to industries in the UK and many other parts of Europe because Nigeria's industrial sector was quite small at the time.

However, the focus on the production of cash crops by both the government and the farmers; for the earning of foreign exchange and for individual financial empowerment respectively, accounted for the shortage in the supply of food crops at different points in time. Also, there were the problems of perennial deforestation of the rain forests as a result of cash crop production as well as loss of biodiversity especially in respect of wildlife (see Bankole and Fatai 2016).

Period of Maximum Government Intervention (1970–1985)

Several socio-economic and political factors accounted for the change from minimum to maximum government intervention in Nigeria's agricultural sector in the late 1960s up to the mid-1980s. On a political note, for instance, the introduction of military rule in 1966 first led to a momentary abrogation of the practice of federalism in Nigeria and, thereafter, when it was restored, it became a largely centralized federal system. In this model that later became peculiarly Nigerian, the central government took over many of the functions hitherto performed by the regions and many others that were fashioned out with the subsequent creation of states in replacement of these regions (Bankole and Fatai 2016)

Not surprisingly, the political factor had overlap effects on the socio-economic sector of the Nigerian system. These effects became more pronounced especially after the discovery of crude oil, the subsequent exportation of the product and its phenomenal foreign exchange earning capacity, which rose further during the oil boom of the 1970s. In 1973, the Federal Military Government established the Nigerian Agricultural and Co-operative Bank (NACB) so as to facilitate the granting of credit and loans to farmers (Bankole and Fatai 2016). The central government also liberalized the importation of certain food items, agricultural machinery and equipment. In 1977, the federal government promulgated the decree that enabled the establishment of six national commodity boards for cocoa, groundnut, palm produce, cotton, rubber and food grains.

There was also the land use decree, which the federal government promulgated in 1978, in order to vest the ownership of land in the government, so as to grant genuine farmers access to farmlands (Adeyeri 2013). It also included agricultural extension and technology transfer policy aimed at enhancing the adoption of improved technology by farmers. Similarly, the policy on input supply and distribution was promulgated to ensure adequate and orderly supply of agricultural inputs notably fertilizers, agro-chemicals, seeds, machinery and equipment.

The civil war of 1967–1970 and the drought, especially in the North Eastern parts of the country, between 1972 and 1974, had massive adverse effects in terms of huge loss of food and cash crops as well as livestock (Bankole and Fatai 2016). Meanwhile, although there were regime and administrative changes in 1975 and 1976, as well as transition to civil rule (the Second Republic) in 1979, there were no fundamental changes in policy direction, both in the agricultural and almost all the other areas of governance. However, it should be noted that the extensive liberalization of import regulations on almost all economic items, which became particularly noticeable in the oil boom years of the early 1970s up to the mid-1970s, continued under the Second Republic albeit for different reasons. Take for example, although Nigeria's revenue, especially from crude oil, had begun to dwindle as at the 1979 commencement of the Second Republic, the then Shehu Shagari administration devised means, through patronage and clientele politics, to enrich many prominent members and supporters of the ruling National Party of Nigeria (NPN). The political patronage of that time mainly involved the scandalous issuance of import licences that were then the major instrument for importations (Joseph 1991).

Incidentally, fertilizer and processed rice, two prominent items on the list of imported products, for which import licenses were abused, came under the agricultural sector. Thus, although the quantity of available fertilizer increased on paper, just as the production of many local food items and the availability of imported rice were supposed to increase, in reality there was a rapid decline in food production with attendant food supply gaps (see Forrest 1995:181–204). All of these and other factors such as the blatantly rigged 1983 general elections as well as the violent aftermath worsened the then unstable polity, the feelings of disenchantment and loss of confidence among the generality of the ordinary citizens. Thus, they partly accounted for the warm reception that the military enjoyed when it struck again in December 1983.

Before proceeding to the next sub-head, it is instructive to note that it was not a mere coincidence that threats to national security, in the form of ideological extremism particularly in several parts of Northern Nigeria that were worst hit because of the drought and poor harvest of that period, also increased at this point in time.

The Structural Adjustment Era (SAP, 1985–1990)

With the 1986 adoption of the Structural Adjustment Programme (SAP) by Nigeria, in line with the growing trend particularly in the developing world, the then military regime shifted focus from the overbearing presence of government in most aspects of life, to a more liberalized and diversified system. However, the programmes were accompanied by a lot of problems, which included increased levels of unemployment and sharp increase in food prices; all of which were not unusual in commercialization and privatization exercises (Bankole and Fatai 2016). Thus, like many other aspects of the programme that sometimes led to protests and riots because of their adverse effects on the living standards and conditions of the ordinary citizens, the agricultural sector did not attain any remarkable level of success. This, in addition to the general feeling of disillusionment in the aftermath of the annulled 1993 presidential election results accounted for the large protests and general pro-democracy activities, all of which culminated in the reintroduction of civil rule in 1999.

The Post-SAP Era

Although SAP effectively terminated in November 1993 with the emergence of another military regime; however, the focus here is on the civilian dispensation, which began in 1999. Altogether, this period covers the different administrations of 1999–2007, 2007–2010, and 2010–2015, with their respective programmes such as the National Economic Empowerment Development Strategy (NEEDS), the Seven-Point Agenda and the Transformation Agenda, all of which had agricultural components.

Broadly, the objectives of the new agricultural policy, first put in place by the Olusegun Obasanjo administration (1999–2007) and largely adopted by the Yar'Adua and Jonathan administrations (2007–2010) and (2010–2015) respectively, were essentially to:

create a suitable macro-environment to stimulate greater private sector investment in agriculture; reorganise the institutional framework for government intervention in the agricultural sector to facilitate the smooth and integrated development of the sector; articulate and implement integrated rural development programmes to raise the quality of life of the rural people; increase budgetary allocation and other fiscal incentives to agriculture and promote the necessary development, supportive and service-oriented activities to enhance agricultural productivity, production and market opportunities; and rectify import tariff anomalies in respect of agricultural products and promote the increased use of agricultural machinery and inputs through favourable tariff policy (*Agriculture Policy 2001*).

There was an attempt by the Yar'Adua administration (2007–2010) to reverse some aspects of the policies on economic liberalization, but the Agricultural Transformation Agenda of the Jonathan administration (2010–2015) re-launched them. Despite this, the country spent between "$7 billion and $11 billion annually to import food", in the period 2011–2014; although the Jonathan administration claimed that it brought the bill down to "$4.3 billion in 2014" (*The Punch* 2015:24). No matter what, this food import bill is excessive and unjustifiable for Nigeria, with its abundant arable land and coastal lines.

In May 2015, President Muhammadu Buhari replaced former President, Goodluck Jonathan in the 2015 presidential election. Although Buhari and his All Progressives Congress (APC) mainly emphasized the intolerably high levels of insecurity and corruption in their campaign, the mutually reinforcing relationship between this and food insecurity should not be overlooked. For instance, it should not be difficult to understand how the scarcity of food items such as livestock, yam, wheat and tomato, among others, that are mainly produced in northern Nigeria, and which became difficult to produce because of the activities of Boko Haram, made them quite unaffordable across the country for a long time due to the group's insurgencies.

Thus, it was a great relief when President Buhari, in his inauguration speech, on 29 May 2015, declared his administration's readiness to revitalize the agricultural sector as one of its programmes of diversifying the national economy (Buhari 2015). Indeed, the administration's "change" mantra, concerning self-sustainability in food production, seemed to have fully taken off with the enthusiasm exhibited by food processing companies, for instance (Odogwu 2016: 20). However, in view of government policies which, so far, still favour the importation of tomato pastes and frozen fish among such other food items, sustainability of food production may still be jeopardized in Nigeria for some time to come. In fact, local food processors, exemplified for instance by *Erisco Foods,* with a "production capacity of 450,000 metric tones of tomato paste and ketchup annually", but which has for one year produced below 20 per cent", have severally lamented over possible close ups due to sundry challenges (Odogwu 2016:20).

Similarly, as reported by *The Punch* on November 15, 2016, Nigeria's presidency also raised an alarm over an imminent famine because of the mass exportation of at least "500 trucks of grains per week", from Northern Nigeria (The Punch 2016:1). Quite disturbingly, this is traceable to surplus in harvest which, although the Buhari administration promised to purchase and keep in government strategic storage, as in the past became a burden for local farmers who needed to dispose and prepare for the next planting season. Why, in spite of all these supposed efforts of successive governments in Nigeria's Fourth Republic, has shortage of food supply, hunger, poverty as well as general deprivation constituted so much threats to national security? What are the probable constraining factors in the ecology of public policies in Nigeria which, apart from the lack of nutrients and undernourishment that food shortage or insecurity imply, account for the danger of anger and, possibly, uncontrollable violence that food insecurity is capable of causing?

Factors and Forces Behind Insecurity in Contemporary Nigeria

There are several plausible explanations and formulations on the causal factors and forces militating against peace and security in Nigeria and beyond (see Eckstein 1965; Crenshaw 1990; English 2009; Adekanye 2003; etc). However, in respect of food production and its effects on national security in Nigeria, the emphasis will be on the impact of such factors as state fragility or dysfunctionality, leadership failure, inconsistency of the followership and uncontrolled corruption, and the interconnections between all of these and policy ineffectiveness in contemporary Nigeria. In the case of state fragility and dysfunctionality, it should be noted as Osaghae (2002, 2007, 2010), Midgal (1988) and Yagboyaju (2014) among several others have argued that a weak state cannot effectively conceptualize, formulate and implement policies to guarantee and enhance food security. And, in order not to confuse issues, it should be useful to note that the strength of a state "is measured not by the unbridled wielding of coercive powers", "but by its ability to make the citizens accept its laws as the standard to which they conform" (Yagboyaju 2008:10).

Meanwhile, this point on the characterization of the weak state and its largely dysfunctional institutions in contemporary Nigeria should be analyzed in conjunction with the impact of leadership failure or deficit that was listed in a preceding part of this section. The thrust of the argument here is that whether in the ancient, medieval or contemporary times, directional and transformational leaders have usually turned around hitherto weak institutions and societies to efficient and progressive ones.

It is at least on record that under the political leadership of Nigeria's immediate post-independence era, the Obafemi Awolowo – led administration in the Western region "instituted free education, using revenue from the export of cocoa" (Baje 2015:26). This was in addition to several other services in the health, transportation and housing among such other key sectors that were comparatively more efficient than they currently are in many of the States that emerged from the defunct Western region. And, although the levels of development differed in this region and the then Eastern and Northern regions, there are evidences that effective political leadership ensured that the proceeds from the cultivation and exportation of rubber and palm oil as well as cotton and groundnut respectively made their own relatively high levels of developmental attainments also possible.

Drawing from the common logic of the interconnections between effective leadership and problem solving, the factor of leadership deficit or failure readily comes to play in Nigeria's paradox of a country so rich, but yet so poor. This expression typifies the country's abundance of human and material resources, including in particular phenomenal "earnings of trillions from crude oil exportation" (Baje 2015:20), spanning almost the entire 55 years of independence since 1960. Despite this, Nigeria is yet to have stable social infrastructure such as uninterrupted power supply, good road networks, affordable health services and clean drinkable water for majority of its ordinary citizens and, above all, a sustainable system of food production.

No doubt, in line with the reciprocal exchanges that should exist and operate between leaders and followers, the latter are supposed to be the main determinant factor for the direction and activities of the former. This takes me to the point on inconsistent followership as a key factor in the general problem of policy failure and, in particular, the contending issue on the relationship between food and national security. For example, while the average Nigerian agonizes about the effects of poor leadership and ineffective governance in almost all facets of life, he also paradoxically often prefers to consider the ethno-religious background of the state officials saddled with key responsibilities, instead of participating in appropriate people's action. These could be in the form of voting out of a non-performing administration and, if the need arises, other symbolic actions such as mass protests and demonstrations.

In Nigeria's heroic past, particularly before the era of noticeable sycophancy that coincided with the height of misrule under the military, between the mid-1980s and late 1990s, there were several examples of people's actions through which unpopular policies and government actions were discontinued. Outside Nigeria, examples of such relevant people's action include the mass protests that ousted President Viktor Yanukovych from power, forced changes in some laws and restored power to the people (Sunday Punch 2014). It should be noted that Ukrainians were also part of the "colour revolutions" that swept autocrats out of power between 2004 and 2010 in former Soviet republics. In Russia itself, ordinary people staged peaceful demonstrations in continuation of the "Snow Revolution" of 2011 against electoral fraud, despite persecution, jailing and police harassment (Sunday Punch 2014:16). In repressive, one-party State of China, activists seeking rights, democracy and halt to corruption, have since the Tiananmen Square protests of 1989, used symbolic walks, blogs and other social media platforms to peacefully press for inclusion, accountability and, in general, policies that guarantee well-being of the people and national security (for more, see Sunday Punch 2014:16).

Drawing from the interconnections between the factors of state fragility, leadership deficit and inconsistent followership analyzed above, it is not surprising that corruption has become such an endemic problem and huge obstacle to development aspirations in Nigeria. Although corruption existed from the colonial and immediate post-colonial periods, it did not constitute a major national problem until 1966 when the plotters of the country's first military coup singled it out as the major reason for their action (Yagboyaju 2014). Since after this exercise, which caused the collapse of the country's First Republic, coups and counter-coups were based on allegations of corruption and other forms of abuse that have generally impeded good governance, particularly in terms of food production and national security. Yet, corruption seems to have grown bolder and more ravenous under successive administrations in the country, whether they are civilian or military (Yagboyaju 2014).

In fact, corruption has over the years remained the single most important obstacle that has confronted national integration, national security and the effectiveness of public policies on agriculture, food production and every other important sector of national life in Nigeria. There are, for instance, evidences that Nigeria's economic recession, which was officially reported in September 2016, is partly traceable to corruption (Tella 2016:20). It is also on record that a large fraction of allocations for arms procurement, particularly in the Jonathan years, was misappropriated. This is confirmed by revelations made during the investigations and trials in the $2.1 billion arms scandal, in which Colonel M.S. Dasuki, former National Security Adviser (NSA) to President Jonathan and several security chiefs were mentioned (Yagboyaju 2016). Obviously, such misappropriations, which meant insufficient funding for the military, contributed in several ways to the prolonging of the battle against the Boko Haram group and the disruption of food supply from areas occupied by the latter, among other related problems.

Similarly, the country's abysmal performance in the attainment of the UN's Millennium Development Goals (MDGs), introduced in 2000 and implemented across the developing countries till 2015, can be traced to the same problem of corruption (Yagboyaju 2008). It should be noted that a critical part of the MDGs, which transformed to Sustainable Development Goals (SDGs) in 2015, is the reduction of poverty and, in particular, lack of access to nutritional food. Meanwhile, the World Development indicator of 2015 shows that the number of people leaving in absolute poverty or on less than $1.90 per day worldwide reduced from "37.1 per cent in 1990 to 12.73 per cent in 2012" (Tella 2016: 20). For Africa, where Nigeria represents more than half of the population, there was "a slight cut from 56.75 per cent to 42.65 per cent" during the same period (Tella 2016:20).

For Nigeria alone, the National Bureau of Statistics (NBS) figures for those living in absolute poverty rose from "54.7 per cent in 2004 to 60.9 per cent", or almost 100 million people in 2010 (NBS 2010). This was despite huge revenues from oil exportation and several other sources such as "borrowing from international markets" (Tella 2016:20). Curiously, this frighteningly high figure was before the commencement of Boko Haram insurgence in 2009 and the "massive fall in oil revenue since 2014" (Tella 2016: 20). Obviously, the percentage must have since increased.

Conclusion

Despite Nigeria's huge arable land area; one of the biggest in Africa, and the country's enormous human population coupled with favourable climatic conditions, the country evidently suffers food insufficiency which, by extension, threatens national security and even the corporate existence of the country. As at 2016, a year after a new government with great emphasis on the need to drastically reduce food importation was inaugurated, Nigeria still imported almost all the quantity of rice and wheat-based products consumed by its citizens. And, as a country where rice and bread (the most popular wheat product in the country) constitute the commonest staple foods, it implies that Nigeria is essentially a food import-dependent country.

Meanwhile, in view of the non-availability of these and many other nutritious food items to the generality of ordinary citizens, partly because they are largely imported as well as because of affordability, it is not surprising as reported by Baje (2015:26) that the World Bank, in 2015, noted "the inexcusably high rates of infant and maternal mortality", as well as the prevalence of "iron and iodine deficiencies amongst the under-5 children". Incidentally, this report by the World Bank, in which Nigeria is said to be responsible for some of the "world's most deplorable figures on Human Development Index" (Baje 2015: 26), is linked to the World Development indicator and such others cited in this chapter.This is apart from the high unemployment rate of 26 per cent as provided by NBS and reported by Baje (2015: 26). Disturbingly, this figure and the ones provided in the 2015 World Development indicator's report on people leaving in absolute poverty are worse than the figures for Egypt, South Africa, Ghana, Angola, Swaziland and even war-ravaged Rwanda, none of which is agriculturally as endowed as Nigeria.

Indeed, the future of Nigeria's national security is threatened so long as the country is unable to effectively address the problem of food insecurity. And, this portends great danger to the country's immediate neigbours as well as the rest of the continent, by way of extension. Although, the way forward is not attainable overnight, the process would automatically commence with the emergence of a transformational leadership, first at the political level and, thereafter, in other sensitive public institutions. Although these institutions, which must be autonomous, strong and functional, would ultimately drive the change needed for sustainable food production and national security in Nigeria, they will initially revolve round some strong personalities.

References

Adamolekun L (2016) The idea of Nigeria: two challenges – unity in diversity and prosperity. Convocation Lecture, Lead City University, Ibadan

Adamu A (2015) Role of food security in achieving national security. In: The Punch. Lagos, August 17, p 24

Adekanye BJ (2003) Terrorism and globalization: how should the international community respond? – An African perspective. Afr J Peace Conflict Stud 1(1):7–44

Adeyeri O (2013) The Nigerian federal experiment and resource control: principle, contradictions and crises. In: Sofela B, Edo VO, Olaniyi RO (eds) Nigeria at 50 – politics society and development. Ibadan, John Archers

Amuwo K (1998) Federal systems: a theoretical perspective. In: Babawale T, Olufemi K, Adewumi F (eds) Re-inventing federalism in Nigeria: issues and perspectives. Malthouse Press, Lagos

Aning K (2016) Negotiating the west African conundrum: developing society through human security and social justice. Keynote address at the international conference, Africa since Independence: Promise, Pugnacity and Failure in the Post-Colonial Contexts, University of Ibadan, 3–5, August

Baje AO (2015) As economic recession looms. In: The Punch. Lagos, November 10, p 26

Bankole SA, Fatai BO (2016) Food production, trade and food security in Nigeria. In: Yagboyaju DA (ed) Reflections on politics, administration and economy in contemporary Nigeria. University Press Limited, Ibadan

Buhari M (2015) Presidential inauguration address, May 29

Crenshaw M (1990) The causes of terrorism. In: Kegley CW (ed) International terrorism: characteristics, causes and controls. St. Martin's Press, New York

Eckstein H (1965) On the etiology of internal wars. Hist Theory 4:133–162

English R (2009) Terrorism – how to respond. Oxford University Press, Oxford/New York

Food and Agriculture Organization (FAO) (2001) State of food insecurity report. FAO, Rome
Forrest T (1995) Politics and economic development in Nigeria. Westview Press, Colorado
Joseph R (1991) Democracy and prebendal politics in Nigeria: the rise and fall of the Second Republic. Spectrum, Ibadan
McNamara R (1968) The essence of security: reflections in office Harper and Row, New York
Midgal J (1988) Strong societies and weak states: state-society relations and state capabilities in the third world. Princeton University Press, Princeton
Mijah E (2008) Security and development in Nigeria: a human security perspective. In: Arts and social sciences research, vol 4. Nigeria Defence Academy, Kaduna, p 3
Morgenthau H (1972) Politics among nations: the struggle for peace and power. Alfred Knopt, New York
National Bureau of Statistics (2010) Annual report of the NBS
Nwaozor F (2015) Combating malnutrition in Nigeria. In: The Punch. Lagos, September 1, p 28
Nwolise OBC (2009) Peace and security. In: Albert IO (ed) Praxis of political concepts and cliches in Nigeria's fourth republic. Bookcraft, Ibadan
Nwolise OBC (2014) Insecurity as a threat to general elections in Nigeria. Strategic Public Lecture in commemoration of the 4th Anniversary of the National Mirror Newspaper, Abuja, December 16
Odogwu G (2016) "Erisco foods" exit: why Buhari must speak up. In: The Punch. Lagos, November 10, p.20
Olayemi JK (1995) Agricultural policies for sustainable development: Nigeria's experience. In: Ikpi AE, Olayemi JK (eds) Sustainable agriculture and economic development in Nigeria. Winrock International, Nigeria
Osaghae E (2002) Crippled giant: Nigeria since independence. John Archers, Ibadan
Osaghae E (2007) Fragile states. Dev Pract 17(4 & 5):122–128
Osaghae E (2010) Revisiting the concepts of state fragility and state building in Africa. In: Akinboye SO, Fadakinte MM (eds) Fifty years of nationhood? – State, society and politics in Nigeria. Concept Publications, Lagos, pp 1960–2010
Sunday Punch (2014) The essence of the people's power. Lagos, March 9, p 16
Tella S (2016) Of recession and debt accumulation. In: The Punch. Lagos, November 10, p 20
The Punch (2015) Buhari's cabinet: putting the nation first. Lagos, November 17, p 24
The Punch (2016) Presidency raises the alarm over imminent famine. Lagos, November 15, p 1
Tzu S (1988) The art of war (trans: Cleavy T). Shambhala Publications, London
Ugwu DS, Kanu IO (2012) Effects of agricultural reforms on the agricultural sector in Nigeria. J Afr Stud Dev 2:51–29
Whynes D (1979) The economics of third world military expenditures. Macmillan Press, London
Yagboyaju DA (2008) Attaining the Millennium Development Goals (MDGs) in a weak state: the Nigerian example. Int Rev Politics Dev 6(1&2):8–20
Yagboyaju DA (2014) Leadership, followership and state dysfunctionality in contemporary Nigeria: an examination of consequences and possible solutions. J Gov Public Policy 4(2):39–51
Yagboyaju DA (2015) Non-military Dimensions of National Security in Nigeria. Paper presented to Course 23 participants at the National Defence College, Abuja, January 19
Yagboyaju DA (2016) Corruption, democracy and development: lessons for Africa and Asia. Paper presented at the Seventh Annual Ibadan Sustainable Development Summit, Making Sustainable Development Goals (SDGs) work for people, University of Ibadan, August 22–25

Chapter 4
Transforming the Bodi from Pastoralists to Outgrowers: Land and State Capitalism in South Omo, Southwest Ethiopia

Fana Gebresenbet

Introduction

South Omo Zone of the Southern Nations, Nationalities and Peoples (SNNP)[1] regional state is among the most underdeveloped and marginalized parts of Ethiopia, by any standard. Historically as well as in contemporary times, the lower Omo valley is hard to reach by physical infrastructure and service delivery is dismally low. This state of affairs remained unchanged after the Ethiopian Peoples' Revolutionary Democratic Front (EPRDF) came to power in 1991 and the ethno-linguistic federalization of the country, *de facto* in 1991 and *de jure* in 1995 (Markakis 2011).

This could be attributed to the geographical fact that the lower Omo valley is located at the southern extreme of the country, very far from the main political and economic power centers. The zone comprises of 16 ethnic groups; nine out of these groups-Mursi, Bodi, Arborie, Brayle, Bacha, Koyegu, Karo, Murle and Dime-have population less than 10,000 people each (Central Statistical Agency 2008) with an expansive mode of livelihood, i.e., agro-pastoralism, practiced by a significant proportion of the inhabitants of the Zone contributed to its marginalization. State making in Ethiopia has been based on extraction made possible by cereal cultivation using the effective ox-plough technology (McCann 1995). This technology does not perform in the arid and semi-arid lowlands, and as such these lowlands were left for pastoralism, shifting cultivation and hunting/gathering with little state intervention.

---

[1] The SNNP regional state is one of the nine regional states created in the federal restructuring of Ethiopia according to the 1994 Constitution (Federal Democratic Republic of Ethiopia (FDRE) 1994). Zone is the third highest administrative level in Ethiopia; and *Woreda* the second lowest, i.e., federal-region-Zone-*Woreda-Kebele*.

F. Gebresenbet (✉)
Institute for Peace & Security Studies, Addis Ababa University, Addis Ababa, Ethiopia
e-mail: fana.g@ipss-addis.org

© Springer International Publishing AG, part of Springer Nature 2019
A. O. Akinola, H. Wissink (eds.), *Trajectory of Land Reform in Post-Colonial African States*, Advances in African Economic, Social and Political Development, https://doi.org/10.1007/978-3-319-78701-5_4

43

The inaccessibility of this mode of production to the state has meant that the state does not cater for the needs of pastoralism and pastoralists (Scott 1998), explaining the severe poverty and marginalization in the lower Omo valley.

The Ethiopian government's policy towards these lowlands significantly changed at the break of this decade. Speaking at the 13th Annual Pastoralist Day celebrations in Jinka, the capital of South Omo Zone, on 25 January 2011, the late Prime Minister, Mr. Meles Zenawi, expressed the 'transformative' changes his government intends to bring to the area (Meles 2011). He stated that "a very huge irrigation project and related agricultural development" was destined to 'develop' the valley (Meles 2011). He argued that the agro-pastoral population would benefit as the proposed project will "help cattle raising to be productive and modern" and ensure a "secure, improved life to pastoralists" (Meles 2011). The intention of his government is to bring "a permanent solution" by transforming the Zone from "backward in terms of civilization" in to "an example of rapid development" (Meles 2011).

This announcement was followed by more detailed plans of establishing the Kuraz Sugar Development Project (KSDP) in the lower Omo Valley and a villagization scheme. The KSDP constitutes about half of the new sugar development projects that the Ethiopian Sugar Corporation has been implementing since 2011, and, if and when successful, will be among the main foreign currency generating sites in the country (see Tewolde and Fana 2014). The KSDP intends to establish sugarcane plantation on 175,000 hectares of land together with five sugar factories. This will create job opportunity for at least 400,000 individuals, mainly expected to come from the densely populated southern highlands to the north of the valley. The benefits of sugar industrialization will be mainly accrued in the highlands, with most of the cultural, ecological and economic costs being left for the agro-pastoral lowlander to bear (Asnake and Fana 2014).

This chapter argues that sugar industrialization is accelerating the pace at which villagized Bodi households are integrated into a monetized, capitalist system by making them out-growers and by advancing a more exclusive land tenure system. The rest of this chapter has four parts. The first introduces Salamago *Woreda*, its people, and state projects there (sugar industrialization and villagization). The second part focuses on the changes these state projects are introducing to the agro-pastoral conceptions and understandings of land and land governance and economic life. The third part dwells on the implications of these changes on land tenure, property rights arrangements and production relations. The last part concludes the chapter.

Overview of Development Interventions in Salamago *Woreda*: Sugar Industrialization and Villagization

Salamago is one of the eight *Woredas* in South Omo Zone. Population projection for 2016/17 puts the *Woreda's* population at 37,074, with close to 95% of the population living in rural areas. With a land area of 4450 km², the *Woreda* is the least dense in the Zone (only 8.33 people found per km²)[2] and among the least densely populated from the country.

The *Woreda* has four native ethnic groups: the Mursi (numbering some 7500), Bodi (6994), Bacha (2632) and Dime (457)[3] (see Central Statistical Agency 2008). The Mursi and Bodi predominantly rely on pastoralism, but also practice shifting and flood retreat cultivation. David Turton (1979: 122) stresses that these three livelihood systems "are spatially separated yet closely integrated, in the sense that each one, although insufficient and precarious in itself, makes a vital contribution to the long-term viability of the [Mursi] economy." A section of the Bodi living on "the wooded western slope at an altitude of 800–1200 m in the western part" the Dime mountain range and the riverbank forest land (Fukui 2001: 2). The Dime practices shifting cultivation. The Bacha mostly rely on rain-fed and retreat agriculture, and complement that with fishing and fishing.

Prior to the establishment of the KSDP, the government only promoted cultural tourism in the area. The lip-plates of Mursi women, body decorations and villages of the Mursi attracted tourists to the area. In 2008, the Ethiopian government initiated the Gibe III hydro-electric project that would have significant impact on lives and livelihoods in the lower Omo Valley: the. Located upstream of the valley, the reservoir regulates flow volume of the River, and thereby simultaneously inhibits flood retreat agriculture and enables irrigated agriculture.

Three years after the commencement of the Gibe III project, the government announced that it would engage in the KSDP and villagization scheme in Salamago *Woreda*, initially in Bodi areas (Meles 2011; Tewolde and Fana 2014). Some 50,000 hectares of land is slotted to be covered by sugarcane plantation and two factories will be erected in the *Woreda* (Yidnekachew 2015). Although officials of the Sugar Corporation[4] argue that the area to be covered by plantation was 'vacant and unused' by the local community, it has been used as pasture land,[5] for honey collection[6] and for some ritual activities.[7] International non-governmental organizations (Human Rights Watch 2012) and researchers with extensive experience in the area have criticized the government for alleged links between the two state projects, taking

---

[2] Based on figures provided by an Expert from the Zone's Finance and Economic Development Department, Jinka (11 August 2016).

[3] This figure from the CSA is not to be believed, as the Dime amount to at least 8000 according to Lucie Buffavand (Personal Communication, 30 August 2016).

[4] Interview: Project Manager, Kuraz Sugar Development Project, Salamago *Woreda* (22 February 2012).

[5] Local government representatives state that the land was only a wet season grazing land, as such not very crucial for the Bodi (Interview: Expert, Agriculture and Natural Resource Office Expert, Salamago *Woreda* (4 August 2016). But Lucie Buffavand (Personal Communication, 30 August 2016), who did extensive field work in Bdi land stresses that it was a dry season grazing land and a route to access the Omo River when it gets too dry.

[6] Interview: Expert, Agriculture and Natural Resource Office Expert, Salamago *Woreda* (4 August 2016).

[7] Interview: Official, South Omo Zone Council, Jinka (24 February 2013).

villagization as a scheme to concentrate the Bodi and Mursi displaced by the sugarcane plantations in new villages.

The government however contends that there was no operational link between the two projects. The argument was that sugar industrialization aimed to benefit the country by creating job opportunities for hundreds of thousands, generating revenues and foreign currency from the hitherto unexploited lowlands, and promoting industrialization and urbanization.[8] On the other hand, villagization aimed to rationalize[9] natural resource use in the valley (i.e., by promoting irrigated agriculture and ranching) and to offer social services. Villagization is a scheme in which households get congregated at a center provided by social services,[10] thereby removing hurdles caused by sparse population density to service the area. The government believes, villagization makes service delivery cost effective, possible and reasonable. At the same time, the services the government intended to provide help the local community to live a 'modern' life from the 'traditional'/'backward' one, according to the government. Thus, according to Li (1999: 302), these services could be regarded as 'modernity packages'.

Villagization also augments the government's intention of converting the local communities from living on expansive modes of livelihood (pastoralism, shifting cultivation and retreat agriculture) to irrigated farming.[11] Three extension agents are stationed in the villages, tasked with the responsibility of skilling Bodi households which joined the villages in ways of doing irrigated agriculture. The skilling starts from distribution of the most basic agricultural tools (such as hoes), improved seeds and also teaching the Bodi to do ox-plowing.[12]

Sugar industrialization and villagization make different aspects of the developmental ambition of the Ethiopian government. While the former promises to increase the size of the nation's economy, the latter intends to create a fairer and equitable distribution of the national wealth. As such, the two state projects in the *Woreda* represent different sides of the same coin, development.

The aims of the state projects could by themselves be commendable, as doing nothing will amount to 'fixing' the local population to poverty and insecurity.

---

[8] Interview: Project Manager, Kuraz Sugar Development Project, Salamago *Woreda* (22 February 2012).

[9] Such arguments were extensively used by Meles (2011). Galaty's (2011) critic of such reasoning, by arguing that it is a justification for "settling, pacifying, or displacing pastoralists in the interests of the state" applies here too. For a critique of Meles' line of argumentation along Galaty's see Tewolde and Fana (forthcoming).

[10] "Eleven infrastructure and social service providing centres will be built in each village: school (Grades 1–4, (5–8 being built in Village II (mid-way to Villages I and III)), health post, veterinary post, mill, drinking water station, police station, *Kebele* office, teachers' house, agricultural extension agents' house, health extension workers' house, and farmers' training station." (Tewolde and Fana 2014: 123–124)

[11] Interview: Expert, Agriculture and Natural Resource Office Expert, Salamago *Woreda* (4 August 2016).

[12] Interview: Expert, Agriculture and Natural Resource Office Expert, Salamago *Woreda* (4 August 2016).

Nevertheless, the implementation and political economy under which these state projects proceed have been criticized by many. For example, the pace with which the government intended to establish villages and sugarcane plantations and factories was too quick for the local community to cope up with. Moreover, the government only went to the extent of *convincing* the local community that these projects are good for them, not to *consulting* them (Tewolde and Fana forthcoming; see also Yidnekachew 2015).

Moreover, as recent as August 2016, villagization was not successful at Zonal level. There is better success in Bodi areas, compared to the rate of success in other parts of South Omo, not when it is compared to the plan held at the time of establishing the villages. The provision of access to irrigation water from the facilities built by the sugar corporation made the relative success so far recorded possible.[13] By the same token, there is poor success in other areas mainly because irrigation facilities could not be built and made operational in time.[14]

Changes in Land Tenure and Production Relations

This section focuses on the changes in land tenure, property rights regime, and production relations of the Bodi through sugar industrialization and villagization. Although a predominantly pastoralist community, the Bodi also rely on shifting farming and flood retreat cultivation. Major decisions relating to land are made by men, and while young men engage in cattle-keeping and it is women who do the cultivation.

These forms of production are not made with market considerations. Sorghum and maize harvests make part of the annual consumption and the subsistence economy of a household. Cattle keeping, in addition to contributing to consumption and the local subsistence economy, makes a major place in Bodi social and cultural relations (Fukui 2001). Herd size determines one's place in the community. Livestock are kept more for these values than the economic, and more value is attached to the number, not quality, of the herds.

The state sanctioned and implemented several projects towards enhancing the performance of these livelihood strategies. As stated above, the Gibe III reservoir inhibits flood retreat agriculture by regulating the annual flow volume and letting the soil brought from the highlands remain in the reservoir (through siltation process). This by itself severely threatens local livelihoods and food security. The sugarcane plantations withdraw land resources from the portfolio of resources accessed

---

[13] Interview: Expert, Agriculture and Natural Resources Expert, Salamago *Woreda* (4 August 2016).

[14] Interviews: Official, Water, Irrigation and Energy Department; Official, Pastoralist Affairs Department; Official and two Experts of the Agriculture and Natural Resources Department of South Omo Zone. Observations and Interviews in Hamer, Dassenech and Nyangatome *Woredas* (6–9 August 2016).

and utilized by the Bodi and other communities downstream, and reduce the effectiveness of their expansive natural resource utilization system.

Villagization, through a range of social services (if delivered), serves to reduce the negative implications of the dam and sugar industrialization; thus, serves as a mitigation strategy (Mulugeta 2014). It promises to make up to the expected losses in consumption/economic gains, and offers additional benefits to the Bodi, primarily by giving villagized households access to irrigation water. All villagized households (the second, third... wife of a man constituting a separate female headed household) get 1.5 ha of land for living (0.25 ha) and cultivation (1.25 ha).[15] Land slotted for cultivation will get connected to the Sugar Corporation's irrigation canals and thus a year-round (according to the plans, but not the case the past years) access to irrigation water.

Officials and experts alike stress that if the Bodi get the necessary skill (through extension services made possible by the villagization scheme) and make the effort (i.e., do away with the traditional 'poor work ethic') they would get significant economic gains, and that they would do better than they used to economically.[16] This depends on the success of the re-skilling component of the villagization scheme, which in turn depends on the skills the development agents (who are trained to function in the highlands dominated by smallholder farmers, where there is basic skill and tradition in doing agriculture) have and the degree to which the local community perceives and takes up irrigated agriculture as an alternative, more productive livelihood. Local officials add that the Bodi are skeptical about any new project whatever its promises are, but would recast their opinion and adopt it after seeing the benefits on the first few risk-takers who had tried it. Thus, the argument is that through positive demonstration effects the Bodi will eventually be turned into agriculturalists.[17]

The Sugar Corporation brought the initiative of economically integrating villagized households with sugar factories to ensure that Bodi benefit from sugar industrialization on its land.[18] The Bodi do not have a choice on whether to become an outgrower or not; they are required to. Neither did they have a legal deed to the land

---

[15] Initially the plan was to provide one hectare for cultivation and 0.5 ha for building houses/backyards per household (see Tewolde and Fana 2014: 124). Now, only 0.25 ha (2500 m²) is slotted for housing area. As is customary the second, third wives live in the same compound, thus increasing the area slotted for housing. Although the government plans that this area will be used to grow vegetables (on backyard gardens), they are rather used for herd camps.

[16] See Tewolde and Fana (2014, p. 124–126); Interviews: Development Agent, Salamago *Woreda*; Expert, Agriculture and Natural Resources Bureau, Salamago *Woreda* (4 August 2016).

[17] Interviews: Development Agent, Salamago *Woreda*; Expert, Agriculture and Natural Resources Bureau, Salamago *Woreda* (4 August 2016).

[18] The turning of villagized households into outgrowers for the sugar corporation also makes them, intentional or not, complacent to the dictates of sugar industrialization and appendages their economic and social life/fate with the sugar factories, thus turn them into supporters of the sugar industrialization or at least appeases them. In Mursi areas, for example, of the same *Woreda* but farther away from the plantation site the government only intends to give 0.5 ha farming land with no possibility of becoming ourgrowers to the factories.

before the sugar corporation planted cane seeds on the land. The decision is made for the villagized Bodi households by the government. They are to *grow* sugarcane[19] on 0.75 ha and maize on 0.5 ha of land. The state is making farming decisions for them, a rare, and a very recent phenomenon, in the highland smallholder areas (McCann 1995).

Getting a certificate is not sufficient to become an outgrower. Individual households with a certificate join the cooperative in their village (the government established one cooperative per village) to be formally considered as an outgrower by the Sugar Corporation.[20] In fact, individuals want to get a land certificate mainly to join the cooperative in their village, and thereby get access to the promised money as outgrowers.

It is expected that all the 1430 households[21] will join the three cooperatives when the villages become populated to the planned level.[22] Till August 2016, only 688 households joined the three villages and of these it is only 513 household heads who collected their land certificates and joined a cooperative.[23] Experts and development agents in the *Woreda* stress that the certification was difficult at the start. They had to work hard to convince the Bodi to take their pictures and give them laminated certificates. Now that trend has changed, and the pressure is presently generated by the yet un-certified 175 households.

---

[19] When it comes to the sugarcane fields, the Sugar Corporation assumed the responsibility of doing all agronomic practices, and the villagized households are becoming outgrowers to the same field tilled and planted some three years ago when they get land certificate and become members of the cooperative in their village. Put briefly, the Bodi are there to get the legal deed over the land which allows them to reap the benefits where they did not sow.

[20] Interviews: Development Agents, Salamago *Woreda*; Expert, Agriculture and Natural Resources Bureau, Salamago *Woreda* (4 August 2016).

[21] These were planned to be distributed among the villages in the following manner: 448 households (HHs) in Koklemeri (Village 1), 173 Male headed household (MHH) and 275 female headed household (FHH); 500 HHs in Arbud (Village 2), 281 MHH and 219 FHH; 500 HHs in Belelong (Village 3), 273 MHH and 227 FHH. (Interview: Official, Agriculture and Natural Resources Department, South Omo Zone (2 August 2016); Expert, Agriculture and Natural Resources Department, South Omo Zone (2 August 2016); Expert, Agriculture and Natural Resources Bureau, Salamago *Woreda*, 4 August 2016).

[22] All villagized households getting 0.75 ha of land to grow sugarcane will translate into having a total of 1072.5 ha being planted with sugarcane. But the total land prepared and planted with sugarcane is about 1600 ha (Interview: Expert, Agriculture and Natural Resources Bureau, Salamago *Woreda*, 4 August 2016).

[23] A total of 182 (115 MHH and 67 FHH) in Koklemeri village, 199 (123 MHH and 76 FHH) in Arbud village and 132 (77 MHH and 55 FHH) in Belelong village have collected their land certificates. The certification started in November 2014, and one will be eligible to get a certificate only if s/he constructs house and clears land (for maize cultivation) after joining a village. (Interview: Official, Agriculture and Natural Resources Department, South Omo Zone (2 August 2016); Expert, Agriculture and Natural Resources Department, South Omo Zone (2 August 2016); Expert, Agriculture and Natural Resources Bureau, Salamago *Woreda*, 4 August 2016).

The Bodi in Transition: Implications of Privatization of Land and Becoming an Outgrower

Villagization and sugar industrialization are bringing significant socio-economic, cultural and political pressure in the *Woreda* (Asnake and Fana 2014; Tewolde and Fana forthcoming; 2014). The Bodi who joined the villages appear convinced that working for (mainly as security guards) and supplying the Sugar Corporation with cane (as outgrowers) is a profitable economic endeavor. This is at the very least hastening the monetization of the local economy. Other more serious changes are occurring in the property rights regime of the Bodi.

The Bodi have a diverse resource use scheme. Fukui (2001) notes that the Bodi practices shifting cultivation, retreat agriculture and cattle keeping. The better resource endowment of their land helped the Bodi to engage in migration mainly for socio-political reasons, than ecological. As a pastoral group, ownership and exclusive use rights over rangelands is not advanced by the Bodi. Communal ownership and expansive utilization of land resources is preferred to adapt to, cope up with and exploit the varying resource endowments. Such a regime of ownership nad utilization of natural resources also helps nurture social and political relationships through migration (Fukui 2001). The government is of the view that villagization, through the promise/actual provision of irrigation water, the government argues, would permanently 'eradicate' ecological uncertainties, thus promote a settled and more intensive mode of livelihood. As the Bodi mainly migrate for socio-political reasons (Fukui 2001), hindrance of migration through sugar industrialization and villagization will severely hinder socio-political and cultural interactions enabled by pastoral migration. By corollary, the processes of land privatization and formalized property rights come into play.

Land classification and use regimes are very complex in Bodi land. Fukui (2001: 6) states that the Bodi classify their land in "extreme detail" and that "when walking through Bodi land not twenty minutes' elapse before arriving at another location with its own unique place-name...it is safe to estimate that a place-name exists within a parcel of land every four to five kilometers." There is also difference in property rights and resource access regimes across their territory. While "the first person to clear a riverbank forest and highland secondary forests by converting them into shifting agriculture fields retains the rights to continued use, but by giving advance notice it is possible for anyone to gain access" (Fukui 2001: 3–4). However, such arrangements do not prevail when it comes to grazing lands.

Despite such differences and complexities in land use and tenure arrangements, the government promotes codified land privatization, in the name of increasing holding security and thereby increasing investment on land.[24] Numerous authors have examined the impact of land certification in highland parts of Amhara, Oromia,

---

[24] Interviews: Expert, Agriculture and Natural Resources Bureau, Salamago *Woreda;* Development Agent, Salamago *Woreda*; Expert, Agriculture and Natural Resources Bureau, Salamago *Woreda* (4 August 2016).

SNNP and Tigray regional states, especially as it relates to land management and investment on land and agricultural productivity (Deininger et al. 2011; Deininger and Jin 2006; Dessalegn 2008; Holden et al. 2011; Mintewab et al. 2011). The reasoning here is that the peasant will have greater security to invest on the land, with positive consequences on productivity and land management.

This reasoning could not be applicable to the case of the Bodi even though local officials take it as the rationale behind the certification. The peasant/pastoralist intends to secure his land mainly from the state and market forces, and in Salamago state and market actors came with vigor (and desire to stay) only after 2011. It is only recently that the state significantly alienated land from, and interfered in the social and economic life of, the Bodi.

Indigenous knowledge and institutions have been utilized to manage the Bodi rangelands well in the past (Fukui 2001). There is ample evidence attesting that common property regimes through a range of norms, institutions and sanctions successfully and sustainably manage resources (for example, Agrawal 2001; Ostrom 2009). Despite the position advanced by those promoting privatization (Hardin 1968) and state actors, pastoralism has proved flexible and adaptive in its response to environmental change and in managing natural resources. This system will be rendered useless and local institutions will be destabilized and dropped in the process of privatizing rangelands (Wily 2011; Maasai in Kenya, Mwangi 2007).

This calls for new institutions and norms which are appropriate to codified property rights and privatized land holdings. These norms and institutions should cater for expected increase in inequality (Mwangi 2007) and contribute to preventing/managing conflicts generated by the exclusivist resource use regimes promoted through privatization. The rise and entrenchment of such norms and institutions takes time, a *luxury* the government does not have due to the securitized understanding of development and the *resolve* to eradicate poverty as quickly as possible (Fana 2015).

Sugar industrialization and villagization constitute part of the modernization project the Ethiopian government is advancing in the lowland periphery (Makki 2012). The outgrower scheme is a par excellence example of this modernizing ambition of the EPRDF and the Ethiopian government. The Bodi are being 'transformed' from practicing a 'backward' agro-pastoral mode of production to becoming outgrowers to a sugar industry in less than a decade. They are being fully integrated into the state's developmentalist projects in the lower Omo valley. One downside of this arrangement is that they have only one buyer, the Ethiopian Sugar Corporation. This clamps down on the possibility of any form of price negotiation. Moreover, as the same buyer does all the agronomic activities for them, the gains the Bodi could get from the arrangement are further reduced (for example by more efficient and cost effective practices). This also creates the possibility that the money the Bodi get from the Sugar Corporation will be regarded as 'easy money' and gets spent on alcohol and other consumables, rather than contributing for meaningful household consumption and asset accumulation.[25]

---

[25] This is from personal observation since 2011.

Furthermore, the codification of property rights allows land to be leased, bequeathed and inherited, not sold, according to land laws of the region (SNNPRS 2007). The Bodi accept hereditary rights through patrilineal line when it comes to flooded land only. Individuals outside this patrilineal line could use the land, provided that they engage in a prior arrangement to share part of the harvest with the landholder (Fukui 2001). Individuals who clear a certain land will have the exclusive right to continually use that land for shifting cultivation (Fukui 2001). However, long fallow years could lead to regeneration of the original vegetation, and changes in ownership of the land if a different person clears the land.

Not recognizing such distinctions and complexities in the land categorization of the Bodi, villagization enables transfer of rights to use a particular land through lease or inheritance (for a similar case in Afar, where the local culture does not support such notions). Codification of land rights implies that uncertified land is 'government land' and that in due time there will be no possibility for the Bodi to clear new forest lands for shifting cultivation. This could result in the fragmentation and subdivision of the land holding after a generation. It remains to be seen if the Bodi will get prepared for such a future and if the 1.5 ha (1.25 for farming and 0.25 for homestead) households get will be enough after getting divided amongst siblings.

On top of this, the villagization and certification of land are bringing a qualitative change to dynamics at the household level. A Bodi man could marry more than one wife, depending on his wealth (i.e., more cattle mean better capacity to pay bride price). The first will be the senior wife, and the second, third will follow her lead and assist her in household chores and cultivation. In the villagization scheme however the second and third wives are considered as separate households.[26] During certification, the government, intentionally or not,[27] went a notch higher and is giving separate certificates for the second/third wife, without the husband being included in the certificate. This practice makes the second, third wives sole owners of the land legally, while that could not be accepted by the culture.

This appears to be giving gender equality often lacking in formal property rights in Ethiopia (Crewett and Korf 2008), but in practice leaves the first wife at a disadvantaged position economically, against the culture. This is particularly the case considering that the Bodi' social organization is centered on the *tui*, the smallest social unit, basically made up of a husband, wife/wives and their children. This unit also "expresses a communal group or lineage principled on the patrilineal line" (Fukui 2001: 5). He further states that "The Bodi greatly fear extinction of their *tui*." By offering the certificates jointly to the husband and first wife and solely to the

---

[26] The number of FHH indicated in footnote 16 and 18 are second/third wives, not female headed households in the real sense of the term. In Afar female headed households, considered incapable to farm equally with men, get smaller land holdings. In Bodi, as there is no clear distinction between MHH and FHH all get equal land holding.

[27] Here the government is disapproving of the local culture and de-legalizing the second/third wife. Zone and *Woreda* experts state that the husband's name and photograph should come first on the certificate of the MHH, while it comes second on the certificate of his second/third wife (wives). Legally speaking, it should not matter whether it comes first or second. In practice however the husband's name and picture does not appear anywhere on the certificates of FHH.

second/third wives, the land certification scheme is countering the basic social organization logic of the Bodi.

Conclusion

The project of building a developmental state in Ethiopia is justifying a greater intervention of the state in the economy. An examination of South Omo's economy immediately reveals that what we have there is state capitalism.[28] The model of state capitalism growing in Ethiopia in recent years is the traditional one, in which the government owns and manages a state-owned enterprise (SOEs), what Musacchio and Lazzarini (2014) dub Leviathan as an entrepreneur. Two such enterprises established to fulfill the developmental ambitions, and often portrayed as embodying the Ethiopian developmental state project, are the Ethiopian Sugar Corporation and the Metals and Engineering Corporation (MetEC). Both are active in South Omo. The former is the main actor, and it brought with it MetEC as a contractor to build some of its factories.

This mode of capitalism is not only alienating land from the native ethnic groups of the area. It is also interfering in their social, political, cultural and economic life. The most important and immediate changes are occurring in the realm of land tenure arrangement and property rights regime, through the villagization scheme. The government is enforcing a codified, privatized and exclusivist land holding system to villagized households, and thereby homogenizing the very detailed and complex classification of land use by the Bodi. With this, local knowledge of land use and classification is being eradicated. Moreover, villagzied Bodi households are made to serve as outgrowers to the Corporation. This is transforming the Bodi, a pastoral community with sporadic monetized market interaction less than a decade ago, into active players in the state capitalist mode of accumulation permissible in their locality.

References

Agrawal A (2001) Common property institutions and sustainable governance of resources. World Development, 29(10):1649–1672

Asnake K, Fana G (2014) The expansion of the sugar industry in the southern pastoral lowlands. In: Dessalegn R, Meheret A, Asnake K, Habermann B (eds) Reflections on development in Ethiopia: new trends, sustainability and challenges. Forum for Social Studies, Addis Ababa, pp 247–268

Central Statistical Agency (2008) The 2007 population and housing census of Ethiopia: statistical report for Southern Nations, nationalities and peoples' region. Addis Ababa, Ethiopia

---

[28] State capitalism is defined here in the manner used by Musacchio and Lazzarini (2014: 2): "*the widespread influence of the government in the economy, either by owning majority or minority equity positions in companies or by providing subsidized credit and/or other privileges to private companies. The new varieties of state capitalism differ from the more traditional model in which governments own and manage state-owned enterprises (SOEs) as extensions of the public bureaucracy. We refer to this traditional model as Leviathan as an entrepreneur*" (Musacchio and Lazzarini 2014: 2).

Crewett W, Korf B (2008) Ethiopia: reforming land tenure. Rev Afr Polit Econ 35:203–220

Deininger K, Jin S (2006) Tenure security and land –related investment: evidence from Ethiopia. Eur Econ Rev 50:1245–1277

Deininger K, Daniel AA, Tekie A (2011) Impacts of land certification on tenure security, investment and land market participation: evidence from Ethiopia. Land Econ 87(2):312–334

Dessalegn R (2008) The peasant and the state. In: Studies in agrarian change in Ethiopia: 1950s–2000s. Addis Ababa University Press, Addis Ababa

Fana G (2015) Securitisation of development in Ethiopia: the discourse and politics of developmentalism. Rev Afr Polit Econ 41(sup1):S64–S74

Federal Democratic Republic of Ethiopia (FDRE) (1994) Constitution of the Federal Democratic Republic of Ethiopia. Addis Ababa, Ethiopia

Fukui K (2001) Socio-political characteristics of pastoral nomadism: flexibility among the Bodi (Mela-Me'en) in Southwest Ethiopia. Nilo-Ethiopian Studies 7:1–21

Galaty JG (2011) (Non) Rational Choice, Paper presented at the Workshop organized on the Occasion of the 60th Birthday of Gunther Schlee, Roundtable on ——Rational Choice and Challenges, 10–12 July 2011

Hardin, G (1968) The tragedy of the commons. Science 162:1243–1248

Holden ST, Deininger K, Hosaena G (2011) Tenure insecurity, gender, low-cost land certification and land rental market participation in Ethiopia. J Dev Stud 47(1):31–47

Human Rights Watch (2012) What will happen if hunger comes?‖ Abuses against the indigenous peoples of Ethiopia's lower Omo Valley. Retrieved from <http://www.hrw.org/reports/2012/06/18/what-will-happen-if-hunger-comes-0>

Li TM (1999) Compromising power: development, culture, and rule in Indonesia. Cult Anthropol 14(3):295–322

Makki F (2012) Power and property: commercialization, enclosures, and the transformation of agrarian relations in Ethiopia. J Peasant Stud 39:81–104

Markakis J (2011) Ethiopia: the last two Frontiers. James Currey, Oxford

McCann J (1995) People of the plow: an agricultural history of Ethiopia, 1800–1990. University of Wisconsin Press, Madison

Meles Z (2011) Speech at the 13th Annual Pastoralist Day of Ethiopia. Jinka, South Omo, Ethiopia (January 25, 2011). Retrieved from 14 January 2014, from: http://www.mursi.org/pdf/Meles%20Jinka%20speech.pdf

Mintewab B, Kohlin G, Mannberg A (2011) Trust, tenure security, and land certification in rural Ethiopia. J Socio-Econ 40:833–843

Mulugeta GB (2014) In: Mulugeta GB (ed) A delicate balance: land use, minority rights and social stability in the Horn of Africa. Institute for Peace and Security Studies, Addis Ababa University, Addis Ababa, pp 309–314

Musacchio A, Lazzarini S (2014) Reinventing state capitalism: leviathan in business, Brazil and beyond. Harvard University Press, Massachusetts

Mwangi E (2007) Socioeconomic change and land use in africa. Palgrave MacMillan, New York

Ostrom, E (2009) A general framework for analyzing sustainability of social-ecological systems. Science 325(5939):419–422

Scott JC (1998) Seeing like a state: how certain schemes to improve the human condition have failed. Yale University Press, New Haven

SNNPR (2007) The Southern Nations, Nationalities and Peoples Regional State Rural Land Administration and Utilization Proclamation (No. 110/2007). Debub Negarit Gazetta

Tewolde W, Fana G (2014) Socio-political and conflict implications of sugar development in Salamago Wereda, Ethiopia. In: Mulugeta GB (ed) A delicate balance: land use, minority rights and social stability in the horn of Africa. Institute for Peace and Security Studies, Addis Ababa University, Addis Ababa, pp 117–143

Tewolde W, Fana G (forthcoming) The developmental state in South Omo: sugar industrialization, politics of development and conflict. In: Dereje F, Tronvoll K (eds) The Ethiopian developmental state: consolidating peace and emerging conflicts. James Currey, Oxford

Turton D (1979) A journey made them: territorial segmentation and ethnic identity among the Mursi. In: Holy L (ed) Segmentary lineage systems reconsidered, vol 4. Department of Social Anthropology, Queen's University Papers in Social Anthropology, Queen's University, Belfast, pp 119–143

Wily AJ (2011) The law is to blame: the vulnerable status of common property rights in Sub-Saharan Africa. Dev Chang 42:733–757

Yidnekachew A (2015) Policies and practices of consultation with pastoralist communities in Ethiopia: the case of Omo-Kuraz sugar development project. In: Yohannes A, Mahmmud A (eds) The intricate road to development: government development strategies in the pastoral areas of the Horn of Africa. Institute for Peace and Security Studies, Addis Ababa, pp 274–297

Chapter 5
The Struggle for Land Restitution and Reform in Post-Apartheid South Africa

Henry Wissink

Introduction

This chapter provides a historical description of the process through which land systematically fell into the hands of the colonial rulers during the 19th and 20th centuries. As with many other post-colonial states in Africa, land reform in South Africa is just as complex and difficult. The complexity does not only have to accommodate the land hunger problem, and agitation for land ownership, but the drafting and implementation of land tenure, restitution and redistribution policies to address the diverse challenges confronting land reform in South Africa. Furthermore, this was a critical requirement in the context of a democratic constitution that was sculpted to transition peacefully into a democratic state or much desired and still illusive "rainbow nation". To prevent post-apartheid conflict and in particular "land-grabbing" actions that would have the potential not only to destabilise the state, but the very productive agricultural economy, these actions were critical to the ruling part and for the country. This chapter also provides an overview of the existing policy frameworks and progress towards the achieving the outcomes that proposes to deal with the vexing problem of land reform and restitution facing South Africa.

H. Wissink (✉)
School of Management, IT and Governance, University of KwaZulu-Natal, Durban, South Africa
e-mail: wissinkh@ukzn.ac.za

© Springer International Publishing AG, part of Springer Nature 2019
A. O. Akinola, H. Wissink (eds.), *Trajectory of Land Reform in Post-Colonial African States*, Advances in African Economic, Social and Political Development, https://doi.org/10.1007/978-3-319-78701-5_5

The Historical Backdrop to the Land Question in South Africa

South Africa is a country consisting of many cultures, today known by its citizens in the post-apartheid era as the "Rainbow Nation", which is a popular slogan that was supported by the first democratic president, Nelson Mandela. South Africa has a history of late colonisation of Dutch, French, and English settlers during the 17th and 19th centuries. Before that there is scant history on how much of the land really belonged to various early indigenous people, tribes and ethnic groupings. The early aboriginal indigenous people – the San Bushmen and Khoikhoi, otherwise known as the Khoisan people were joined by the arrival of Black tribes and later Europeans to make up what is currently known in present day South Africa's multi-cultural population, with thirteen official languages, all stemming from the multi-cultural and -linguistic groups. Briefly speaking, the Khoisan lived in the region for millennia, while black Africans are descendants of immigrants who have migrated from the more northern regions of Africa, and who started entering the region currently known as South Africa about 1700 years ago (RSA 2015/16). People who are generally referred to as Coloured descended from these groups, as well as people who were brought to South Africa as slaves from Madagascar and the East Indies by the Dutch East Indian Company. Furthermore, South African mining and agricultural entities (farmers) also brought in slave labour from India and China who arrived in the nineteenth and early twentieth centuries, and today make up significant groupings in the country.

Early Migration and Habitation in South Africa

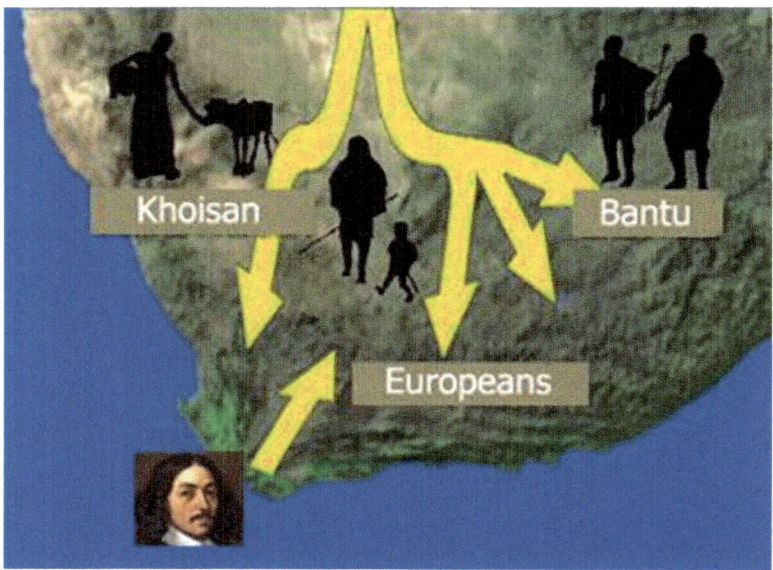

Source: SA Yearbook (2011/12)

Apart from the fact that European settlers colonised South Africa, and gained significant control of huge portions of the land during this period, South Africa has had a long history of conflict and wars that ultimately determined what we find today as a much skewed dispensation of land ownership, use and beneficiation of the elements associated with land ownership amongst its various population groups.

The question of land ownership and history remains a sensitive and highly emotional one, and started during the early period of colorial domination and early political and military driven campaigns (wars) to gain control of land. This situation was reinforced when exacerbated during the dispossession programme given effect by the 1913 Natives' Land Act No. 27, and worsened during the era of apartheid when a similar forms of legislation effectively impoverished the non-white population, and in particular banished black people from their land to the far less fertile areas of the country. In 1936 the Trust and Land Act No. 18 was promulgated. According to Fourie (2000:1) these laws earmarked 87 percent of the land surface of the country for Whites, Indians, and Coloureds, but mostly for White European settlers. Black South Africans that on average generally made up 75 percent of the population, were given 13 percent of the country's land to occupy.

According to Fourie (2000:1) South Africa has created "…the largest ratio in the world of discriminatory land holding, either between races" or between 'haves and have-nots." She continues to state that these circumstances, aligned with the, and aligned with the reality of small portions of land made available for Black people, meant that the agrarian problem was exacerbated, and ultimately led to large informal settlements (squatter settlements), coming into existence in and around the larger cities and towns close to rural areas. For instance, the largest city in South Africa - Johannesburg, has approximately 360 separate informal settlements, resulting in the fact that the upgrading and formalisation of ownership and services, poses a major cadastral challenge, and continues to be the greatest challenge for South African land surveyors. The policy of apartheid also resulted in the situation where generally formal housing provision was not implemented for the whole population, creating enormous housing shortages in the cities and towns for poor citizens.

In the post 1994 period of the country's reconstruction and development the situation has improved quite significantly, but the set objectives of the government have not been achieved by far, as the struggle continues to redistribute the land legally, and to restore inequalities of the past. For instance, the government intended to build a million houses within 5 years. By early 1999 745,717 houses had been completed or were under construction, with 350,000 houses being completed alone in 1998. According to Fourie (2000), this compares very well with other large scale housing programmes in the world, for instance in Cuba they built 500,000 over 25 years and 85,000 in the first 5 years; and even in developed countries dealing with developmental issues such as Sweden, they built one million houses in 10 years, 250,000 in the first 5 years.

The 1913 and 1936 Land Acts allocated around 13 percent of the national land surface for Black South Africans, and following the formal establishment of Apartheid in 1948, these same areas were declared Homelands or 'Bantustans.' The South African government planned for these homelands to become independent states separate from the Nationalist South African state. This ideology was designed and promoted to relocate Black citizens from South Africa to these states. In addition, from 1950 onwards - a new ruling was superimposed on the 13 percent land allocation. Xhosa speaking Blacks could only live, own or occupy land in the former Transkei (name of the homeland – on the eastern seaboard below KwaZulu), whereas Zulu speakers could only live, own or occupy in the KwaZulu Homeland. Tswana people were limited to Bophutatswana. Subsequent to this arrangement, many Homelands were offered the 'independence' option. The Transkei, Bophutatswana, Venda and Ciskei, and started changing their cadastral systems, with different systems, giving rise to very complicate systems problems and creating multiple problems and implications for re-uniting these areas into the jurisdiction of South Africa in April 1994.

Sub-standard forms of land titles for Blacks, not already accommodated for in the freehold system were available in terms of the 1913 and 1936 Land Acts. In 1936 the South African Development Trust was created to keep in trust all the unallocated land within the allotted 13 percent. Only about 5 percent of KwaZulu Province was held by Black freehold owners, whereas the rest was assigned to the South African Development Trust as referred to above. The function of the Trust was to then allocate land to Blacks only, by virtue of a set of very restrictive title deeds. Firstly, the occupiers were granted permissions to occupy; secondly 99 year leaseholds which could be cancelled administratively; thirdly, the use of customary rights, and house and property rentals. The requirement was that a Black person needed to be the primary occupier, and often the state could reverse such allocations based on unacceptable 'political' behaviour or misrepresentation. Outside of these designated areas for the allocation of land to Black people, to those who did have possession of freehold that they had purchased or acquired prior to 1913. According to Todes (1997), it is estimated that approximately 3.5 million people, were removed from this land and land was consequently reallocated to white farmers, or entrusted to the South African government.

Other race groups such as the Coloured people also experienced forced removals from urban areas designated for White group areas, and businesses, and were forcibly removed as well. In some instances, people who have claims to ancestral land, taken by the early Afrikaner settlers during local wars, became indentured labourers on farm lands, and lost any form of entitlement over land, as the land was registered under the cadastral system in the name of White farmers. By implication, there were very few records or formally registered rights of such ancestral claims, other than oral history in many instances, and some recorded history in archives and other records. This would ultimately prove to make the process of land claims even more complicated. The situation was even more complicated by the fact that the Apartheid government wanted and needed Black labour in their cities and on their farms, and were forced to allow many Black people to work in and around major city centres and on farms. Around cities, land had to be made available for the creation of townships, with very little provision for formal registration of land deeds and the appropriate services and infrastructure within these areas such as Soweto (close to Johannesburg), KwaMashu close to Durban.

In 1991, on the eve of the establishment of the new democratic order in South Africa, the 1913 and 1936 Land Acts were abolished. This happened through the process initiated by the transitional government following the release of Nelson Mandela and the unbanning of the ANC and other political parties. The promulgation of the Abolition of Racially Based Measurements Amendment Act No. 133 followed. This was the start of a long and very arduous and complex journey of a new government, as there were more than 17,000 separate portions of legislation and public policy involved in effectively banishing racially based settlements and life in South Africa.

According to a study by Jacobs et al. (2011:6–8) tenure patterns in South Africa "…are complex and varied, due, in part, to the coexistence of statutory and communal (traditional) systems." The following forms of tenure can be distinguished:

Freehold Tenure Freehold tenure places full ownership rights to landowners. This implies that individuals, married couples in terms of the law, legal entities, such as companies or trusts, may own land in a "freehold tenure" and have a formal title deed as private landowners. This implies that they have the right to develop, sell the land, rent the land to any entity or person, bequeath the land in a will, use as collateral, and transact as a legal entity in which the land is registered, and/or exclude other persons from occupying the land within the limits of legislation.

Leasehold Land is assigned to an individual(s) or an organization for a specified period of time (including lengthy periods such as 99 years generally applied to the management of state or public land). Leaseholds are granted in lieu of a specified amount of money, and aligned with written lease agreements between the government (lessor) and the lessee.

Permission to Occupy (PTO) The Native Land Act of 1936 allowed a magistrate to grant rural Africans (Natives) applying for land a so called "Permit to Occupy" (PTO) as evidence that a portion of land can be occupied and utilised by the applicant. The PTO system operated independently and parallel to the deeds and cadastral land administration system in place today. Traditional leaders and/or authorities (tribal or community leaders) issued PTOs to occupants on public land. Although PTO's provided rights to occupy and utilize the land, the state still remained the owners of the land. The PTO system was declared unconstitutional during the mid-1990s, but PTO certificates are still awarded in some areas by traditional authorities. The problem with PTO's is that it is not recognized by banks as collateral property, and therefore renders the occupants unable to be empowered to pursue commercial and productive agriculture with the support of loan capital from the private sector.

Customary Land Land allocation and access to land, as well as the management and conflict resolution are done by community authorities. They are often tribal chiefs, or other traditional authorities according to customary norms of various people groups within what was known as the homelands. These norms are based on specific traditions, or previous decisions of local and traditional authorities, rather than the officially promulgated legal documents (laws). Allocation of lands by the local chief normally involves neighbors or other local leaders as witnesses. A membership fee may be charged. The application of the land as well as community rules are determined by the chief. Numerous forms of such customary land tenure processes and procedures exist in South Africa. Traditional systems, generally allocate land to men but not to women, which also impacts on the empowerment of women in agriculture.

Rental Land In both statutory and communal land tenure systems, landowners rent out their land, or portions of their land to tenants, formally or informally. These arrangements are made between the lessor and lessee, and determine period and rental amounts the tenant will pay. The landowner maintains ownership of the land, regardless of the period of occupation of the land.

Informal Occupation/Squatting Informal occupation and squatting may also be prevalent on land in either statutory or communal systems. However, people occupy land to which they have no formal or legal claim. The main difference between informal occupation and squatting is that squatting occurs on land belonging to a particular registered person or entity. Informal occupation on the other hand, happens on land not known to belong to anyone in particular, for example, and land under the state control.

Land Reform and Restitution in South Africa

According to Hall (2004:214–215), the issue of land reform and the factors that determine the political economy of land reform in most contexts, relate to the relations and distribution of resources among the three classes, namely "the proprietor of the land, the owner of the stock or capital necessary for its cultivation, and the labourers by whose industry it is cultivated". These relations are critical in determining land reforms and restitution (land policy), and how political decisions determine the allocation of public resources among these competing classes or uses. This approach to land policy is quite a challenge, as the government committed itself to de-racialisation of land ownership, but at the same time to commit the state to optimalising commercial farming in order to ensure that the maximising of food security and the gross domestic benefit within South Africa is maintained. At the same time the agrarian situation in South Africa are calling for serious attention, as rural development and the contribution that agricultural and other land uses can make to growing and ensuring job and sustainable employment and food security in the previous homelands is critical for the future of dealing with the land issue in South Africa, which is an important aspect of resolving one of South Africa's major issues. The mere fact that the inequity of land ownership can be addressed is an important aspect of transforming South Africa into a truly democratic state, and ensuring that all of its citizens feel that they have a stake in the future of the economy, and in this case the land based ownership economic opportunities. This needed to translate into new socio-economic relationships and opportunity to close the gap between the rich/privileged and the poor/disadvantaged members of our state, especially in the light of the lingering rural poverty situation.

According to Hall (2004:214), around 70% of people living in rural areas, lived in poverty, and among them there were around one million farm workers and their dependents, also resulting in a third of the population of South Africa living in of the land, mostly former homelands. According to a report of BSA (2015) between 1994 and 2011, South Africa transferred over 6.8-million hectares of land to people who were dispossessed under the system of Apartheid. This statistic represents 27% of the government's original target of transferring 24.5-million hectares by 2014. To refer to some of the details, that from 2009 to December 2011, about 823,300 hectares of land that was attained and allocated to 20,290 beneficiaries, as an improvement over previous years of performance. In addition, 76,368 land claims for approximately 2.9-million hectares of land in line with the stipulations of the Land Restitution Programme were dealt with. Of these claims 712 against 1845 claims amounting to 292,995 hectares, were settled between the period 2009 and 2011.

Evaluation of the Overall Progress of the Land Reform and Restitution Process

There are multiple problems associated with the multifaceted land issue in South Africa. According to the report of the BSA (2012):

> The process of acquiring and distributing a particular piece of land is often lengthy, and this escalates the cost of redistribution because the former owner stops investing in the land. Many of the farms are therefore in a poor state of repair at the point of acquisition.

In addition, there is often a decline in the productivity and development on these farms. This situation culminated into a recapitalisation programme (November 2010) aimed at increasing food production and job creation through a programme of commercialisation of small farmers. According to the BSA (2012), by December 2011, 595 farms were in programme of being rehabilitated, with the focus on reconstructing and improving infrastructure. The concerns of government were that without adequate and continuing support for and the development of farmers, the situation could again deteriorate in future.

In addition, the policy of a 99-year leasehold land allocation created an impediment to investing capital in the land, and that these farmers would choose to be given full ownership. The concern that government proffered in return was that it would often result in beneficiaries selling the land. More investigation is needed to determine the extent to which this situation will be limiting the success of the leasehold based transfer. Regardless of the dispensation of land reform being pursued, according to (Philips 2016) it appears that generally insufficient post-settlement support and the lack of suitable agricultural marketing means that most land reform recipient farmers are not developing their opportunities into sustainable farming entities. Philips (2016) continues to state that less than 5% of beneficiaries have benefited from either Comprehensive Agricultural Support Programme (CASP) grants or Micro-Agricultural Finance Institutions of South Africa (MAFISA) loans. Furthermore, only 11,000 new smallholder farmers have been established since 2009, against a target of 50,000.

In addition, much support has been provided to both emerging and established farmers through programmes such as CASP, Letsema, the Recapitalisation and Development Programme and MAFISA. Sadly, only a small number of the 5381 smallholders are involved in agribusinesses and only 3910 smallholder farmer are linked to significant commercial outlets and markets. It is proposed by Philips (2016) that to achieve the outcomes required, the small farmers require a more inclusive agri-business support programme platform that includes:

1. Favourable commodity pricing
2. Access to finance, that take into consideration the unique challenges these farmers face, including an overall risk assessment and plan to ensure the success of such financing operations.
3. Provision of technical expertise, farming and technological mentorship and training, and:
4. Contracted markets – that ideally should give preference to small farmers acting in a cooperative manner.

According to the report "…no convincing support package is yet in place; government initiatives tend to cause dependency, and the sector is struggling."

It is suggested that the government should rather consider providing improved and well-structured incentives for existing commercial farmers who are willing and declared proficient to mentor emerging smallholder farmers. It is also proposed that more support is needed for farmers who are struggling and inducements are needed for innovations and interventions to expand existing services and boost production and processing models that are aimed at conserving and natural resources and utilizing green and clean energy. From a food security point of view, it should be a priority to invest in agriculture and agro-processing in South Africa, taking into consideration that increasingly farmers and the viability of their farming operations are very dependent on global economic conditions and markets.

This, combined with challenges such as climate change, continuing droughts and insecurity around the future of land reform, the number of commercial farmers are declining with a resultant decrease in levels of production levels. This in turn has resulted in higher volumes of food imports and with the weakening exchange rate, rising food prices. New entrants into the agricultural sector are discouraged and naturally this has also lead to the decline of job opportunities and employment creation. It appears that South Africa's agricultural sector is now part of the downward spiral resulting from the combination of negative impacts and extremely difficult situation that has no easy solution.

On the other hand, and from a positive point of view, it appears that the current SA government is engages with the Agricultural Business Chamber[1] on policy and

---

[1] More information is available online at https://agbiz.co.za/

legislation that directly affects the agricultural sector, and in particular land reform and restitution issues. Agbiz engages in draft policies and may offer recommendations prior to promulgation of legislation. It provides government with advice on commercial and emerging farmers, agri-businesses, and on national food security problems and issues. It is not clear if government, Agbiz, and other key role players always agree on the direction and solutions encapsulated in policy proposals.

The National Development Plan - Policy Directives, Plans and Programmes for Land Reform

Broadly speaking, the SA Government strategy is currently informed by their Medium Term Strategic Framework (MTSF) for the years 2014 to 2019. This strategy is also informed by the National Development Plan (NDP) and by the New Growth Path (NGP), the South African Government principal policy plan and economic development programme. The MTSF focuses on achieving 14 outcomes generated from the NDP and the NGP, of which three are related to agriculture. They are:

1. Outcome 4: decent employment through inclusive growth;
2. Outcome 7: comprehensive rural development and food security; and
3. Outcome 10: protect and enhance our environmental assets and natural resources.

The South African economy already in recession due to two consecutive terms of negative growth. In addition, South Africa has an unemployment rate of 26.6% of employable persons, and has also recently been downgraded to a credit junk status during 2017, and according to Le Cordeur (2017),

> It is the second rating agency to downgrade South Africa to junk status, meaning certain international investors will have to pull their investments from South Africa or else they will be in breach of their portfolio mandates. It takes two rating agencies to make a country officially junk status for these rules to kick in.

On the bright side, agriculture and mining industry contributed positively to growth, but not enough to avoid the recession. In particular, the plans focus on agriculture and the agro-processing value chains as the major driver of future economic growth. The Agricultural Policy Action Plan (APAP) and the Strategic Infrastructure Project 11 (SIP 11) – Agri-logistics and Rural Infrastructure – are specifically poised to assist agriculture to produce this growth.

One of the limitations to agricultural development in South Africa is the problems related to land reform policy and legislation, which has a direct impact on investor confidence in the sector. It is widely accepted, in post-colonial and developing countries with skewed land ownership dispensations, that land reform is undeniably important. This matter is a highly complex, sensitive and problematic issue against the backdrop of our history. It is therefore imperative that we pursue land reform and restitution. The question is how to achieve equitable land ownership in line with the demographic realities of South Africa, without compromising agricultural development, productivity, and probably one of the biggest challenges that lie ahead of us - food security.

To date, the SA Government has implemented a few approaches or policy-models for land reform. They are as follows:

1. Department of Rural Development and Land Reform's (DRDLR) Green Paper
2. National Reference Group (NAREG) process on Land Reform
3. National Development Plan Model on Land Reform, and the;
4. Inter- Departmental Task Team on Outcome 7 of the MTSF.

The first principle essential to successful land reform is deracialising the agrarian economy. The second is in line with this transformative programme, and to create democratic and equitable land allocation, distribution and use within the rural areas primarily. This reform needs to include considerations of race, gender and class. In terms of the plan concerns were raised regarding the use of the term around the term 'land allocation', implying that government would still own large parts of agricultural land, but allocate it in accordance with a set of criteria and legal requirements, such as a 99-year leasehold. The third principle is sustained production discipline for food security. The other contention is that agriculture cannot be driven alone from a policy perspective, but needs to be driven by entrepreneurs who are prepared to risk investing their capital and skills with a strong profit motive. At the same time the important gaols are achieved such as food security and increased tax income to the state.

From an ideological perspective, there are still a few differences between Agbiz, but the important point is that these negotiations are taking place, even though there are many issues that still needs to be addressed in the relationship. By and large The SA Government has a political agenda to please its supporters, in terms of promises made for reconstruction, development, transformation and empowerment of previously disadvantaged communities.

According to Le Cordeur (2017), "…the goal of government in land reform negotiations is to promote social cohesion and development that is based on shared growth and prosperity, relative income equality, full employment and cultural progress." He continues to state that from 2012 to 2014, the NAREG on land reform, involving Agbiz, the government created 14 policy proposals. Agbiz conditionally supported 12 because they argued that they met the criteria for an open and competitive market based agricultural system.

According to Le Cordeur (2017), the first of the two policy positions which they had a problem with was:

• Implementing limits for private agricultural land ownership, and regulating ownership of agricultural land by foreigners. It is believed that foreign investment in agriculture is critical for the country and the land market. This position will be explored later when policy proposals are made in the final chapter of this book.
• The second policy proposal that is a concern is the idea of cementing the rights of people working the land. This was initially referred to as the '50:50 model'

that stirred up a lot of emotions among farmers, and became very polemic. Although the 50:50 model may have been abandoned for the moment the proposal for a farm equity scheme remains. The percentage ratios and the management model will be revisited, as proposed.

- Other policies have been developed from NAREG's 14 policy positions.

    a) The first one is the Spatial Planning and Land Use Management Act 16 of 2013. The law gives the Department of Rural Development and Land Reform (DRDLR) the power to pass Regulations in terms of SPLUMA (Spatial Planning and Land Use Management Act 16 of 2013) to provide additional detail on how the law should be implemented.

    b) The second is the Property Valuation Act 17 of 2014. This legislation "… provides for the establishment, functions and powers of the Office of the Valuer-General; and to provide for the regulation of the valuation of property that has been identified for land reform as well as property that has been identified for acquisition or disposal by a department."

    c) The Restitution of Land Rights Amendment Act 15 of 2014, which is now operational, and in particular provides for the amendment of the cut-off date for lodging a claim for restitution, which initially expired in 1998.

    d) The Expropriation Bill, passed by the SA Parliament on 27 October 2017, is designed to protect the state from having to pay 'extortionate amounts of money' to effect land restitution. The Expropriation Bill sets out the rules and administrative procedures by which the government can claim land 'in the public interest' and 'for public purpose'.

    e) The Extension of Security of Tenure Amendment Bill [B24–2-15] is currently being approved.

- Additional land reform-related legislation is also in the process of being drafted and considered. These draft bills still have to go through cabinet and the National Economic Development and Labour Council process before tabled before Parliament. These include the following:

    a) Electronic Deeds Registration Systems Bill that proposes electronic deeds registration process and system to fast-track property ownership and registration.

    b) Communal Property Associations Amendment Bill, to provide for clarity on the objective of communal property associations; to extend the application of the Act to certain labour tenants who acquired land; to provide for the establishment of a Communal Property Associations Office.

    c) Communal Land Tenure Bill, to predominantly provide for the transfer of communal land to communities; to provide for the conversion into ownership of land rights of communities that own or occupy such land; to provide for the transfer of ownership to communities and community members of land acquired by the State to enable access to land on an equitable basis.

    d) Regulation of Land Holdings Bill, which addresses land ownership ceilings and ownership of land by foreign persons or entities, and the concepts of an "offer" and "a right of first refusal" that may result in confusion. The Bill purports to attempt to grant the Minister a right of first refusal but places an obligation on a foreign owner to "offer" the right of first refusal to the Minister.

e) Preservation and Development of Agricultural Land Bill. This last aims to protect agricultural land from, among others, mining and urban sprawl, and to provide for agricultural regulation pertaining to subdivision and rezoning applications on high potential cropping land and on medium potential agricultural land, respectively; to provide for Protected Agricultural Areas; to provide for the use of agricultural land; to provide for other applications on agricultural land.

- One of the policy approaches according to Le Cordeur (2017), are alternatives suggested is for to consider the Namibian land reform approach of 'government right of first refusal'. This concept gives the Namibian government the first option to buy or not to buy commercial agricultural land that becomes available. Namibia has successfully transferred roughly 28% of its commercial farmland to emerging farmers. This success has been achieved by following the land market mechanism and was not due to land expropriation or other potentially harmful interventions.
- Many believe that it was necessary to suspend the original farm equity scheme concept, and to have it reviewed, and that an appropriately amended farm equity scheme concept still holds potential for orderly land reform. It proposes benefits for the creation of opportunities for commercial farmers to participate in land reform and help establish black farmers in partnerships. These commercial farmers will then in future be exempted from further land reform obligations and responsibilities. According to Thom (2006: 73), the nature of the schemes does not accommodate the financial interests of most farm workers, due to the fact that capital appreciation usually takes a long-time to realize. In addition, "…the clash of financial interests within equity schemes is an indication of the fundamental problem of partnerships between unlikely business partners… and farm workers do not know who to turn to when their rights on paper are not realized."
- Agbiz and the rest of the private agricultural sector are proposing a land reform system that enables an expedited transfer of land to black or previously disadvantage beneficiaries without significant interference and effects on land markets or investor confidence. At the same time, sustainable production on transferred agricultural land needs to be ensured through appropriate and effective training and support structures.
- The other issue that still needs quite a bit of attention is the notion of women and gender inequality as far as land and land ownership is concerned. This matter is also addressed elsewhere in this book, and should be given priority as a tool to empower in particular women who struggle with ownership issues, in a predominantly "patriarchal-agricultural" culture in South Africa. According to Jacobs (2004), in a study conducted among NGO's, states that "…despite some encour-

aging state initiatives, most informants felt that poorer rural women remained marginalized within the land reform programme and more generally. Needs for independent income, health, and personal security were emphasised, with secure access to land seen as potentially beneficial although not as strong a priority." She states that this should not be construed as a reason for ignoring the existing gains land rights for women, and that a "rural women's movement" is needed to continue to campaign for the rights of this group.

- Finally, whilst land reform and restitution is a policy area with its own set of specific objectives, it can be generally considered to also form part of the government policy and programme for broad based black empowerment (BBBE). Many proponents however argue that although it is critical that land ownership is addressed, and the continuing inequality and skewing of the land pattern in South Africa should be addressed, it may not be the most effective vehicle to assist the majority of South Africans to attain economic empowerment. According to Rumney (2005:17) "…Ownership of intellectual property, and the ability to use modern technology to advantage, is a source of wealth often neglected in discussions on ownership…"

Current Ownership Patterns in South Africa – What Has Been Achieved Since 1994?

The racial classification of land as 'white' and 'black' is still a reality in South Africa, but the current economic, demographic and environmental conditions do show a change in line with the South African government policies and programmes aimed at transforming the state. In the early 1990s just under 60,000 white-owned farms reflected 70% of the total area of the country (approximately 122,081,300 hectares of land). As per statistics below, in Table 5.2, we have seen the decline of farms that are commercially viable, and today there are just under 40,000 farming units covering about 67% of the land in the country (Walker and Dubb 2013). Increasingly quality of this land varies, with only 13% classified as being commercially and agriculturally productive. Just over a third of this land is located in the arid Northern Cape where 2% of the population lives. Most of these commercial farmers are white, and a small number of black farmers now own farms who have gained access to capital. Apart from some farmers who have been granted land through the reform and restitution (LRR) process, other black farmers are obtaining land outside of the provisions of LRR (Table 5.1).

State owned land is constituted from the following:

- 1% Other provincial, including schools, hospitals, agricultural
- 1.6% Other national, including Home Affairs Justice, Agriculture
- 0.4% Military, police, prisons
- 7% Conservation Areas

Table 5.1 Land ownership in
South Africa

122,081,300 ha	Percentage
Total	100
State (Other)	10
White Commercial	67
Black Communal	15
Remainder, including Urban Areas	8

Source: Walker and Dubb (2013)

Black communal areas are constituted from the following:

- 1% Former 'coloured' reserves
- 2% Ingonyama Trust (former KwaZulu)
- 2% Other customary lands held in trust by the state
- 10% Ex 'homelands' other than KwaZulu

Whereas other public land (remainder), including urban open space is constituted as follows:

- 2% Metro
- 6% Other, including non-metro urban areas

In accordance with a report and speech by the Minister of Rural Development and Land Reform in 2012, it was often claimed that in 1994, as a result of colonial occupation, followed by Apartheid, 87% of the land was owned by whites and only 13% by blacks. At the end of 2012 post-apartheid driven land reform policies and actions had transferred 7.95 million hectares back into black ownership, approximately equal to 7.5% of previously white-owned land (Nkwinti 2012). Redressing the historical and racial imbalances in land ownership is still one of the land reform's most vexing issues, and is still receiving urgent priority. However, it is also stated that the post-apartheid state currently owns 25% of the land (see Table 5.1 above) and redistributing this should be a first priority. According to Walker and Dubb (2013) if this can be added to the existing 7.95 million hectares in black ownership already acquired and a relatively unknown amount of land that black farmers are acquiring privately, the differences between white and black ownership will be quite dramatically reduced and in some provinces may even become come close to equitable ownership.

A very remarkable fact regarding the nature of and size of commercial farms, is that the number of commercial farms have declined quite dramatically over the past 100 years. Approximately 48_50% (half) of commercial farms have disappeared, with farm sizes increasing by approximately 100% (doubling in size). This is largely due to the fact that commercial farms are only viable when they are operated on a large scale or where the benefits of scale are optimal. The growing global pressures (export standards) and technological demand for agriculture to be globally and locally competitive has forced South African farmers to either consider selling or adding to their farmland in order to remain competitive (Tables 5.2 and 5.3).

Table 5.2 The changing agrarian structure of the South Africa 1910–2010

	1910s	1930s	1950s	1970s	1980s	1990s	2000s	2016+
Farm no.	76,622	101,299	112,305	79,842	64,540	59,289	43,322	<40,000
Total area '000 ha	77,042	84,339	88,150	86,814	85,862	82,404	84,301	+/− 84,000
Ave. farm size (ha)	1006	833	788	1094	667	1260	1946	>2000 ha +

Source: Moyo (2013:27). (2016+ added statistic sourced from Walker and Dubb (2013))

Table 5.3 Unemployment Statistics

	African	Coloured	Indian	White
1993	17	15.7	8.3	3.2
1997	27.1	15.2	9.8	3.9
2001	35.1	21.1	18.7	5.6
2005	31.1	22.3	15.6	4.9
2008	27	17.3	6.6	10.3
% change between 1997 and 2008	−0.3	13.4	−32.6	164.1

Source: Moyo (2013:27)

In the light of the statistics above, it is clear that the state does not own the majority of the land, and in some respects the land under its jurisdiction is either allocated to nature conservation, or forestry, and/or conditions not appropriate for farming purposes. The idea of further redistribution of these lands, may be possible in theory, but not in reality. Looking at the large and even recently growing number of Black South Africans that are still unemployed, the land reform and restitution drive is still not making a significant difference to their socio economic inequality and plight.

Conclusion

Land reform and restitution in South Africa has been a slow and somewhat painful and onerous process. What seemed like a moderately attainable task, and in particular for government to transfer land to previously disadvantaged people, using a variety of policy instruments, and hopefully a generally acceptable "willing seller – willing buyer" process, proved to be far more vexing and difficult to accomplish. Apart from the complexity of the process, South Africa is also guided by a constitution with enshrined rights and responsibilities, and promotes justice and equality for all in a new democratic dispensation. Inasmuch as some of the constitutional imperatives should receive priority, such as dealing with poverty and inequality, the Constitution is also the guardian of human rights, and promotes the Rule of Law in its broad sense. Land grabbing or expropriation without due processes, legal guidelines, and appropriate compensation becomes a very difficult and arduous process. Land grabbing in desperation and for the purposes of political expediency, may have occurred in some of South Africa's neighbouring states, but it has all proven to be disasterous when state leaders take matters into their own hands and force issues without appropriate and evidence based policy analyses on the issue. Amidst the recent debates on land exproprition without compensation, it appears that South Africa has adopted a healthy process of consultation between government and agri-business, NGO's and many other stakeholders in order to manage and resolve these issues, without compromising on the Rule of Law, food security and other constitutional requirements critical to a modern and liberal democracy. The process still remains painfully slow. Perhaps the future will be more effectively shaped if in the medium-term, the realities of skewed land ownership, inequality, poverty, combined with the increase in skill provision, and more efficient utilisation of people power can be utilised to optimise employment and economic development. Although responsible land reformation and restitution of land can never be abandoned, urbanisation trends point to increasing demands for sustainable livelyhoods within 'urban political economies' based on the accelerated development of professionally skilled people, the development of innovations and new technologies, and ownership of intellectual property. These factors can be combined with the promotion of entrepreneurial skills to take some of the pressures of government to ease land hunger issues, primarily stemming from unemployment and economic inequality. In the long term, this approach may be a far more sustainable solution to provide for improved employment and economic development opportunities to remedy the problems of inequality in South Africa, as land reformation and restitution actions have not produced the desired results to achieve significant socio-economic development in the majority of countries of the developing world.

References

Brand South Africa (BSA) (2012) Land reform: progress, challenges. Internet, https://www.brandsouthafrica.com/investments-immigration/business/economy/development/land-050612. Retrieved on 5 October, 2017

Constitution of the Republic of South Africa, No.108 of 1996. Pretoria: Government Printers

Fourie C (2000) Land and the cadastre in South Africa: its history and present government policy. Paper presented as a Guest Lecture at the International Institute of Aerospace Survey and Earth Sciences (ITC), Enschede, The Netherlands, 1st November 2000

Hall R (2004) A political economy of land reform in South Africa. Rev Afr Polit Econ 31(100):213–227. Available at: https://www.researchgate.net/publication/228855795_A_Political_Economy_of_Land_Reform_in_South_Africa

Jacobs S (2004) Livelihoods, security and needs: gender relations and land reform in South Africa. J Int Women's Stud 6(1):1–19. Available at: http://vc.bridgew.edu/jiws/vol6/iss1/1

Jacobs P, Lahiff E, Hall R (2003) 'Land redistribution', Programme for Land and Agrarian Studies. University of the Western Cape: Evaluating Land and Agrarian Reform in South. Africa Occasional Paper Series, No. 1

Jacobs K, Namy S, Aslihan K, Bob U, Moodley V (2011) Gender differences in asset rights in KwaZulu-Natal, South Africa

Landman JP (2003) Breaking the grip of poverty and inequality in South Africa 2004–2014. Current trends, issues and future policy options. Available at: http://www.sarpn.org.za/documents/d0000649/P661-Povertyreport3b.pdf

Le Cordeur M (2017) Breaking: fitch downgrades SA to junk status, Fin24. Available at: http://www.fin24.com/Economy/breaking-fitch-downgrades-sa-to-junk-status-20170407

Le Roux A, Augustijn PWM (2017) Quantifying the spatial implications of future land use policies in South Africa. S Afr Geogr J 99:1

Lipton M (1985) Capitalism and apartheid. David Philip, Cape Town

Marcus T, Eales K, Wildschut A (1996) Down to earth: land demand in the new South Africa. Indicator Press; Durban.

May J, Roberts B (2000) Monitoring and evaluating the quality of life of land reform beneficiaries 1998/99. Summary report prepared for the Department of Land Affairs.

Moyo S (2013) Land ownership patterns and income inequality in Southern Africa. Background paper prepared for World Economic and Social Survey. Available at: http://www.un.org/en/development/desa/policy/wess/wess_bg_papers/bp_wess2014_moyo.pdf

National Treasury (1996) Government Printers, PretoriaGovernment Printers, Pretoria

NDA (National Department of Agriculture) (2001) Strategic plan for agriculture. Government Printers, Pretoria

Nkwinti G (2012) Speech by the Minister of Rural Development and Land Reform, 2012 Policy Speech

Philips L (2016) The current status and future of land reform in South Africa. Farmer's Weekly, Volume 2016, Issue 16009, p. 6–7

RSA (1996) Land Affairs Vote 30; Estimates of National Expenditure 2003. Government Printers, Pretoria

RSA (2001) Determination of employment conditions in South African agriculture. Report by the Department of Labour, Regulation Gazette No. 7159; Government Gazette Vol. 435, No. 22648; Pretoria: 13 September

RSA (2015/15) Pocket guide to South Africa. History of South Africa. Available at: https://www.gov.za/about-sa/history

Rumney R (2005) Who owns South Africa: an analysis of state and private ownership patterns? In: State of the Nation 2004–2005. HSRC Press, Pretoria

Steyn L (2002) Land occupations in South Africa. Unpublished report to African Groups of Sweden, June

Thom B (2006) Reviewing farm worker equity schemes: a case study of Saamwerk wine farm in the Overberg region, Western Cape. Mini-thesis submitted in partial fulfilment of the requirements for the degree of Master of Philosophy (Land and Agrarian Studies). University of the Western Cape (UWC), Cape Town

Todes A (1994) Urbanisation and urban management in KwaZulu-Natal. Dev South Afr 11:541–554

Todes A (1997) Restructuring, migration and regional policy in South Africa: the case of Newcastle. Unpublished Ph.D. Thesis. University of Natal, Durban

Van der Walt L (2015) Beyond 'white monopoly capital': who owns South Africa? S Afr Labour Bull 39(3):39–42

Walker C Dubb A (2013) PLAAS – Fact Check No1. (ND). The distribution of land in South Africa: an overview. Available at: http://www.plaas.org.za/sites/default/files/publications-pdf/No1%20Fact%20check%20web.pdf

Wolpe H (1972) Capitalism and cheap labour-power in South Africa: from segregation to apartheid. Econ Soc 1(4): pp. 425–456

Wonnacott R (2010) 90 Years of surveying and mapping. Position IT, Nov/Dec

Chapter 6
Land Policies in Africa: A Case Study of Nigeria and Zambia

Merioboroghene Mowoe

Introduction

Land, especially hoe land, which is a source of conflict, is seen as a primary factor of production in the agricultural sector. It plays an important role in developing and sustaining agricultural production, Hence, the importance of land in state's developmental agenda cannot be down played. The role of land is determined by land attainment, management and arrangement for the use of land ownership (Arusa 1998). However, the fact remains that land is the primary factor in the agricultural sector, which is the biggest contributor to the African economy. Therefore, issues of land policies do not focus only on the policies enacted, they also examine how government authorities manage land resources. In addition, these policies are directed at re-adjusting the institutional landscapes of rural and urban areas, which were distorted by foreign domination during colonialism (Lund and Boone 2013).

During the pre-colonial epoch, land in the traditional rural areas of Nigeria and Zambia, were seen and known as common properties, because it was owned by all who lived in the community (Helliker and Murisa 2011). Land was seen as a joined property owned by families and clans, which left no space for privatization. In addition, land was believed to belong to the rich and the poor, the young and the old, the living, the dead and the unborn. In some ways, there was an ancestral lineage clinging to the lands of Africa, and were only acquired through inheritance and user rights of households (Helliker and Murisa 2011). Additionally, land administration varied across regions, because they were governed according to the norms, and needs of the tribes in the regions.

Currently, land issues in Africa generally, especially Nigeria and Zambia, have become a political, as well as an economic issue. This is due to the conversion of

M. Mowoe (✉)
Nelson Mandela Metropolitan University, Summerstrand, South Campus. Habede Road.,
Port Elizabeth 77000, South Africa

© Springer International Publishing AG, part of Springer Nature 2019
A. O. Akinola, H. Wissink (eds.), *Trajectory of Land Reform in Post-Colonial African States*, Advances in African Economic, Social and Political Development, https://doi.org/10.1007/978-3-319-78701-5_6

customary lands into leasehold lands, in order to increase land markets that currently exists. Such conversions are often motivated by ideologies of capitalism and industrialization (Brown 2005b). Thus, land conflicts in Zambia and Nigeria are deep rooted in the countries' history of colonization by the British. During this period, changes began to occur drastically in the areas of land, due to the expanding mining and agricultural industries that were taken place (Ekechi 2002). Once Britain extended her colonial rule to these societies, it began to divide the lands into Crowns, Reserve, and Trust lands. In Nigeria, the northern part was designated as crown lands, and the southern part became the Reserve and Trust lands. The same type of land division also took place in Zambia, and the purpose was to separate the natives from the white settlers (Mamdani 2008).

The crown lands were taken by the white settlers, because they were rich in minerals and natural resources, while the Reserve and Trust lands were given to the blacks for their livelihoods (Brown 2005b). The purpose of this division was to turn communal or customary lands to farm blocks for commercial use, and this was done at the expense of the native people losing their lands, and becoming landless. The European domination on African soil was motivated mainly by economic, political and social reasons, as they tried to expand their economy, as well as increase their political power in the world (Prothero 1913). In the past, customary land could not be traded or sold, but, ever since the invasion of colonialism on Zambian and Nigerian soil, the conversion of customary land has become a means of transferring land to a land administration system that recognizes land as a commodity, to increase their land markets.

Due to colonization, Nigeria and Zambia are experiencing land alienation, and concentration of landed capital in the rural areas, because of the conversion of land as commodity. In addition, insecurity of land tenure systems, land subdivision, informal land markets, and land dispossession have increased as a result of conversion (Lund and Boone 2013). According to Lund (2008), "the openness and contingency of land issues in Africa, focuses intently on questions that aim at knowing how, and to whose benefit settlements are reached, who has the capacity to enforce and endorse them, and how, and by whom they are challenged". With these questions in mind, Bernstein (2002) believes that there are two agrarian questions that need to be taken into consideration. The first is capital, which looks at industrialization and capitalism, and the second is labour, which looks at those who work manually on the lands (user rights).

Debates on agrarian change and rural politics have overlooked rural forms of mobilization, and action for land agrarian reform. Moreover, demands for lands by the poorer population are ignored, because they are seen as being morally and economically problematic, due to low productivity from small scale farmers, as a result of lack of support from governments and Non-Governmental Organizations (Helliker and Murisa 2011). Owing to land management predicaments at large, politics of land is seen to be saturated by a 'neo-patrimonial' culture, which derives from standards of arbitrary rule, which was established under the colonial regime (Ekechi 2002). This 'neo-patrimonial' culture, which appears to put women at a vulnerable position in acquiring land, seems to be ironic in the case of Zambia because, during pre-colonial times, their acquisition of land was based on inheritance of land through the matrilineal lineage, and not just the patrimonial lineage.

Nevertheless, there has been increased interest in research, and policy debates about Nigeria and Zambia's land tenure system, especially those that seem to be related to rural impoverishment. Despite the conversion of lands from customary lands to market-based lands, occasioned by colonialism, it looks like most of Africa, (especially Nigeria with the Bakassi incident, due to contested oil that was found in Peninsula along the Gulf Guinea), is under siege for land grabs, which is resulting in land insecurities (Tariebbea and Baroni 2010). Colonial-inspired dispossessions have created a new category of propertied agrarian capitalists in Nigeria and Zambia, which in most instances; were made up of minorities who dominated land policy. This is owing to the fact that governments since colonial period, continue to allocate land to settlers who had no prior claim to land on the basis of ancestral use, established occupation of the land, sweat equity, or market principles (Oshio 1990).

As a result, land redistribution and land reforms, are very important in Nigeria and Zambia, because it dilutes the influence and control of the propertied agrarian class, and enlarges the scope of economic and socio-political participation of a larger set of farmers, with smaller pieces of land (Lund and Boone 2013). Given the history of colonial land alienation, land reform is a prerequisite for agrarian reform, as well as economic development in Africa. However, until now, land issues of Nigeria, and Zambia continue to involve property that have implications of social and political relationship struggles, in addition to 'commodization' of land (Lund and Boone 2013).

This land-development nexus, and its associated effects have attracted scholars and public debates in the contemporary political economy of nation states, particularly in post-colonial societies like Nigeria and Zambia. It was soon discovered that equitable land distribution and management, are essential corollary of sustainable development. Apart from these, land has constituted a threat to enduring peace in these countries. Moreover, there has been ongoing competitions over ownership, resources, delaminating jurisdictions, and property divisions, due to the weak ownership of land, as a result of transfer of land control from local heads to colonial governments (Lund and Boone 2013). Consequently, to improve Nigeria and Zambia's land management and understand the evolution of current land issues, it is important to examine the history of land tenure system in these societies, so as to grasp the factors responsible for the policy shift. For this reason, this paper will focus on examining the historical colonial context of land tenure systems in Nigeria and Zambia, and exploring how institutional pluralism affects land tenure system in Nigeria and Zambia.

The land-development nexus is important because, improvements in Zambia's economy and Nigeria's economy is drastically needed to increase well-being of the people. One way of looking at this is to ensure proper management of these lands, and the establishment of land policies, because land is the biggest contributor to the African economy, due to their agricultural and mining industries. Moreover, when looking at land, the focus is not only on the policies and management of land. Jurisdiction, land governance, property rights, the positions of authorities over land,

land resources, institutional landscapes of national and local governments are important aspects that must be taken into consideration. In addition, some scholars such as Sam Moyo, Mahood Mamdani have shown that African countries could only move forward by completely dismantling the policies they inherited from their colonial powers and starting again.

Theoretical Framework

There are two established theories of land tenure systems that need to be considered when undergoing a country-specific case study. The first is the neoclassical theory, which supports, and looks at the issue of land tenure from a methodological individualist's point of view. It stands on the idea that economic and market forces will allocate land, as well as natural resources to their most efficient users, through a market mechanism (Walrasian auctioneer) within a general equilibrium analysis. Accordingly, land would be sold or allocated to the highest bidder, which would be determined by the equilibrium price vector, where the amount of land available in a country, equates with the amount demanded by the people of that country. In the long run, this would ensure the efficient use of land (Dadzie 2007).

The second theory of land tenure system, which is the institutionalist theory or view, supports the traditional approach to land tenure system. In this case, it is believed that the traditions, or institutions that exist within a culture, are very significant to the active roles of a nation. Furthermore, they argue that, land tenure systems originated from the heritage of African societies and the ceremonies that ensure that land is used in accordance to the laws, or code of the society (Dadzie 2007). Furthermore, institutionalists believe land tenures are found within cultures, and they are part of factors of production, and that it is both instrumental, (in the sense of feeding the community and contributing to life) and ceremonial, (in the sense of how they govern the way land is passed through lineages) (Dadzie 2007).

It becomes important to first conceptualize land tenure before determining the most applicable theory. This is because land tenure, as a concept, "is the relationship between people whether customarily, or legally defined, or groups with respect to land" (FAO 2002). Nonetheless, land tenure systems only work once there is an understanding of its rights, interest, and property, because "it is an institution invented by societies, and nations to regulate, and govern behaviour" (FAO 2002). Land tenure is an important part of social, economic, and political structures of a country, making it very multi-dimensional. Moreover, when looking at land tenure systems of a country, one has to look at the interests it constitutes in the country. This is so, whether it is overriding (when a country has the power to allocate land), overlapping (when different parties have different rights to the same land), and complementary (when different groups or parties share the same interest to the same land) (FAO 2010).

According to Johnson (1972), a supporter of neo-classical approach to land tenure systems,' for land to facilitate wealth in a country, three things must be present; there must be a clear definition and allocation of property rights, the income generated from the lands must create incentives for people to value the use of their land, and there should be a reduction in the number of land sold to increase the equilibrium level of investment in a country, which in the long run, will increase consumption, expanding the economy. Nonetheless, land tenure systems do not only affect rural household livelihoods, and the ability to produce for their subsistence and markets. It also affects their socio-economic status, their incentive to work and use sustainable land resource, as well as their ability to self-insure, and have access to financial markets (Tikabo 2003; Platteau 1992). This issue of land tenure systems in Africa and other developing countries has resulted in a debate on how to encourage economic, social, and environment goals of land (Tikabo 2003). The institutional theory, which supports traditional land systems of land tenure, will be used in this paper to provide understanding and perspective on the allocation, and use of land.

Overview of Land Tenure Systems

Land is an important natural source that supports human activities, and it is linked to people's economic, and social interests. It is from land that a lot of nations, especially developing nations, derive most of their economic resources from. For countries to properly utilize their lands and land resources, proper land policies and tenure systems need to be governed efficiently, and facilitated appropriately. Land policies, and tenure systems are seen, as an integral part of socio-cultural framework of every country (Bashar 2008). Therefore, it becomes pertinent to understand the term, land tenure system. Land tenure refers to legal regimes or organizations in common law systems, and represents the planned change in the terms and conditions (Adams et al. 1999). It is related to land that is held by an individual, and determines who uses the land resources for a specific time. Under these conditions, these resources are employed (Garvelink 2012). 'Land tenure system is seen, as a right to hold property, and it is part of an ancient hierarchical system of holding land' (Garvelink 2012).

According to Famoriyo (2002), "land tenure is a systematization of the rules, which function by specifying what different classes of persons may, or may not, or can, or cannot do with reference to the occupancy, use and mistreatment of land, or disposition of land." These rules define the rights, privileges and duties of people in relation to each other with reference to land. According to FAO (2002), there are four concepts of land that need to be considered, when looking at land tenure systems in Africa. The first is freehold, which is a western concept that implies a country's absolute control over the management, use, or dispossession of a piece of land. Leasehold, which is the second concept, stipulates that land can belong to one person through contractual agreement, and at the same time be leased to another entity for a fixed period of time. The third concept, statutory allocations, holds whereby state land is held by virtue of some statutory provisions, and is allocated for the use of some legally constituted body. The last is customary systems, whereby tenure rights are controlled and allocated according to traditional practices.

There is an integral need for land reforms in Africa. Land tenure reforms are needed for the redistribution of lands, which results in a change in the size of ownership, and improve the quality of tenancy contracts. Moreover, land tenure reforms were proposed for eradicating the obstacles to economic and social development, which arose from the shortcomings in agrarian structure. In addition, land reforms build the path to achieving economic growth, ending income inequality, achieving food security, and political, social and economic stability. However, for land reforms to be implemented successfully, land tenure reforms must be built on a meticulous understanding of livelihood strategies of those intended to benefit, the adequacy of land tenure laws, and how administrative support should be practiced (Adams et al. 1999). The administration of land tenure systems required an assessment of the structure and processes for the determination, archiving and delivery of land rights, and the systems through which general oversight of the performance of the land sector, is managed (African Union 2009). However, this is not the case for most African countries.

Land Tenure Systems and Policies in Africa

Africa comprises of 54 countries, most of which have boarders that were drawn during colonialism. In pre-colonial African communities, land tenure systems of Africa were shape by traditions of ancestral lineage. Since then, the traditions have been affected by decades of colonialism, and 'post-independence government interventions'. Also, these traditions continue to evolve and change due to cultural interactions, demographic pressures, socio-economic change, and political processes, which seems to be a major contributor (Cotula 2007). These wild changes affected land tenure systems across the regions of Africa, and created room for modern policies that allowed investments and agricultural developments, at the expense of landowners' tenure security. Furthermore, African States have taken it upon themselves to regulate land relations, either through nationalization or registration programmes that aim at promoting privatization (Delville 2007).

Recently, energy crises, and high food prices have been seen, as global scramble for Africa's cheap available lands; hence, the importance of land and property rights for all can no longer be ignored, particularly in Africa (Wachira 2008). With lack of access to secured land tenure for all Africans, the spirit of universal declaration of Human rights cannot be achieved. Land ownership represents more than security and status to people. It is seen as a source of livelihood, and the key to further economic developments in Africa. Due to the failure of African governments, to ensure the availability and accessibility of land to its people, with properly established tenure reforms, this has locked African nations into cycles of poverty marginalization, feeding discontent, thus fueling discord and highlighting divisions in society (Wachira 2008). There is a widespread argument that Africa can only develop, if the land tenure, consisting of 90% of Africa's land resources, are integrated into the leasehold tenure system, which is founded on the principles of individualism

(Brown 2005a). Owing to the overlapping of rights over ownership of land resources, it is believed that the idea of implementing the leasehold tenure system would be efficient.

Regardless of this, the problem with African government's land tenure reform is that, it does not pay close attention to the legal status and economic activities of the people, especially the poor and the defenceless, who are often disproportionately dependent on land resources. Despite the complications, tenure reform is needed for people to sustain gained access to land and its resources (Adams et al. 1999). Moreover, the sensitivity and complexity of land tenure issues, and concentration on land redistribution, have caused some governments in Africa to neglect tenure reform. According to the FAO (2010), access to arable land in Africa is declining, due to uneven land redistribution, which seems to be persistent in the delivery of equitable land reform in Africa, especially Southern Africa. Land markets, which are seen as serving a purpose in the African economy, are distinguished by large disparities between countries and sub-Saharan region, which seems to be revealing diverse trends in rates of the land distribution, and various land tenure systems employed. These disparities range from radical land distribution to government, using moderate to low measures in protecting the land rights of marginal groups.

Consequently, due to the disparities, Africa's land economy mirrors a multi-faceted, and complex array of land governance, and administration systems (FAO 2010). The need for reform in Africa's land tenure system is needed, as land is significantly essential to the economies of African regions, contributes a major share of 65% to GDP and employment, and responsible for the livelihoods of the majority of the African population (Cotula et al. 2004). Due to inadequate land tenure systems and policies, land is becoming increasingly scarce as a result of pressures like demographic growth, commercialization and urbanization, that African land policies have been unable to deal with. For these reasons, there has been increased competition and strife for land between different groups, such as multiple land users like farmers, herders, fishermen urban elites and foreign investors (Cotula et al. 2004).

For example, the Migingo Island dispute, which has been brewing between Kenya and Uganda since 2004, has to do with the ownership of the Island that both countries claim. As a result, residents of the island, who have chosen to live on the island for fishing, have been suffering. Though most of the residents on this island are Kenyans, most of them have been arrested, and have been detained for fishing in 'Ugandan territorial waters' (Shaka 2013). Due to unreformed land policies and tenure systems, diplomatic efforts have been unsuccessful, and tension continues to be endemic between Kenya and Uganda over this fishing Island. This has furthermore threatened to spill over into military action between the two African nations (Shaka 2013). In relation to commercialization and capitalism, at the forefront of Africa's land policies and tenure reform, is the fact that African states have begun to lease out community lands to foreigners. Consequently, the lands that Africans fought to reclaim from foreign colonizers are being taken away from them through the system of purchase (Naluyaga 2013).

In Ethiopia, about 70,000 people from western Gambela region have been re-allocated against their will to new villages that lacked adequate food, farmland, healthcare, and educational facilities, due to the purchase of the land by Bangalore-based Karuturi Global Ltd., which will further lease 311,000 hectares of land from Ethiopia (Naluyaga 2013). Furthermore, "socio-economic change in many societies in Africa, have eroded the customary rules, and institutions that have traditionally administered land rights and policies, because of the misunderstanding of land reform by African governments" (Cotula et al. 2004). African governments have paid little attention to the distributive philosophies underlying tenure security. This is the case in South Africa, whereby the focus of land reform, adopted by the African National Congress (ANC), is to distribute 30% of arable land to the blacks, at the expense of white farmers, without regards to how this may impact badly on the economy of the country, and tenure security of the white farmers (Nicolson 2012). The complicity of the policy has resulted into food insecurity and land unproductivity in the Rainbow nation.

Owing to the misunderstanding of land reform, many countries, such as Zimbabwe, have experienced land tenure insecurities, whereby white farmers were forcibly removed from their homes and land, for inexperienced black farmers, who claim these lands as their own, forcing the white commercial farmers to leave the country. This has led to economic collapse and widespread poverty in the country (Aljazeera 2013). Dispossession of land from white farmers as witnessed in Zimbabwe and partly in South Africa, without pragmatic policy options in land utilization and sound management, would not resolved the land-development question. As noted by Nicolson (2012), Africa still has a lot of work to do, and a long way to go in reforming their land policies and tenure systems. From the different corners of Africa, it has been observed that, there were persistent struggle for land legislation to be properly implemented, and those who are dependent on land, such as farmers, rely on their country's local tenure system to gain access (Cotula 2007). Thus, when it comes to land tenure systems of African nations, there is usually a combination of statutory and customary entitlements, and numerous overlapping rights over the same land resources. Presently, African countries have sought to replace customary land policies with the modern ones they inherited from their colonial masters, which has made governments realize that laws that they make, must be built on traditional practices of the past (Cotula 2007). With the idea that traditional policies are as important as modern policies, there has been a shift in the policy thinking of African nations, to protect local land rights. There seems to be a better understanding of what should happen to the land tenure systems of Africa.

Land Tenure System: The Nigerian Experience

Nigeria, a West African nation, which is located in the tropics, is made up of a federation of 36 states, with a central government that plans for, and coordinates the economic programmes of all the states. Presently, Nigeria has a population density of 178.39 with a total land use area of 923,770 kilometers squared. According to the 2011 Worldstat, the available arable land of Nigeria, is about 365,000 kilometers squared, and land used as farmland, is about 785,000 kilometers squared. Traditional land tenure in Nigeria was based on customary laws under which land was considered communal property. In such system, and an individual could have 'user' rights to the land, and possesses the land he cultivated in his lineage or community area, as long as the land that was at use, benefitted tghe individual's family and the community (Bisong 2010). In addition, land was inherited, and the organization, and order of land rights were vested in the community through traditional authorities like the chiefs or clans, in accordance to the customary laws established (Oshio 1990).

Nigeria's land tenure system was controlled by several disparate legal systems during the period of 1900 to about 1978. During the 78 years, these disparities included customary law in the South, which promoted the idea of collective ownership among family and communities, Islamic law, and custom in the North, and the statutory land systems during Britain's colonial rule. The two land systems under Britain's colonial rule were mainly, private ownership in the South, which authorized the legal conveyance of land to be registered with government, and crown ownership in the north and south (Butler 2012). These disparities, according to Nigerian rulers, lacked a national land system and unification of land (Butler 2012). Before the 1978 Land Use Act, there were two principal land tenure systems. The first was Northern Land Tenure system (NNLTS), which was founded on the principle that, land belongs to the government, and private ownership of land should be prohibited. This freehold system of land was believed to promote economic growth and development, because land was accessed by government and investors, and compensation was paid for the development of land (Kayode 2010).

In the case of NNLTS, the premise of neoclassical theory of land system would stand, as it supported the idea of market forces allocating the land to the best user, in which case these best users would be the government and investors (Johnson 1972). The second was Southern Nigeria Land Tenure System (SLTS), and it was based on the principle that land belongs to communities, families and individuals. According to Kayode (2010), the SLTS did not aid development and economic growth, because access to land was both difficult, and costly, and also because of the 'Caveat Emptor rule', (which is a principle that states that the buyer is responsible for making sure that the property he or she is buying is in good condition and works properly) was present at the time. In this case, according to Johnson's (1972) premise on the neoclassical theory of land system, there was no best user. According to Barrow and Roth (1990), when looking at the SNLT and NNLT there was an interaction between the tool-using heritage of the Nigerian society, and the ceremonies that it had put in place after colonialism, to ensure that land is used in accordance with Nigeria's prosperity code.

Due to the potential crisis of land dissemination, which was caused by the establishment of multiple land systems in Nigeria, in 1977, the federal military government enacted the Land Use Act of 1978, which was later integrated into the constitution in 1979, to amalgamate the various land tenure systems of Nigeria

(Barrow and Roth 1990). Under the land use act of 1978, all lands were vested in the state through the office of military governor of each state, and all management, and administration of land use was through Nigeria's governments, which held land in trust (Mabogunje 2007). Thus, due to the nationalization of Nigerian lands, allocation of land rights in urban areas were administered by the governor's office while land rights in rural areas were administered by local governments.

In Nigeria, unlike most countries, chiefs were not used to administer land rights in rural areas, because it was believed that, "all forms of customary tenure systems, were backward, and not able to follow the demands of a fast changing agricultural sector" (Mabogunje 2007). It also prompted people to get a certificate of occupancy, in order for them to keep hold of their lands, which made land tenure in Nigeria unbearable (Butler 2012). This Land Use Act of 1978, had five principles that would constitute a major change in the structure of Nigeria's land tenure system (Famoriyo 2002). According to Famoriyo (2002), the principles of the Land Use Act of 1978 were:

1) To make possible, swift economic and social transformation of Nigeria through a 'rationalization' of land use.
2) To allow the state governments to bring about appropriate control and management of land for the benefit of the people
3) To curtail the incidence of high land prices from speculators
4) To remove a cause of social and economic inequality
5) To provide an incentive to development by providing easy access to land for the state and the people.

Although the Land Use Act of 1978 was meant to protect the rights of all Nigerians to land, and to promote both economic and social development, Mabogunje (2007) saw it as a clog in the wheel of Nigeria's development over the years, because it was embedded in the constitution, and he believed that the only way to reform was through an amendment of the constitution. The Constitution, as modified under the 1999 Constitution (sections 43 and 44), gave every citizen a right to immovable property, which included land, and could only be appropriated by government for public use, provided appropriate compensation is paid. It has also been found that there had been problems of resource degradation in common lands and property resource use (Bisong and Andrew-Essein 2010). However, Butler (2012) also realized that the Land Use Act of 1978, had significant effect on land market development, such as ending private ownership per se, and instituting statutory and customary rights of occupancy, that may be ignored in land market transactions. The second significant effect that Butler (2012) pointed out was that the Land Use Act contributed to the growth of informal markets in Nigeria.

According to Oseni (2012), the promulgation of the Land Use Act of 1978, was due to the diversity of customary laws on land tenure, and complication of applying the various customs of the different communities, as well as the rampant practices of fraudulent land sales. However, despite the Land Use Act (LUA), corruption still seemed to be rampant in Nigeria, when it came to administering land ownership and sales. As a result, the Land Use Act of 1978, failed to live up to its five principles

(Oseni 2012). The LUA of 1978 failed because the government was not efficient in its use of polices. Moreover, the act was not established to address the lack of uniformity in the laws governing land use and ownership, the issue of uncontrolled speculation in urban areas, the question to land rights by Nigerians on equal basis, and fragmentation of rural lands arising from the application of traditional principles of inheritance to population growth.

Consequently, the LUA began to restrict communal access to land, as state governors' had full control and trusteeship of land (Oseni 2012). Over the years, since the implementation of the LUA in 1978, there has been a series of bedeviled issues, which have resulted in injustices of land allocation, loss of land market, lack of equity, transparency, and inaccessibility of land to the urban and rural poor (Bashar 2008). Moreover, the implementation and application of the LUA with regards to access to land, has been rather inappropriate in terms of ownership. It has also engendered inadequate distribution of land among the Nigerian population, especially when it came to the underprivileged (Bashar 2008). By 2009, there was an amendment of the LUA of 1978 due to its failings.

The LUA was amended because of the exclusive power of the governor in relations to the alienation of, or possession of property. It was reviewed that the exclusive powers of the Governor, over ownership of land, had entitled only private persons and governments to a leasehold interest through the right of occupancy (Adefulu and Esionye 2009). The 2009 amendment aimed at removing the consent of the government in issues such as, sublease of land, transfer of land ownership, and customary and statutory right of occupancy. Moreover, it allowed a statutory and customary holder of land to alienate his rights to his own land through mortgage, transfer of ownership or sublease, without getting permission from the governor (Adefulu and Esionye 2009). In this case, the idea of a leasehold tenure system, in a country like Nigeria, seems more plausible and reasonable. According to Adefulu and Esionye (2009), "the proposed amendment seeks to restrict the requirement of the Governor's consent to solely alienation, via an assignment (which is an act of making a legal transfer of property or right), or sale." Despite the amendment of the 1978 Land Use Act in 2009 and the control the government had over land in Nigeria, land-related issues continue to be a problem today.

Land Tenure System in Zambia

Zambia, a Southern African nation located in the Sub-Saharan, has a total land mass of 752,614 kilometers squared. Of this land mass, customary land is estimated to be about 94 percent, while state land is estimated to be about 6 percent. The customary land area is occupied by 73 tribes led by 240 Chiefs, 8 of which are senior chiefs, and 4 are paramount Chiefs (Muleya 2006). Under the customary land tenure system, no one can claim to own land as a whole, because it is believed that land belongs to the community, and not the individual (leaving no place for privatization). In this case, the freehold system is emphasized. It is the duty of the Chiefs to ensure that every member of the community, capable of owing land, is given land. The issue of capability only applies to the state land, which uses the leasehold tenure system to allocate lands to individuals (Muleya 2006).

Zambia, like Nigeria, has two types of land tenures. The customary land tenure and the leasehold land tenure. Throughout history, Zambia has operated dual land systems. In 1924, during the colonial rule of the British, land was divided into three categories, Crown land, Natives reserves, and Trust land. The Native reserves and Trust lands were designated for the Africans, while the Crown lands, (which are very fertile and rich in soil) were given to the white settlers and farmers (Tagliarino 2014). Land rights in the Reserves and Trust lands were based on customary law, and the chiefs controlled the use and allocation of these lands. However, with the approval of the chiefs and central government, white farmers were given permission to cultivate, and to farm Reserves, for the duration of five years. Though, the British Government carved out portions of the Crown lands for Native trusts in 1947, Native Trusts remained under the customary tenure, and could not be converted to Crown land. However, after Zambia's independence, Crown lands were converted to state lands, and administered by the Ministry of Lands. All states' land was vested in the President, and state land transactions required the President's approval. Moreover, freehold tenure rights were converted to statutory leaseholds. However, Native Reserves and Trust remained under the customary tenure system (Tagliarino 2014).

In terms of statutory leaseholds, before a landowner or farmer can acquire land, they must first register their deeds. After registration, a consent to an application of ownership of land from the president, and a certificate of title, which is conclusive evidence of land ownership, must be attained. Unlike the customary tenure system, which uses a freehold system, statutory leasehold ensures that the owner of land is protected against ejectment or adverse possessions. However, in the case of the customary land tenure system, land ownership is assured only through a letter from the Chief, stating that the person in question has rights to a particular land (Loenen 1999).

Customary land is crucial to the survival and well-being of rural communities in Zambia, because it is the source of food, shelter, power and social status. However, in 1995, the Multiparty Democracy established a Land Act. This was done on the basis of new land reforms, and a more efficient system of tenure conversion in Zambia. This land act was established to attach economic value to under-developed lands, and reward productive use of the Lands through the creation of Private titles. The conversion of customary lands was justified on the basis that customary land tenure systems were insecure, and subject to severe limitations. Under the Land Act of 1995, all lands in Zambia, including customary lands, became vested absolutely in the president (Tagliarino 2014).

According to Loenen (1999), it seemed inevitable that customary rights would be replaced by statutory rights, due to the defects (lack of documentation) encountered, in the securing of land rights. For example, if the chief dies, or changes his opinion about ownership of land, there is a possibility that someone in the community, perhaps a foreigner, will be evicted. However, the conversion of customary tenure to leasehold tenure is both a long, and difficult process. It requires a cadastral survey, and the approval of both the local authorities and the President.

Moreover, ever since the Land Act of 1995 allowed for the conversion of tenure rights, it became uncertain whether the leaseholds on customary land would remain subject to local customs and traditions (Loenen 1999). However, despite the conversion, the Lands Act of 1995 has not made any significant changes to the land tenure system in Zambia. All lands in Zambia remain vested in the President, and it allows for land to be administered under two tenure systems, statutory and customary tenure (ZLA 2016). Furthermore, the Lands Act established a Land Development Fund, and introduced the Lands Tribunal, which is on the same level as the High Court, and handles all land related cases (Brown 2005a). This tribunal was established to encourage development of land through the provisions of funds.

The Land Act of 1995 was a necessity because customary tenure was characterized by different levels of transparency and accountability, which was dependent on the traditional leader, therefore creating space for corruption. Yet, there are no provisions for the reverse (Brown 2005a). Zambia is a heavily rural low-income population with widespread poverty. About eighty percent of its rural population make a living through subsistence farming on customary land. The adoption of the Land Act of 1995 led to some large agri-businesses, industrial and tourism businesses investing in local communities, providing them with benefits such as employment, out grower schemes, small-business opportunities, and infrastructural development. However, this has rendered some communities landless, eroded their rights to common pool resources, and enclosed communal land. Moreover, the Land Tribunal has become underfunded, and inaccessible to most of the population (ZLA 2008). As a result of the failings of the 1995 Land Act, Zambia's government has initiated a process to implement a new land policy that would encourage, and support investments in rural areas of Zambia. The policy was intended to address the weaknesses in the operation of the current legal framework for land, such as imbalances in the alienation of land and the need for security of the customary land tenure system (ZLA 2008).

Conclusion

Africa is well endowed with land and natural resources. This includes farmlands, range lands, forests, wildlife, minerals and water. These resources need to be harnessed because they are crucial in achieving socio-economic development. Nonetheless, Africa, especially Nigeria and Zambia, has failed to harnessing their lands and natural resources efficiently, equitably and sustainably, for the eradication of poverty, and the creation of wealth (Barraclough 1999). Apart from the two countries, other African countries like South Africa and Zimbabwe are still at a cross-road in respect of converting the large land mass to instruments of development. What the Nigerian and Zambian governments need to realize is that, for their land policies to work effectively, they need to be well informed about the issues surrounding land tenure in their country, which is germane to the enactment of effective land policies.

Furthermore, land tenure institutions should be continually adapted and regulated for the benefit of all the stakeholders in the land scheme, more important are the rural poor and the landless. The government also has the responsibility to balance the land hunger from the vulnerable population with sustainable development, which is the ultimate goals of the modern state. Moreover, the land policies that are enacted should account for the poor, people earning below the income margin and future generations. A more flexible approach to land policies in Nigeria, and Zambia, that benefits both the rural and urban population is needed. These policies should take into consideration the dichotomy between public and private properties.

References

Adams M, Sibanda S, Turner S (1999) Land tenure reform and rural livelihoods in southern Africa, vol 39. Natural Resource Perspective, Overseas Development Institute, London. https://www.odi.org/sites/odi.org.uk/files/odi-assets/publications-opinion-files/2883.pdf

Adefulu A, Esionye N (2009) An overview of Nigeria's land use amendment bill. http://www.mondaq.com/article.asp?articleid=81844

African Union (2009) Land policy in Africa: a framework to strengthen land rights, enhance productivity and secure livelihoods. AUC-ECA-AfDB Consortium, Addis Ababa

Aljazeera (2013) Are land grabs an opportunity for Africa? 13 November. http://www.aljazeera.com/programmes/south2north/2013/09/2013920101434517250.html

Arusa EO (1998) Multidimensional analysis of land tenure systems in Nigeria. Centre of Rural Development, Nsukka

Barrows R, Roth M (1990). Land tenure and investment in African agriculture: Theory and evidence. The Journal of Modern African Studies, 28(2), pp.265–297

Barraclough SL (1999) Land reform in developing countries: the role of the state and other actors. UNRISD, Geneva. Discussion Paper No.101. http://www.unrisd.org/80256B3C005BCCF9/(httpPublications)/9B503BAF4856E96980256B66003E0622

Bashar M (2008) Public land policy, new trends: challenges in Nigeria institutional frameworks for state and public sector land management. FIG/FAO/CNG International Seminar on State and Public Sector Land Management, Verona, Italy, September 9–10

Bernstein H (2002) Land reform: taking a long (er) view. Journal of Agrarian Change, 2(4):433–463

Bisong FE (2010) Nigeria Strategic Investment Framework for Strategic Land Management (NSIF-SLM). National Fadama Development Office, Abuja, Nigeria.

Bisong F, Andrew-Essien E (2010). Indigenous Land tenure reforms in the conservation of common property resources in the high forest regions of south-eastern Nigeria. Journal of sustainable development, 3(4), p.256

Brown T (2005a) Competing jurisdiction: settling land in Africa. Brill Academic Publishers, Leiden, Netherlands

Brown T (2005b) Contestation, confusion and corruption: market based land reform in Zambia. Brill Academic Publishers, Leiden, Netherlands

Butler S (2012) Focus on land in Africa brief: Nigeria land markets and land use. World Resource Institute. https://agriknowledge.org/downloads/0c483j41b

Cotula L, Toulmin C, Hesse C (2004) Land tenure and administration in Africa: lessons of experience and emerging issues. International Institute for Environment & Development (IIED), London

Cotula L (2007) Changes in customary land tenure systems in Africa. International Institute for Environment & Development (IIED), London

Dadzie R (2007) Neoclassical versus Institutionalist views on land tenure systems: implications for economic development. University of Missouri, Kansas City

Delville PL (2007) Changes in 'customary' land management institutions: evidence from West-Africa. In: Essays on the law of Botswana. Juta & Co, Cape Town, pp 196–202

Ekechi F (2002) The consolidation of European rule 1885–1914. In: Falola T (ed) Colonial Africa, 1885–1939, vol 3 of Africa. Carolina academic Press, Durham

Famoriyo S (2002) Land tenure, land use and land Acquisition in Nigeria. Institute for Agricultural Research, Nigeria

FAO (2002) FAO land tenure studies: land tenure and rural development. Rural Development Division, Food and Agricultural Organization of the United Nations (FAO), Rome

Food and Agriculture Organization (2010) Global forest resources assessment main report. FAO Forestry Paper 163, http://www.fao.org/docrep/013/i1757e/i1757e.pdf

Garvelink WJ (2012) Land tenure, property rights and rural economic development in Africa. Centre for strategic and international studies. https://www.csis.org/analysis/land-tenure-property-rights-and-rural-economic-development-africa

Helliker K, Murisa T (2011) Land struggles and civil Society in Southern Africa. Africa World Press, Trenton

Johnson OE (1972) Economic analysis, the legal framework and land tenure systems. The journal of law and economics, 15(1), pp.259–276

Kayode OD (2010) Land acquisition compensation and resettlement in developing economies: Nigeria as a case study. FIG Congress 2010, Facing the Challenges – Building The Capacity, Sydney, Australia, 11–16 April

Lund C (2008) Local politics and the dynamics of property in Africa. Cambridge Press, New York/Cape Town

Lund C, Boone C (2013) Introduction: land politics in Africa – constituting authority over territory, property and persons. Africa 83(1):1–13

Mabogunje AL (2007) Land reform in Nigeria: progress problems and prospects. Available online at http://siteresources.worldbank.org/EXTARD/Resources/336681-1236436879081/5893311-1271205116054/mabogunje.pdf

Mamdani M (2008) Lessons of Zimbabwe. London Book Rev 30(23). https://www.lrb.co.uk/v30/n23/mahmood-mamdani/lessons-of-zimbabwe

Muleya M (2006) The challenges of customary land tenure in Zambia, XXIII FIG Congress

Naluyaga R (2013) Land issues plague Africa as state lease out community lands to foreigners. The East African. Saturday 25th May 2013. Online: http://www.theeastafrican.co.ke/news/Land-issues-plague-Africa-as-stateslease-out-community-land/2558-1862728-b4n3iuz/index.html

Nicolson G (2012) South Africa: Who controls the land anyway? Daily Maverick. Online: https://www.dailymaverick.co.za/article/2012-04-16-south-africa-who-controls-the-land-anyway/#.WsDjh-tXerU. Accessed: June 15 2014

Oseni B (2012) "Summary of the Land Use Act Decree No. 6 of 1978 in Nigeria" in Environment of Nigeria at http://nigeriaenvironment.blogspot.com/2012/11/summary-of-land-use-act-decree-no-6-of.html (accessed 21July 2014)

Oshio P (1990) The indigenous land tenure and nationalization of land in Nigeria. Boston Coll Third World Law J 10(1):43–62

Prothero GW (1913) The colonization of Africa. Cambridge University Press, Cambridge

Platteau JP (1992) Land reform and structural adjustment in sub-Saharan Africa: controversies and guidelines (No. 107). Food & Agriculture Org

Shaka J (2013) Mgingo Island: Kenya or Uganda territory? J Conflictol 4(2):34–39

Tagliarino N (2014) Conversion of customary lands to leasehold titles. Indiana University Maurer School of Law, Brief

Tariebbea NK, Baroni S (2010) The Cameroon and Nigeria negotiation process over the contested oil rich Bakassi peninsula. J Altern Perspect Soc Sci 2(1):198–210

Tikabo MO (2003) Land tenure in the highlands of Eritrea: economic theory and empirical evidence. Dissertation no. 27. Agricultural University of Norway, Norway

Van Loenen B (1999) Land tenure in Zambia. University of Maine: Department of Spatial Information Engineering. https://www.researchgate.net/publication/242672704_Land_tenure_in_Zambia

Wachira G M (2008) Vindicating Indigenous People's Land Rights in Kenya. Doctoral Dissertation, University of Pretoria, Pretoria. https://repository.up.ac.za/bitstream/handle/2263/24411/Complete.pdf?sequence=8

Zambia Land Alliance (ZLA) (2008) Land policy options for development and poverty reduction: civil society views for pro-poor land policies and laws in Zambia. http//www.sarpn.org/documents/d00029/index.php

ZLA (2016) Ministry of lands, Natural resources and environmental protection. Draft land policy. Lusaka, Zambia

Chapter 7
Land Governance in the Context of Legal Pluralism: Cases of Ghana and Kenya

Fayth Ruffin

Introduction

Land governance, legal pluralism, African indigenous knowledge systems (AIKS) and gender constructions are independent concepts from disparate bodies of knowledge. The chapter examines the intersection of these concepts in the trajectory of post-colonial land reform. Differentiated epistemologies undergirding living African law, westernised rule of law orthodoxy, and 'official' customary law as constructed during and sustained after colonisation are explored. It is argued that legal pluralism tends to suppress AIKS of land governance, constitutionalism and gender complementariness. In this chapter, conceptual treatment of land governance intersects with these bodies of knowledge but converges into different focuses on Kenya. For Ghana, the lens of the institution of traditional leadership (IoTL) is utilised. As to Kenya, the focus is on women's land rights on the one hand and communal land ownership on the other hand. In both the Ghana and Kenya cases, African ways of knowing are the guiding theme for conceptualising land governance. This chapter contributes to bodies of knowledge on AIKS, land governance and legal pluralism.

The chapter is organised as follows. First, a brief historical context of land governance and gender constructions highlights epistemological views. Second, an overview of customary international law treatment of indigenous peoples is followed by a discussion of legal pluralism. Fourth, an AIKS of Ghanaian land governance is considered before land dilemmas during and after colonisation are examined against the backdrop of the IoTL. Fifth, unintended consequences for women from an imported land titling policy adopted in Kenya are highlighted and current-day gender constructions questioned. Then the landmark Endorois case decided by the African Commission on Human and People's Rights is explored in light of AIKS.

F. Ruffin (✉)
Public Governance, University of KwaZulu-Natal, Durban, South Africa
e-mail: Ruffin@ukzn.ac.za

© Springer International Publishing AG, part of Springer Nature 2019
A. O. Akinola, H. Wissink (eds.), *Trajectory of Land Reform in Post-Colonial African States*, Advances in African Economic, Social and Political Development, https://doi.org/10.1007/978-3-319-78701-5_7

Overarching lessons are learnt from Ghana and Kenya in terms of the role of indigeneity in the land reform trajectory. Finally, the chapter is concluded and recommendations presented on how to ease tensions between seemingly irreconcilable epistemologies underlying land governance in the context of legal pluralism.

Historical Context of Land Governance and Gender Constructions in a Consensus Constitutional Democracy

In his more than sixteen years of fieldwork across Africa in the twentieth century, Chancellor Williams gleaned through oral histories, the framework of an AIKS[1] of constitutional democracy. In this AIKS, lineage was the organising force and the age-grade system obtained fundamental governance in so-called 'stateless' societies (Williams 1974:174, 180). Boys and girls received the same intellectual training, while ommunity consensus was the supreme law. Dispute resolution was handled first by the family council, then the age-grade council before the Council of Elders. One could ignore prescriptions from these bodies but only at the risk of one's own peril (Williams 1974:180). As governance evolved, kings or queens, chiefs or chieftesses became mouthpieces of communities as opposed to autocratic rulers in the Western epistemological sense. British scholars noted a "wild and most primitive system of democracy" whereby Africans would remove from office a king or chief commissioned by the British to carry out British laws to effect indirect rule of villages (Williams 1974:26; Makahamadze et al. 2009:35, 36).

While Williams (1974: 178, 181) found variations and modifications of ancient African constitutional law across various African societies, all societies converged on such points as constitutional group duties and rights perceived as inseparable oneness, that 'land belongs to no one' and that African spirituality is an actual way of thinking and knowing inherent in all governance institutions. This is contrary to Western epistemology entrenched with private property mandates, individual rights discourse and separation between church and state. On the one hand, in ancient Africa, land is considered sacred heritage, 'a bond between the living and the dead' and political power of kings or queen rest in ancestral influence (Makahamadze et al. 2009:35). On the other hand, westernised land disposition politics generally do not take ancestral worship and divination practices into account. Further, 'certain land groves, lakes and rivers' are set aside as sacred and used for innumerable spiritual rituals and festivals in African societies

[1] AIKS can be defined as systems designed and executed by original African people historically attached to a particular land and fundamentally expressive of their civilization inclusive of sociopolitical, economic, scientific and technological identity, culture, values and ways of knowing (Dei 2012:111; Odora Hoppers 2001:4).

(Williams 1974:181, 184). This is diametrically opposed to John Locke-inspired individual land use and ownership to the exclusion of others. Contemporary liberal democracy separates the political from the economic to ensure the 'sanctity of private property' beyond the control of democracy (Pierson 1992:98). In contrast, AIKS of consensus democracy epistemologically view the political and economic as interwoven. This is the non-dualism of 'forms and things' expressed by ancient Egyptians (Nabudere 2011:27) and found in Williams' (1974) fieldwork.

Just as types of constitutionalism are underpinned by different epistemologies (Keevey 2009), so are gender constructions. Historically, unlike women in westernised society who were often relegated to the domestic sphere, indigenous African women participated politically and economically in public life (Oluwagbemi-Jacob & Uduma 2015; Makahamadze et al. 2009; Weir 2007; Amadiume 2007). This was based on lineage and independent economic success. Ancient Igbo society included a "dual sex" political system through men's and women's associations whereby members of the queen's council were represented on the king's council to democratically protect the interests of women in an egalitarian way (Oluwagbemi-Jacob & Uduma 2015:230; Nzegwu 2012:15). Makahamadze, et al. (2009) explain the normative reign of female chiefs in Shona society as does Day (2007) with reference to Sierra Leone. Weir (2007) highlights the role of Zulu women during the regime of Shaka Zulu, including his mother and paternal aunt. Olugwagbemi-Jacob & Uduma (2015:232 and Chuku (2013:272) point out how the Igbo girl child was empowered with a trade to facilitate independence after marriage.

The public life of indigenous African women extended beyond political and socio-economic arenas into the military realm. Williams (1974:276–289) explains how Queen Nzinga led Angolan militarism against the Portuguese in the 17th century for over thirty years. Similarly, Weir (2007:12–15) draws upon archives of 19th century Zululand and Natal history to show that female chiefs such as MaChibise, MaNthatisi and MaMthunzini, amongst others, led their respective polities in battle against male-led polities. Makahamadze, et al. (2009:35) document the same militarism by Shona female chiefs such as Nyamazana who organised armies against the male chief who refused to be guided by ancestors.

As to land governance and inheritance, indigneous African polities were organised as matrilineal or patrilineal societies. These systems are not to be confused with partriarchy, just as societal gender roles are not to be conflated with biology or sexism. Rather, epistemological perspectives should be distinguished and modes of land governance and inheritance underlying African ways of knowing recognised. Even in patrilineal societies, women could inherit land as communal land ownership was attributed to a family (Ndima 2003; Amadiume 1987). Amadiume (1987) explains how women who did not marry and remained on the family homestead 'inherited' the property as 'male daughters'. Again, gender roles governed African ways of knowing in consensus constitutional democracies, not biology. Gender complementarity in AIKS is another example of non-dualism epistemologies, which was reconstructed or (mis)understood by Plato as dualism (Nabudere 2011:27).

Land Governance: International Law and Post-Colonial Legal Pluralist States

This chapter pays attention to indigenous communities. Indigenous people inhabit rural, and peri-rural vast lands of African countries that are legally, politically, socially and economically under the concurrent jurisdiction of a nation-state and the IoTL within common geographical boundaries. While national governments in Africa and elsewhere struggle with post-colonial land governance concerning indigenous populations, the international human rights regime addresses this phenomenon. The United Nations Declaration on the Rights of Indigenous Peoples (UN DRIP 2007) provides in pertinent part:

> Indigenous peoples have the right to own, use, develop and control the lands, territories and resources that they possess by reason of traditional ownership or other traditional occupation or use, as well as those which they have otherwise acquired (UN DRIP 2007: Article 26).

Article 26 further indicates that states shall respect customs, traditions and land tenure systems of indigenous peoples. Besides living on their traditional lands, practicing their culture and autonomous self-governance, indigenous peoples are distinguished from other groups by their "collective spiritual relationship to their land" (Wiessner 2011:129). This resonates with the ancient African constitutional theory and practice found by Williams (1974). Simultaneously it is in contradistinction to "those who are confident of the hegemony of private property in the West" (Boone 2009:195).

In relation to customary international law, the International Law Association (ILA) Committee on the Rights of Indigenous Peoples' 2010 Interim Report points out the rights of indigenous peoples to autonomy, self-defined cultural identity and entitlement to traditional lands and natural resources as well as reparation and redress for dispossession by conquerors (ILA Interim Report 2010). Similarly, the African Commission on Human and Peoples' Rights (ACHPR) recognises the relationship between indigenous peoples and their traditional lands and natural resources in light of a landmark decision in favour the Endorois people in Kenya as subsequently discussed. Although international instruments promote land entitlement of and land governance by indigenous people, African states continue to struggle with the phenomena of land dispossession and restoration on a national level.[2] This is particularly the case in legal pluralist African countries like Ghana and Kenya.

As previously described, legal and constitutional systems existed in African countries before conquests by Europeans (Williams 1974; Ndima 2003:330). These complex indigenous legal systems are termed living African law since they are dynamic and indicative of the socio-cultural context in which they are embedded. Law and morality are seen as interwoven. Oral transmission of law and morality originate in the family unit and resonate with judicial processes that include public participation. Similarly, land governance is communal with the family homestead system as central and family head as manager. Ndima (2003:333) explains "the concept of ownership as individualised in Western law was imposed upon African

---

[2] A notable exception is the South African Constitutional Court's restoration of indigenous lands in Alexkor Limited v. The Richtersveld Community and Others, 2003 (19) SA 48–51 (CC).

law, disregarding the communal nature of the indigenous traditions and experiences". It is the imposition of British and Roman-Dutch law in countries such as Ghana and Kenya that gave rise to legal pluralism in these countries. Large scale efforts were undertaken to bring living African law in line with English and Roman-Dutch law, despite the divergent values and epistemologies underlying the two legal systems. A third legal system emerged during colonisation which was used as a system of indirect rule. This indirect rule included inventing chieftaincies to carry out rules of the colonisers, creating paramount chiefs through a process of centralisation to gain oversight and dominion of what appeared to Europeans to be vacant lands or stateless societies (Schmid 2001), and changing gender roles to more closely reflect westernised patriarchy (Ubink 2011).

Pimentel 2011:73–81) identifies three types of legal pluralism: equal dignity approach, colonial approach and superior state approach. The equal dignity approach could be analogous to living African law, termed unofficial, informal, folk or non-state law yet prioritised by adherents who do not wish to succumb to state law. Here, rule of law orthodoxy runs parallel to the AIKS. This is considered strong legal pluralism. The colonial approach is the system of 'codified' or 'official' customary law shaped by colonisers in collusion with elite leaders to project westernised legal theories and practices through indirect rule. It persists today through state court interpretation of 'official' and unofficial customary law through a westernised lens, devoid of socio-cultural context. The superior state approach involves constitutional recognition of living African law and 'official' customary law so long as it does not conflict with state law at which time the indigenous law or 'official' version must give way to the supremacy of state law (Ndima 2003). Both the colonial approach and the superior state approach are considered weak legal pluralism. Each of these legal pluralist approaches are pitfalls of neo-colonial propagation due to conflicting epistemologies underlying customary and state legal systems. Simultaneously, some theorists and practitioners do not deem living African law, the 'unofficial' or 'official' versions of customary law as law at all (Twining 2009).

In contrast to defining legal pluralism on its own merit, some scholars perceive legal pluralism as a species of normative pluralism (Twining 2009; Tamanaha 2008; Griffiths 2005). Twining (2009:488–489) advocates that recognising the existence of different norms warrants conceptualising legal pluralism as a social fact. For Twining's (2009:488–489), social fact legal pluralism encompasses state legal pluralism (weak legal pluralism), legal polycentricity (different sectors of law within a single state system) and coexistence of two or more autonomous or semi-autonomous legal orders in a single nation-state. Twining further argues that social fact legal pluralism moves away from questions of state centrism and vitality of state law without minimising liberal democracy, human rights and the rule of law. Hence, state and non-state legal orders would be perceived as social facts thereby downplaying debates about the validity and legitimacy of what counts as a legal system. Yet, protections of westernised individual rights-based ideals are analogous with a perceived superiority of state law over other legal orders. Similarly, Galligan (2007) argues for the supremacy of state-centric legal orders in modern democratic societies.

Twining's (2009) advocacy of social fact legal pluralism devalues the epistemological outlook of living African law. Social fact legal pluralism valorises the superior state model. It promotes dualism (separation of doctrinal law from its socio-cultural context), individualism (individual rights as opposed to collective duties and rights), and materialism (rule of law orthodoxy emphasises individual material-based winners and losers). In contrast, living African law metes out justice in light of the socio-cultural context of the parties and the situation, searches for communal-oriented decision-making to holistically promote community interests, and seeks restorative justice relationship-building taking ancestors into account (Ntlama and Ndima 2009). To perceive legal pluralism in African countries as nothing more than a species of normative pluralism is to deny the epistemological foundation of living African law. Hence, for African countries, social fact legal pluralism does not move away from state centrism and vitality of state law. Instead, it obliterates indigenous ways of knowing and prioritises westernised liberal democracy over consensus democracy as known in African polities. This point is further borne out with reference to land governance in Ghana and Kenya which are next discussed. Land governance in Ghana is explored through the lens of the IoTL. The Kenyan case is examined first through the gender dimension of land titling policy and then the landmark Endorois case in light of AIKS.

Land Governance Dilemmas: The Ghanaian Institution of Traditional Leadership

> *With independence...a new harmony needs to be forged, a harmony that will allow the combined presence of traditional Africa, Islamic Africa and Euro-Christian Africa, so that this presence is in tune with the original humanist principles underlying African society (Nkrumah 1964:70).*

Ancient autonomous polities that would later become part of present-day Ghana fit the brief historical overview of AIKS described at the outset of this chapter. The "original humanist principles underlying African society", to which Nkrumah (1964:70) referred means an egalitarian society where indigenous inhabitants abided by social, political and economic prescripts that included attaching spiritual significance to land. Asante (1965:852) explains that, indigenously, land belongs to the ancestors; oneness of land title was indivisibly vested in the 'the stool' which means the ancestors. Materially, the stool is an intricately designed wood carved seat engraved with certain insignia that are associated with particular polities and rituals. The stool physically rests with the royal family and spiritually connects the deceased and living communities through the king and Queen Mother.[3] Put another way, the land belongs to the stool which links the embodiment of the community –

---

[3] For comprehension of the institution of Queen Mothers see: Stoeltje BJ. 1997. Asante Queen Mothers. *Annals of the New York Academy of Sciences*, 810(1):41–71; Steegstra M. 2009. Krobo Queen Mothers: gender, power, and contemporary female traditional authority in Ghana. *Africa Today*, 55(3):105–123 and Mensah CA, Antwi, KB and Dauda S. 2014. Female Traditional Leaders (Queen Mothers) and Community Planning and Development in Ghana. *Environmental Management and Sustainable Development*, 3(1):205.

the living, the living dead who remain involved with the living (Mbiti 1990) and unborn generations. Asante (1965:856) confirms that traditional leaders generally had no authority to sell land or to make other socio-political and economic decisions without consultation with the Council of Elders and the ancestors. Even then a decision was not considered the decision of the traditional leader but a consensus decision of the polity in the best interests of the polity. The king could be 'destooled' as was the case when British used the IoTL to institutionalized indirect rule (Williams 1974).

Simultaneously, distribution of land to community members – to which all were entitled – was accomplished through a usufructuary right to stool land which is the "right to occupy, till, or otherwise enjoy an unappropriated portion of stool land to appropriate the fruits of such user" (Asante 1965:853). Usufructuary rights were usually granted to a family although it could be allotted to an individual, were perpetual and transferable to a community member and such rights were held exclusive of benefits to others, including the stool (pp. 853–854). Furthermore, such rights holders were expected to present fruits of the land to the stool as a political arrangement. Reversion of land interests rested in the stool. Other land interests included grant by the stool for public concerns such as community development, grant rights to strangers for particular reasons and by the institution of *guaha* (Asante 1965: 856). Although alienation of property from the stool could be accomplished through the institution of *guaha,* this was rare and frowned upon mainly because of the indivisibility of the stool, sacredness of heritage and ancestors thereby linking the living, living dead and those yet unborn. In that case, extensive rituals and ceremonies would be performed to oblige ancestors to leave that land (Asante 1965: 860). Land governance was administered through living African law in the customary judicial system. As indicated in the section on legal pluralism, living African law is dynamic and fluid, an AIKS which changes in light of socio-cultural realities and political circumstances in which that legal system is embedded and administered (Ndima 2003; Asante 1965). This is epistemologically contradistinctive to rule of law orthodoxy with statutory mandates and case precedents founded on *stare decisis* which would bring legal pluralism to Ghana through European colonisers.

In the nineteenth century, with the onset of commercialisation of agriculture, mining expeditions and other forms of land exploitation along with erection of concrete structures as homes on land held pursuant to usufructuary rights, land governance began to change. Land dilemmas such as land dispossession and restructuring on the IoTL occurred. English ideas of land alienation through freehold estates and vesting of property interests through written documentation were imported (Asante 1965:858–859). Several attempts at land dispossession were successfully resisted by the Aborigines Rights Protection Society (ARPS) and British speculators. The ARPS was "an alliance of chiefs and business and intellectual elites on the Gold Coast" (Amanor 2008:58).

The ARPS argued that the 1894 Crown Lands Ordinance was unconstitutional since the Gold Coast had not been established by conquest, but by an 1844 treaty between Europeans and Africans on equal footing. The following year Ghana was declared a colonial protectorate (Amanor 2008). In 1897 a Public Lands bill was introduced by a British governor to transfer family holdings to individual holdings, to allow settlers to own land to the exclusion of the stool and to declare vacant land as British 'Crown Land' (Amanor 2008:58–59). Here, the ARPS contended that the taking of land was unlawful since the land was vested in the stool where geographically located (Asante 1965:858 n. 38). However, Amanor (2008:58–59) argues that the ARPS was more concerned with protecting their own interests in transacting land deals on parity with European settlers and investors than maintenance of customary land tenure. British speculators opposed the legislation out of an interest in free markets and non-interference by the colonial government.

During this time, the IoTL was disrupted. It was reconstructed with British invention of chiefs and chiefdoms as well as a hierarchical structure of paramount chiefs and sub-chiefs with alloidal (ultimate) rights as a matter of indirect rule (Busia 1951:105–106). Land transactions came to be solely between the chief and the colonial administration or the chief and foreign investors who received concessionaire contracts across large tracts of mineral rich Ghanaian land. The role of the earth priest and propitiation of ancestors declined or was eliminated (Tonah 2008). Rather, the colonial government attributed to chiefs the sole authority to transact stool land (Amanor 2008:60, 61) irrespective of consultation with the Council of Elders, community members or ancestors of the jurisdiction of the stool. Alongside the rise of commoditisation of land, widespread dispossession of land occurred by enactment of the Land and Native Right Ordinance of 1927. This law determined certain Ghanaian lands 'public lands' under dominion of the colonial government and without compensation to occupiers or owners, thereby making chiefs and earth priests subservient (Tonah 2008:116, 119).

Simultaneously, the colonial approach to legal pluralism emerged. A series of case law precedents effectively reshaped usufructuary interest as a freehold estate for indigenous people and foreign settlers alike, eliminating any reversionary interest in the stool (Asante 1965). This was despite the fact that the institution of *guaha* permitted alienation of land through certain indigenous procedures that predated European presence in Ghana. This led to the ascendancy of 'lawyer's customary law' in land governance (Crook 2008; Schmid 2001) and arguably, the concomitant suppression of AIKS of constitutionalism, law and consensus democracy. The colonial approach to legal pluralism, means land cases and other legal matters were handled by chief-led Native Courts pursuant to the 1935 Ashanti Native Courts Ordinance and the 1944 Colony Native Courts Ordinance. These courts were deemed part of the state hierarchical legal system with right of appeal thereto. Cases that reached state courts were interpreted from a westernised lens. The IoTL seemingly devolved into an aristocratic sect rather than a mouthpiece for the stool in olden days. Yet strongholds of consensus democracy in Ghana remained as Amanor (2008:67) highlights the "spasmodic waves of 'destoolment' of chiefs which swept the country between 1949 and 1952". The Native Courts were abolished in 1958 but land management and governance by traditional leaders remained intact.

In 1957, Ghana became the first African country to gain independence. Under the Nkrumah regime, the State Lands Act (125) of 1962 transferred 'allodial' title to the state. The Administration of Lands Act (123) of 1962 vested administration and management of stool land in the state as trustee for the stool to safeguard the public interest. The Office of the Administrator of Stool Lands (OASL) was established for oversight, revenue collection from transactions involving stool lands and disbursement of funds to customary communities for public purposes. On the one hand, Nkrumah limited the legislative and judicial authority of chiefs given the nature of the IoTL that emerged during colonialism. On the other hand, Nkrumah created greater institutional links between indigenous people and the state (Berry 2008:30, 41). Once Nkrumah was deposed by the military, the Chieftaincy Act Number 370 of 1971 was enacted – declaring in section 15 that the government has no jurisdiction in chieftaincy affairs. This is sustained by the 1992 Constitution of the Republic of Ghana, Chap. 22 meaning, *inter alia*, that land matters involving chiefs as well as nomination, appointment, election or destoolment of chiefs remain outside the jurisdiction of the state (Republic of Ghana 1992). First instance non-chief related land matters, however, are vested in the state.

Post-colonial land reforms include the 1979 repeal of the 1927 Land and Native Right Ordinance in an effort to restore land rights hitherto dispossessed. Constitutionally, Articles 36(8) and 267(1) confirm that allodial title of stool land is governed by chiefs with consent of councillors and indigenous communities pursuant to customary law. While Article 11(2) of the 1992 constitution recognizes customary law, Article 272 mandates that National and Regional Houses of Chiefs interpret and codify customary law. The question becomes whether these contemporary constitutional mandates, in effect, restore the indigenous constitutional and legal framework under which traditional leaders were a mouthpiece for families and clans upon consultation with the Council of Elders and ancestors. Some scholars (Amanor 2008; Crook 2008; Ubink 2008) argue that, although alloidal title is supposedly vested in the state, chiefs manage to reap excessive personal economic benefits. These include compensation for land expropriated from locals and sold to investors (Amanor 2008: 68, 70, 77) and receipt of so-called 'drinks money', land taxes or rents (Crook 2008:131). Rather than a socio-cultural and political act to appease the stool (ancestors) when demarcated land was leased or alienated in olden days, 'drinks money' now amounts to chiefs receiving market value for land sales to ready buyers upon dispossessing occupants of land resource. This post-colonial dispossession of land for conveyance is often claimed to be done in the interests of community development. Land taxes or rents are established by the IoTL since limitations envisaged by the Rents Stabilization Act Number 109 of 1962 was subsequently repealed. Hence, land transactions by the IoTL may fall short of the "original humanist principles underlying African society" (Nkrumah 1964:70) and therefore outside epistemologies of AIKS. Twenty-first century land reforms include *inter alia* a new Land Administration Project that restructures state land sector agencies, decentralises land management, regional land courts and dispute resolution mechanisms, and creates Customary Land Secretariats (CLSs) which work in conjunction with the IoTL in land governance (Crook 2008:135).

As to post-colonial land governance and legal pluralism, Ghana at once exhibits both weak and strong legal pluralism. It is weak to the extent land matters decided in customary courts are ultimately disposed of in state courts through statutory enactments or through judicial interpretation of customary law from a westernised lens thereby evolving 'lawyer's customary law' (Woodman 1996:45). It is strong to the extent that indigenous people continue to seek customary law and other forms of community-based dispute resolution mechanisms outside the confines of the state. Customary law is also strengthened by the insulation of the IoTL from the state. Yet unresolved questions exist as to whether the quality of such customary law reflects AIKS of constitutional, legal, political, economic and socio-cultural ways of knowing that once evidenced a holistic approach inclusive of the living, the living dead and posterity protection.

Ubink (2008:162) argues that since pre-colonial checks and balances to hold the IoTL accountable such as meaningful consultation with the Council of Elders and the option of de-stooling a chief are no longer effective, the state should inter-vene. To Ubink (2008:163) British colonisers held the IoTL to account while the post-colonial state does not. This point brings to bear epistemological distinctions. It supports the argument that legal pluralism suppresses AIKS of governance. Apparently some traditional leaders may have abandoned the original epistemo-logical outlook of AIKS in favour of a westernised version of the IoTL leadership created during colonisation and sustained post-independence that promotes dual-ism, individualism and materialism. With the CLS now under the auspices of the IoTL, it remains to be seen as to whether African epistemologies will be advanced. The discussion now turns to the case of Kenya after which the chapter is concluded.

Kenyan Land Titling: From Marginalisation of Women's Rights to Communal Land Ownership

The harmony and stability of the African's mode of life, in political, social, religious, and economic organisations, was based on the land which was, and still is, the soul of the people...The land not only unites the living members of the tribe but also the dead ancestors and the unborn posterity (Kenyatta 1970:27).

In ancient times, autonomous polities existed throughout African societies with governance, legal and constitutional systems intact (Williams 1974). As indicated by Kenyatta in the above quote, the African's mode of life was inextricably bound to land as a unitary force of generations. Kenyatta (1970:27), the first post-colonial president of the autonomous polities centralised into Kenya, describes the early Kikuyu governance experience consistent with Williams (1974) as set forth in this chapter. As with other polities, the family unit and age-grade system were the foun-dation of governance. This was expanded by clans and councils of elders at village, district and national scales ensuring family representation. Traditional leaders were elected at the various scales, positioned as mouthpieces of the community and con-nected through ancestral heritage and communication (Kenyatta 1970:22–23). There was a system of rotational governance whereby succeeding generations, prepared through the age-grade system, uptake the leadership function of government. According to Kenyatta:

> The spirit of itwika, namely, the changing of government in rotation through a peaceful and constitutional revolution, is still ingrained in the minds of the Kikuyu people. About 1925–1928 was the time when the itwika ceremony was to take place corresponding to the last great itwika ceremony which was celebrated about 1890–1898. The irungu or maina generation, whose turn it was to take over the government from the mwangi generation, organised in 1925 and began singing and dancing itwika ceremonial songs and dances to mark the termination of rule by the mwangi generation. But after a short time the itwika ceremonial dances and songs were declared illegal, or in other words, "seditious," by the British government (Kenyatta 1970:24).

Kenyatta (1970:24–25) questions underlying assumptions of Britain's Kenya White Paper of July 1925 in which the British government committed itself "to work continuously for the training and educational of the African towards a higher intellectual, moral and economic level than that which they had reached when the Crown assumed the responsibility for the administration of this territory". This British mission suggests an unawareness of pre-existing AIKS of education and democratic constitutional governance in Kenya including the ontological, epistemological and axiological underpinnings of such practices as the *itwika* ceremony for rotational governance. This could be seen as the onset of hegemony of the European frame of reference which was perceived as universally superior and culturally higher than African worldviews and fora which were deemed backward and lacking in validity and authenticity.

This suppression of AIKS of governance extended to the indigenous legal system. For example, English common and statutory law were imposed in Kenya. As is the case with Ghana, legal decisions in Kenya based upon living African law in its socio-cultural context were reconstructed through British judicial reinterpretation and misinterpretation thereby giving rise to 'official' customary law (Joireman 2008:8). Land governance and land tenure in Kenya are no exception to the westernisation project. Kenya, a country with vast rural lands inhabited by indigenous people as both agriculturalists and pastoralists, was among the first countries to begin massive efforts toward individual land titling and registration in the 1950s (McAuslan 2005). This was done through the Swynnerton plan while Kenya was still a British colony and protectorate (Meinzen-Dick and Mwangi 2007; Kenya Colony and Protectorate 1955). This type of land tenure reform was adapted by many African countries, particularly after the work of economist Hector de Soto became prominent and provided the ground stone for the Commission on Legal Empowerment for the Poor (CLEP).

Pursuant to that line of thinking, indigenous people as landholders possess 'dead capital' as land and, once such land moves from customary tenure to individual ownership titled and registered, capital is activated and can be used as a tool of poverty alleviation through, *inter alia*, land alienation and collateral for credit. Although the CLEP approach is supported by global governance organisations such as the World Bank and the International Monetary Fund, the CLEP and de Soto's theories have been subject to criticism (Otto 2009). These criticisms include impracticality for indigenous people in legal pluralist societies where local realities differ from the values and belief systems from the imported discourses of neoliberalism.

Meinzen-Dick and Mwangi (2007) draw upon Kenyan case studies to identify ways in which an imported policy focussed on deed titling and registration can marginalise women's rights. Under customary land tenure, land was held in trust by the family or lineage head for the community – meaning the living, living dead and those yet unborn as previously described (Meinzen-Dick and Mwangi 2007:8). As wives and widows, Taita women in Kenya were endowed with land use rights and access to natural resources in the agricultural community. This included the right to alienate land on behalf of minor heirs pursuant to the patrilineal system of inheritance. Upon implementation of the land tenure reform, title deeds were drawn and registered solely in the names of husbands. As a result, women were denied land allocation and access to natural resources in both the customary system and rule of law orthodoxy (Meinzen-Dick and Mwangi 2007:5).

As to pastoralists among the Maasai, customary tenure included dynamic land-holdings in light of age-grade sets and cattle holdings. However, this land reform of titling and registration led to grouping of ranches and then subdivisions within the groups (Meinzen-Dick and Mwangi 2007:6). The rotation system was annihilated. Women were excluded from the land reform process. Claims of youths who were ordinarily entitled to common Maasai land as a birthright, were denied that birthright by the land reform. The subdivision element of the land reform changed the socio-economic and cultural entitlement to access to land and resources by virtue of being part of the Maasai community as a whole. Instead land inheritance vested in a particular family, limiting access to resources to a specific plot of land (Meinzen-Dick and Mwangi 2007:7). This suggests that the imported policy suppressed AIKS.

In other words, AIKS of land governance for agricultural and pastoral communities are effectively undermined through such a land reform. The protection of collective rights and connection to ancestral heritage inherent in customary land tenure are obliterated by private property ownership titled in the names of men (Meinzen-Dick and Mwangi 2007:8) against the grain of AIKS. Strong land use and management decision-making rights and reciprocal duties for women upon land allocation is lost (p. 7) contrary to some of the protections afforded in the foregone system of gender complementarity. Socio-economic networks that permitted grazing of livestock herds and access to natural resources that bolstered the ecological balance were curtailed by land being fenced-in by property owners in accordance with ranch subdivisions (p. 7). This suppression of AIKS likewise diminishes human relationships among the living and tends to weaken ancestral relations and posterity of future generations (p. 8) – thereby breaking the bond articulated by Kenyatta at the outset of this section on Kenya.

Some scholars argue, however, that customary institutions of AIKS work injustice against women as a matter of course (Daley and Englert 2010; Chopra and Isser 2011; Hellum 2000). According to Daley and Englert (2010: 98):

> There is currently a relative consensus, or "received wisdom", that customary social and political institutions, being rooted in patriarchal social, political and economic relations, are virtually by definition bad for women...Reliance on customary institutions, with all their

inherent biases, is therefore now more widely recognised as being potentially detrimental to women in land matters ...

Similarly, Chopra and Isser (2011: 23–24) state, "it is widely assumed that customary systems are based on patriarchal social norms that reaffirm a subordinate role for women". While these scholars cite reputable sources including academics and practitioners affiliated with major regional and global governance organisations, attention does not seem to be directed toward the fact that the customary institutions and customary laws studied were those reinvented by colonisers. Living African law still exists but is seldom studied. It should be recognized that European settlers did not grasp the ontological, epistemological and axiological distinctions between the European and African worldviews and mind-sets from the outset. While Hellum (2000:657) argues that dichotomies such as Western and African are not useful, the point here of highlighting distinctive epistemologies is to demonstrate how the former projects its understandings of law, constitutionalism and governance – including land governance – onto the pre-existing disposition of the latter which has historically worked toward the detriment of the latter. For example, westernised feminism has the tendency to universalise female subordination through patriarchy to all women. Mohanty (1988, 2003) began correcting this with her seminal work "Under Western Eyes: Feminist Scholarship and Colonial Discourses", explaining the importance of context. Not unlike, Daley and Englert (2010) and Hellum (2000), Mohanty (2003) calls for micro-level studies to contextualize, theorise, and problem-solve issues women face in local societies. Yet, indigenous gender constructions as discussed earlier in this chapter are seldom of focus. Rather, there seems to be a tendency not to distinguish European ways of knowing patriarchy from indigenous African ways of knowing gender complementarity.

As John Henrik Clarke puts it, rather than African women being perceived as subordinate to men, "the Africans had produced a civilization where men were secure enough to let women advance as far as their talent, royal lineage and prerogatives would take them" (Diop 1978:iii). Nevertheless, in postcolonial African countries, westernised ontology, epistemology and axiology continue to be perpetuated by Africans themselves – as being co-opted into westernisation does not come without personal benefits – including economics and perceived higher social status as seen in the Ghanian case of the IoTL. Unless AIKS are taken into consideration, the same westernisation that imposed colonialism in an effort to disintegrate indigenous law, consensus constitutionalism and land governance; and the same westernisation that typically underlies the development project; will be the same westernisation that penetrates twenty-first century land reforms. For example, phrases from Daley and Englert (2010) are insightful.

Drawing upon a number of research findings from other scholars, Daley and Englert (2010:99–100) suggest it is best to view "custom and customary institutions as first and foremost local practices and institutions rather than necessarily "traditional" practices and institutions"; "update and reform rather than replace custom"; "build on what is already there while simultaneously seeking to change it"; "be open to updating as local context changes"; "land laws can be amended and reformed later on as custom catches up". In addition, a "gender equitable society...

must be of mutual benefit to all, and, importantly, must not alienate men". From an indigenous knowledge perspective, customary and customary institutions are local ways of knowing, practices and institutions yet global phenomena considering the existence of indigenous communities all over the world. Living African law, for example, is reflective of local societal change and it is not a matter of being behind or catching up because it is reflective of legal dispositions in socio-cultural context in a given space in time. It includes public participation with legal decisions made in the interests of holistic communalism inclusive of spirituality and the role of ancestors. Hence, an AIKS epistemological understanding is critical for at least two reasons. First, there must be an awareness that AIKS were suppressed by colonialism, and both the colonial state and superior state approaches to legal pluralism; yet living African law still exists. Non-recognition and lack of empirical inquiry into living African law – as opposed to 'codified' customary law is to continue to perpetuate epistemological colonialism. Second, gender complementarity is at the heart of AIKS of justice meaning that gender equity is not new to AIKS but inherent in it, as earlier discussed in this chapter. In fact, a distinguishing factor of African feminisms from western feminisms is the former's inclusion of men in women's liberation (Hudson-Weems 2001) which is consistent with AIKS.

AIKS are central to land reform. National governments still struggle with land reform – in the midst of commoditisation of land and land grabbing in a global economy steeped in neoliberalism and in constant search for new markets and land acquisition. Westernised epistemologies seem to have survived colonisation, persisting in post-colonial African states. However, international customary law and regional governance by the African Union seem to support AIKS in land governance and restitution. For instance, the ACHPR overturned the Kenyan government's 1973 dispossession of the Endorois community of "ancestral land it had occupied since time immemorial" (Morel 2014:1). Titled Minority Rights Group International and the Centre for Minority Rights Development (on behalf of the Endorois Welfare Council) v Kenya and adopted by the African Union in 2010, this landmark decision holistically merges religious freedom, cultural rights, property rights, the right to natural resources and the right to development to restore communal ownership of land to the Endorois indigenous community.

The Endorois community successfully argued, *inter alia*, that (1) indigenous people are entitled to recognition under the African Charter as a 'legal personality' ripe for communal ownership of land; (2) said 'legal personality' is inextricably bound to ownership and beneficial interests of their ancestral homelands; and (3) such communal ownership of land is required for religious freedom on sacred ground including ceremonies, rituals and festivals that, from time immemorial are convened in certain areas in light of ancestral homage (Morel 2014:2–6, 8–10). The Endorois community was granted restitution of ancestral lands. In addition, the Endorois community victoriously demonstrated that (4) the state had a legal duty, under the African Charter, to protect the Endorois' cultural and physical existence; and (5) cultural activities on the game reserve expropriated from the Endorois community did not harm the ecosystem but instead promoted authenticity of Endorois culture in peaceful co-existence with the game reserve (Morel 2014:6–8).

These rights to communal land ownership, religious freedom and cultural activities extended to the Endorois community's right to natural resources of their ancestral land and the right to development beneath, on and in such land. During the protracted struggle of the Endorois community against the Kenyan government, the Kenyan government had denied the Endorois community access to medicinal saltlicks and fertile soil, thereby debilitating livestock of this pastoral community. The Kenyan government failed to consult the Endorois community regarding concessions for ruby mining and excluded them from benefits from such concessions as well as from benefits generated by game reserve revenues and employment opportunities. This the ACHPR declared violates the right to natural resources, wealth and property (Morel 2014:10–12). As to the right to development, although the ACHPR ruled that the right of indigenous people to natural resources is not absolute, the ACHPR found that state governments must adequately and timely consult indigenous communities, obtain knowing and voluntary consent for activities that could adversely affect the survival of such communities and that indigenous communities are entitled to equitable distribution of benefits from activities that so affect natural resources (Morel 2014:12–14).

Once the ACHPR held that the Kenyan government had violated the following sections of the African Charter: Article 8 (religious freedom), Article 14 (property rights), Articles 17(2) and 17(3) (cultural rights), Article 21 (right to natural resources) and Article 22 (right to development); land governance changed. The new Kenyan Land Policy of 2009 (Section 3.3.1.2) and Kenyan Constitution of 2010, Chap. 5 recognise communal land ownership (Morel 2014:22, note 96). Hence, the land trust regime that existed as a matter of land restoration and restitution in many African countries was abolished in Kenya. Therefore, the more AIKS-oriented form of communal land ownership now stands equal to public and private ownership of land. In light of the monumental Endorois case decision, Kenyan public organisations such as the National Environmental Management Authority and Department of Mining, regional governance organisations such as the European Union and global governance organisations such as the United Nations and World Bank have taken action that recognises and tries to implement the Endorois decision (Morel 2014:15). Hence, taken as a whole, Kenya provides an example of how assignment of individual property rights to women disadvantaged women, while recognition of communal land ownership sustains indigenous communities. The Endorois case provides a unique example of how AIKS can inform twenty-first century land governance in post-colonial African states.

Conclusions and Recommendations

In this chapter, the author has tried to conceptualise the intersection of land governance, legal pluralism, AIKS and gender constructions as pertinent to the land reform trajectory in post-colonial African states. The driving theme in the conceptualisation lays in epistemological differentiation – African and western perspectives. It was suggested that westernised ways of knowing are not reserved for Europeans but could be embodied, for example, by traditional leaders who may not meaningfully consult the Council of Elders and ancestors when transacting land deals in Ghana on behalf of the stool which is in contravention of AIKS. It was indicated that the weight of literature on gender constructions in customary institutions fails to acknowledge indigenous constructions of gender complementarity. It was argued that legal pluralism in Ghana suppresses AIKS while an imported land policy for individual land titling suppresses AIKS in Kenya. The latter also wreaked unintended consequences of marginalising women's land rights. However, customary international law and AIKS yielded communal land ownership rights in Kenya given the monumental decision by the ACHPR in the Endorois case. This is instructive for other African states.

The overarching lesson from both Ghana and Kenya is the unrealised role of indigeneity in the land reform trajectory of post-colonial African states. Recommendations on how to ease tensions between seemingly irreconcilable epistemologies underlying land governance in the context of legal pluralism are as follows:

1. Recognise, acknowledge and be informed by epistemological differentiation on land governance as a method of designing land reform.
2. Use AIKS to inform contemporary land governance as accomplished in the Endorois case.
3. Teach living African law in law schools and in the management sciences from its own ontological, epistemological and axiological perspective to empower a generation of African land court jurists and land governance and management experts aware of indigeneity.
4. Infuse the IoTL with indigenous African ways of knowing through outcomes of socio-legal action research conducted by post-graduate students of law and the management sciences.
5. In the judiciary, situate and decide living African law cases and 'official' customary law cases in their socio-cultural context even if these cases are decided in venues of rule of law orthodoxy. Recommendations 3 and 4 above would facilitate this endeavour.
6. Include ancestors through divination practices in the post-colonial land reform trajectory as spirituality and the cycle of the living, living dead and posterity protection connected to land is a sign post of African ways of knowing.

References

Amadiume I (1987) African matriarchal foundations: the Igbo case. Karnak House, London
Amanor K (2008) The changing face of customary land tenure. In: Ubink JM, Amanor KS (eds) Contesting land and custom in Ghana state, chief and the citizen. Leiden University Press, Leiden, pp 55–79
Asante SKB (1965) Interests in land in the customary law of Ghana. A new appraisal. Yale Law J 74(5):848–885

Berry S (2008) Ancestral property: land, politics and 'the deeds of the ancestors' in Ghana and Côte d'Ivoire. In: Ubink JM, Amanor KS (eds) Contesting land and custom in Ghana state, chief and the citizen. Leiden University Press, Leiden, pp 27–5?

Boone C (2009) Electoral populism where property rights are weak land politics in contemporary sub-Saharan Africa. Comp Polit 41(2):183–201

Busia KA (1951) The position of the chief in the modern political system of Ashanti: a study of the influence of contemporary social changes on Ashanti political institutions. Oxford University Press, Oxford

Chopra T, Isser D (2011) Women's access to justice, legal pluralism and fragile states. In P Albrecht, HM Kyed, D Isser, E Harper (eds) Perspectives on involving non-state and customary actors in justice and security reforms. International Development Law Organisation, Rome, Italy pp 23–38

Chuku G (2013) Nwanyibuife. In: Chuku G (ed) Igbo intellectual tradition: creative conflict in African diaspora thought. Palgrave Macmillan, New York, pp 257–293

Crook RC (2008) Customary justice institutions and local alternative dispute resolution: what kind of protection can they offer to customary landholders? In: Ubink JM, Amanor KS (eds) Contesting land and custom in Ghana state, chief and the citizen. Leiden University Press, Leiden, pp 131–154

Daley E, Englert B (2010) Securing land rights for women. J East Afr Stud 4(1):91–113

Day L (2007) Nyarroh of Bandasuma, 1885–1914: A reinterpretation of female chieftancy in Sierra Leone. J Afr Hist 48(3):415–437

Dei G (2012) Indigenous anti-colonial Knowledge as 'heritage knowledge' for promoting Black/African education in diasporic contexts. Decolon Indigen Educ Soc 1(1):102–119

Diop CA (1978) The cultural unity of black Africa. Third World Press, Chicago

Galligan DJ (2007) Law in modern society, Clarendon law series. Oxford University Press, Oxford

Griffiths J (2005) The idea of sociology of law and its relation to law and to sociology. Law Sociol Curr Leg Issues 49(8):63–64

Hellum H (2000) Human rights and gender relations in postcolonial Africa: options and limits for the subjects of legal pluralism. Law Soc Inq 25(2):635–655

Hudson-Weems C (2001) Africana womanism: an overview. In: Aldridge DP, Young C (eds) Out of the revolution: the development of Africana studies. Lexington Books, Lexington, pp 205–217

ILA Interim Report (2010) ILA Committee on the rights of indigenous peoples, 2010 Interim Report to the 74th ILA Conference in The Hague, 15–20 Aug. 2010. Available at: www.ila-hq.org/en/committees/index.cfm/cid/1024. Accessed 23 Feb 2016

Joireman SF (2008) The mystery of capital formation in sub-Saharan Africa: Women, property rights and customary law. Political Science Faculty Publications Paper 70. Available at: http://scholarship.richmond.edu/polisci-faculty-publications/70. Accessed 22 Feb 2016

Keevey I (2009) Ubuntu versus the core values of the South African constitution. J Juridicial Sci 34(2):20–58

Kenya Colony and Protectorate (1955) A plan to intensify the development of African agriculture in Kenya. Government Printer, Nairobi

Kenyatta J (1970) The Kikuyu system of government. In: Cartey W, Kislo M (eds) The Africa reader: independent Africa. Vintage Books, New York, pp 19–23

Makahamadze T, Grand N, Tavuyanago B (2009) The role of traditional leaders in fostering democracy, justice and human rights in Zimbabwe. Afr Anthropol 16(1, 2):33–47

Mbiti J (1990) African religions and philosophy. Heinemann, Portsmouth, NH

McAuslan P (2005) Legal pluralism as a policy option: is it desirable, is it doable? In: Proceedings from the UNDP-international land coalition workshop: land rights for African development: from knowledge to action. Nairobi, Kenya 31 October–3 November 3, 2005. Available at: http://www.undp.org/drylands/lt-workshop-11-05.htm. Accessed 3 Mar 2016

Meinzen-Dick R, Mwangi E (2007) Cutting the web of interests: pitfalls of formalizing property rights. Land Use Policy 6(3):2–11

Mohanty CT (1988) Under western eyes: feminist scholarship and colonial discourses. Fem Rev 30:61–88

Mohanty CT (2003) "Under western eyes" revisited: feminist solidarity through anticapitalist struggles. Signs 28(2):499–535

Morel C (2014) Indigenous peoples as equals under the African charter: the Endrois community versus Kenya. In: Laher R, Sing'Oei K (eds) Indigenous people in Africa: contestations, empowerment and group rights. Africa Institute of South Africa, Pretoria, pp 1–23

Nabudere DW (2011) Afrikology, philosophy and wholeness: an epistemology. Africa Institute of South Africa, Pretoria

Ndima D (2003) The African law of the 21st century in South Africa. Comp Int Law J South Afr 36(3):225–345

Nkrumah K (1964) Consciencism. Monthly Review Press, New York

Ntlama N, Ndima D (2009) The significance of South Africa's traditional courts bill to the challenge of promoting African traditional justice systems. Int J Afr Renaiss Stud 4(1):6–30

Nzegwu N (2012) Widows and daughters in inheritance disputes. In: Nzegwu N (ed) Family matters feminist concepts in African philosophy and culture. Sunny Press, New York, pp 103–156

Odora Hoppers CA (2001) Indigenous knowledge and the integration of knowledge systems: towards a conceptual and methodological framework. HSRC, Pretoria

Oluwagbemi-Jacob D, Uduma CE (2015) Gender equality, gender inequality, and gender complementarity: insights from igbo traditional culture. Philoso Stud 5(5)

Otto JM (2009) Rule of law promotion, land tenure and poverty alleviation: questioning the assumptions of Hernando de Soto. Hague J Rule Law 1(1):173–194

Pierson C (1992) Democracy, markets, and capital: are there necessary economic limits to democracy? Pol Stud 40(Supplement s1):83–98

Pimentel D (2011) Legal pluralism in post-colonial Africa: linking statutory and customary adjudication in Mozambique. Article 2. Yale Hum Rights Dev J 14(1):59–104

Republic of Ghana (1992) Constitution of the republic of Ghana 1992. Ghana Publishing Corporation, Tema

Schmid U (2001) Legal pluralism as a source of conflict in multi-ethnic societies. J Leg Pluralism Unofficial Law 33(46):1–47

Tamanaha B (2008) Understanding legal pluralism: past to present, local to global. 30 Sydney L Rev. 375

Tonah S (2008) Chiefs, earth priests and the state: Irrigation agriculture, competing institutions and the transformation of land tenure arrangements in Northeastern Ghana. In: Ubink JM, Amanor KS (eds) Contesting land and custom in Ghana state, chief and the citizen. Leiden University Press, Leiden, pp 113–130

Twining W (2009) Normative and legal pluralism: a global perspective. The seventh annual Herbert L. Bernstein Memorial Lecture in International and Comparative Law, Duke University School of Law, 7 April 2009. Available at: http://scholarship.law.duke.edu/cgi/viewcontent.cgi?article =1049&context=djcil. Accessed 22 Mar 2016

Ubink J (2008) Struggles for land in peri-urban Kumasi and their effect on popular perceptions of chiefs and chieftaincy. In: Ubink JM, Amanor KS (eds) Contesting land and custom in Ghana state, chief and the citizen. Leiden University Press, Leiden, pp 155–181

Ubink J (2011) Gender equality on the Horizon: the case of Uukwambi Traditional Authority, Northern Namibia. In: Harper E (ed) Working with customary justice systems: Post-conflict and fragile states. International Development Law Organisation (IDLO), Rome, pp 52–71

UN DRIP (2007) United Nations Declaration on the Rights of Indigenous Peoples, GA Res. 61/295, 13 Sept. 2007. Available at: http://www.un.org/esa/socdev/unpfii/documents/DRIPS_ en.pdf. Accessed 22 Mar 2016

Weir J (2007) Chiefly women and women's leadership in pre-colonial southern Africa. In N Gasa (ed) Women in South African history: they move boulders and cross rivers. HSRC Press, Pretoria

Wiessner S (2011) The cultural rights of indigenous peoples: achievements and continuing challenges. Eur J Int Law 22(1):121–140

Williams C (1974) The destruction of Black civilization: great issues of a race from 4500 B.C. to 2000 A.D. Third World Press, Chicago, IL

Woodman GR (1996) Legal pluralism and the search for justice. J Afr Law 40(2):152–167

Chapter 8
Cultural Practices and Women's Land Rights in Africa: South Africa and Nigeria in Comparison

Bolanle Eniola and Adeoye O. Akinola

Introduction

Gender parity has been the subject of intellectual debates worldwide, particularly in Africa. The last few decades have witnessed public enlightenments, through policy makers, scholars and activists, towards the actualization of women empowerment and land rights in Africa. This became more intense due to the global activism of the gender and development movement, which links socio-economic development with gender equality in relation to societal resources like land (Wanyeki 2003). This has given rise to a shift in global and national policies towards women capacity building and gender equality, especially in accessing societal resources like land. The United Nations' Millennium Development Goal (MDG 3 - promotion of gender equality and empowerment of women) underlines the need to liberate women from social-economic and political exclusion (UNDP 2015).

In Africa, the denial of women's property rights has been a major impediment to gender equality and development (Yeboah 2014). The continent groans under the weight of poverty, gender disempowerment and socio-economic underdevelopment; and land-related issues are one of the drivers of these inequalities. Furthermore, there are cases of conflict over land due to the convergence between land distribution patterns and increasing levels of poverty in Africa (Lahiff n.d.). This lends credence to the importance of land in Africa. Despite the diversification of African economies to different sectors and endeavours, land still constitutes a significant factor of production, means of livelihood and source of security against impoverishment in Africa. Based on the importance of land, an unequal land right that relegates some

B. Eniola (✉)
Ekiti State University, Ado Ekiti, Nigeria

A. O. Akinola
Department of Public Administration, University of Zululand, KwaDlangezwa, South Africa

© Springer International Publishing AG, part of Springer Nature 2019   109
A. O. Akinola, H. Wissink (eds.), *Trajectory of Land Reform in Post-Colonial African States*, Advances in African Economic, Social and Political Development, https://doi.org/10.1007/978-3-319-78701-5_8

sections of the society to the background explains the persistent poverty and inequality prevalent in most African societies (Lahiff n.d.). As presented by Odeny,

> Land is one of the cornerstones of economic development on which farmers, pastoralists and other communities base their livelihoods. Land is also a significant component of business assets, which play significant role in business investment strategies. Thus, securing land rights can have a profound impact on economic development...land is a source of identity and cultural heritage (Odeny 2013: 4).

Land resource, land arrangements and policies has a profound impact on socio-economic and political development of Africa. In South Africa, land policy and politics has become one of the most significant public discourses in the post-Apartheid era. Land reform in the country was premised on the perception that agrarian transformation was required to reallocate capital assets which were distorted by the 1913 Natives' Land Act that produced a landless majority (Hall 2004; Cousins and Walker 2015). The land reform was centred on redressing the skewed land arrangements between the white and landless black, and not necessarily bridging the gender gap in land tenure system. Similarly, Nigerian land reform was specifically targeted at transferring most land under state ownership. Therefore, it becomes pertinent to have a grasp of the place of gender in the African land project.

Women are persistently denied of land rights due to African indigenous practices that reinforces man as the custodian of properties; hence, "land-related gender inequalities are culturally created" (Yeboah 2014). According to Odeny (2013), gender has assumed an important issue in women's land rights due to the direct relationships between accessing land resources, security of land rights, securing food security and improvement in livelihood. According to SOFA (cited in Odeny 2013), women actually produce about 80% of the agricultural products in the continent, yet they can only claim ownership of a mere 1% of the land. For instance, Guijt (cited in Odeny 2013) revealed that during the irrigation project in Gambia, 87 percent of the quality lands were recorded in men's names, while only 10 percent were under women's control, despite the women's higher productivity and holding claim as a major producers of rice on swamp lands. Even with the diverse forms of land reforms in many African countries, its impact on improving women's land rights was very marginal.

Some African countries (Nigeria, Uganda, Mozambique, and South Africa) have managed to integrate women's land rights into their legal frameworks, in reality this did not bring feasible outcomes with respect to equitable access and control over land as a result of poor implementation and enforcement of the laws. Women are unable to benefit from these provisions and even where there are equitable laws, women in Africa's rural areas lack adequate knowledge about their rights (Odeny 2013: 4–6); although, Kenya enjoys a slightly different land relation. Odeny (2013) presents how Kenya's constitutional and institutional arrangements provide for women's land rights. The 2010 Constitution and the National land policy (2009) have adopted the African Union's principle on land policy by recognizing women's land rights, giving consideration to other challenges in the attainment of their rights land ownership and create the required legal and institutional framework to promote the realization of these rights. Also, Land Registration Act, Land Act and Land

Commission Act 2012 reinforce gender parity in respect of land ownership and use in the country. The question of institutional support is very germane to the success of land policy. For instance, institutional weakness has been identified as one of the deficiencies of the South Africa's land policy.

This chapter examines women's land rights (access and control) in Africa, focusing on the Nigeria and South Africa's experiences. It assesses African traditional practices and norms that limit women's property rights and explores how gender inequalities in terms of land ownership and rights have jeopardized attempts at sustainable development in Africa. The chapter is divided into six sections, starting with the introduction, and followed by an examination of land arrangements in South Africa and Nigeria. The third section provides an overview of women's property rights in South Africa and Nigeria, followed by an assessment of women's land rights in the two countries. Section five identifies those cultural and customary practises that restrict the implementation of women's land rights in Africa, and the chapter concludes by reiterating the urgent need to promote gender equality, which is an essential corollary for Africa's survival and sustainable development.

Land Tenure Systems in South Africa and Nigeria

Prior to the colonial era, Africa operated communal land tenure system does not significantly reflect patriarchal land arrangement. The skewed land arrangement in terms of gender inequality was part of Africa colonial heritage. As noted earlier, South Africa and Nigeria both experienced colonial subjugation. Nigeria became an independent state in 1960; South Africa's experience is different as it proceeded from colonialism to apartheid before becoming a democratic state in 1994. The historical antecedents of the two countries have greatly influenced their legal systems as they operate plural legal systems, which was projected in their respective land tenure systems. Land was a major means of production, and required by the colonial administrations to achieve their economic purpose in the colonized countries (Udoekanem et al. 2014; Odeny 2013). The land regimes, introduced by the colonial powers, were not in consonance with the existing African indigenous land tenure system. While tenure was communal, it had a patriarchal bias (Yeboah 2014). After independence, Nigeria and South Africa sought to redress the injustices perpetrated by the colonial and Apartheid regimes respectively.

Conquest and forced dispossessions during the colonial and Apartheid eras in South Africa resulted in the reservation of just about 13% of the land as 'homelands' that are presently referred to as communal lands for the black majority (Walker and Dubb 2013; Kaarhus et al. 2005). The remaining 87% of the land was controlled and owned by the white minority and the white-controlled Apartheid government. The successive democratic governments sought to redress the lopsided land pattern by adopting different strategies: the enactment of different Land Acts, establishments of institutions of land like the Reconstruction and Development Programme (RDP) in 1994, adoption of the 'willing buyer willing seller' approach, and other subsequent land reform initiatives (Department of Land Affairs 1997; Hall 2004; Anseeuw and Alden 2011; Walker and Dubb 2013; Cousins and Walker 2015). One of those that directly address women's land rights is the RDP. It identifies land and agrarian reform, particularly women's land rights, as an important socio-economic policy for development (Rangan and Gilmartin 2002: 633). Since then, the governments have intensified their efforts at ensuring equal land rights, particularly for women, through various programs, legislation and policies. These include the Growth, Employment and Redistribution (GEAR) strategy, and the Communal Land Rights Act, 2004 which spearheaded land tenure reform and redistribution of land rights. However, land reform projects in the country continue to attract criticism because of its very slow progress (Satgé 2013).

One of factors hampering land tenure reform and women's land rights is the role played by traditional leaders in the redistribution of communal land. Section 21(2) of the Communal Land Rights Act, 2004 provides that "if a community has a recognized traditional council (in terms of the Traditional Leadership Act), the powers and duties of the land administration committee of such a community may be exercised and performed by such council". This has been one of the constraints to women's equal access to land as there is no gender parity in the traditional council that redistributes the land. Even in modern political institutions, men dominate (Abati 2016). The traditional authorities operate on the principle of hereditary, and this reinforces the patriarchal nature of the society.

Furthermore, the principle of equality in terms of property ownership is alien to the customs and traditions that regulated the conduct of the traditional council (Rangan and Gilmartin 2002: 638). Hence, women cannot fully benefit from redistribution as their rights to land are subsumed under that of their husbands'. Even in cases where women have been listed as independent household heads, and as beneficiaries in their own right, their access to land has been mediated by membership of patriarchal households. While some of the land reform strategies emphasizes individual rights to land, this might not benefit women as many are too poor and too dependent on male authority to be able to assert their rights(Razavi 2003: 28).

In the case of Nigeria, a plural land tenure system was in operation during the colonial dispensation. It was a broad-based land policy that combined the British and African indigenous land systems. It was not until about 12 years after independence that the military regime realized the necessity to effect a change in Nigeria's land arrangement; hence, the enactment of the Land Use Act (1978) of Nigeria. The Act, which nationalized land in the country, was adopted to regulate the use and ownership of land. Broadly, the land act was passed to reconcile the problem of urbanization in respect of land availability, promote easy accessibility of land to the citizens irrespective of gender, unify land tenure system, abolish the traditional practices of land inheritance, and ensure equity and justice in land distribution, use and ownership (Odeny 2013: 10).

Under the provision of the Act, Section 5(1) empowers the Governor of a State to grant a statutory right of occupancy to any person for all purposes in respect of land, whether or not in an urban area and issue a certificate of occupancy as evidence of such rights in accordance with the provisions of Section 9(1). The land law also vests control of all non-urban land on local government. Local government can thus grant customary rights of occupancy (Section 6 of the Land Use Act). According to its provisions, the customary right of occupancy includes the right of a person or community to lawfully use or occupy land in accordance with customary law. Most of the land for agricultural purposes was located in non-urban areas which are mainly regulated by customary law. As such women's land rights in these areas are subject to customary law which does not recognize women's right to land. Also reinforcing the limitations of the Land Act, Mabogunje (cited in Odeny 2013: 11), adds that the act also failed to ensure adequate compensation for land that was hitherto acquired arbitrarily; rather it reinforces discriminatory traditional and customary practices that impede women access to land.

Women's Property Rights in Africa: South Africa and Nigeria

In terms of history and women's property rights, Nigeria and South Africa have many factors in common. Like other African countries, both are products of colonial invasions or under foreign minority rule and distortion of their cultural practises. Generally, Odeny puts this in context,

> Expropriation of land by colonial masters, introduction of tenure systems alien to Africa and concentrating African population to designated areas significantly contributed to landlessness in Africa. The development of extractive industries such as mining, introduction of land markets, and large-scale agriculture, bio-fuel plantations and tourism are displacing people in large numbers (Odeny 2013: 6).

In the case of South Africa, Kariuki historicizes the South African experience and notes that "the process of settler occupation entailed the alienation of fertile agricultural lands and the creation of exclusive reserves for African occupation that were least arable and environmentally degraded" (Kariuki 2009: 1). Therefore, the quest for land reform outweighs ideological rhetorics, rather, it is a decisive conditions of socio-economic and political stabilization of societies (Anseeuw and Alden 2011).

Furthermore, as with most African states, the two societies' are of heterogeneous cultural entities. Their constitutions were drafted and adopted at relatively similar periods (South Africa's in 1996 shortly after the demise of apartheid and Nigeria's in 1999 after the exit of military dictatorship) and experienced similar trajectories towards democracratization. Although the evolution of their constitutions differ, both constitutions contain extant provisions that guarantee equality and human dignity and forbid discrimination on the grounds of gender, including the right to own property (Chap. 2 of the South African 1996 Constitution and Chap. 4 of the Nigerian 1999 Constitution). All citizens have the right to own both movable and immovable property (Section 25 of the South African 1996 Constitution and Section 43 of the Nigerian 1999 Constitution).

Although, the constitutions of South Africa and Nigeria hold cultural rights in high esteem (Sections 30 and 31 of the South African 1996 Constitution and Section 21 of the Nigerian 1999 Constitution), the culture envisaged is one that enhances human dignity. Any customary practice that fails to meet this criterion will be deemed invalid. The various provisions of these constitutions seek to resolve the conflict between customary laws and the constitution (Sections 2, 30 and 31 of the South African 1996 Constitution and Section 1(3) of the Nigerian 1999 Constitution). The constitution is the supreme law of the land and any law, including customary law that is inconsistent with its provisions shall be null and void. As noted by Justice Langa in the case of *Bhe V Magistrate Khayelitsha* 2004(1) SA 580 CC para41, customary law "is protected by and subject to the constitution in its own right".

Nigeria and South Africa have both signed and ratified international human rights instruments on discrimination against women. Among others, these include the Universal Declaration of Human Rights (UDHR), 1948, the International Covenant on Economic, Social and Cultural Rights (ICESCR), 1966, the International Covenant on Civil and Political Right, the Convention on the Elimination of all Forms of Discrimination against Women (CEDAW), 1979, the African Charter on Human and Peoples' Rights, and the Protocol to the African Charter on Human and Peoples' Right (ACHPR), 1981. All these instruments guarantee equality between men and women and prohibit discrimination based on gender.

In addition to the provisions of these treaties, several resolutions that focus on women's land rights have been adopted by UN committees. These include the UN Committee on Economic, Social and Cultural Rights which states that "women have a right to own, use, or otherwise control housing, land and property on equal basis with men and do access necessary resources to do so"(UN Committee on Economic, Social and Cultural Rights, 2005). The UN Committee on the Elimination of Discrimination against Women recognizes that a woman's right to own, manage, enjoy and dispose of property is central to a her right to enjoy financial independence (UN Committee on the Elimination of Discrimination against Women, 1992).

The Committee further enjoins countries undergoing redistribution of land or agrarian reform programs to embrace the principle of equality irrespective of women's marital status (Paragraph 27, UN Committee on the Elimination of Discrimination against Women, 1992). In November 2013, the African Commission on Human and Peoples' Right adopted a resolution *(262: Resolution on Women's Right to Land and Productive Resources)* on women's right to land and other productive resources (ACHPR 2013). This resolution seeks to ensure that women have equal access to land. Among other things, it calls on states parties to repeal discriminatory practices that hinder women from access to, use of and control over land and other productive resources. The protocol also recognises the immense contribution of women to the productive use of land in terms of ensuring food security, agricultural sustainability and community development in Africa.

However, the various international human rights instruments on women's right to land and property rights have not made an appreciable difference in the lives of women due to the influence of cultural practices. This limits women's participation in economic development, especially in the area of food production. They are unable to produce food crops for family subsistence. As noted by Yeboah, "gender mainstreaming and women's empowerment are increasingly becoming integral elements of development interventions. Persistent gender-related inequalities with respect to land go against other efforts towards inclusive development and good governance" (Yeboah 2014). Women cannot fully realize their fundamental human rights without equal rights to property. As noted by the UN Commission on Human Rights (cited in Gbadamosi 2007: 285), property and land rights are important indicators of women's empowerment and human development. Therefore, countries with poor records of women's land rights are far from accomplishing the women empowerment and gender parity project.

Women's Land Rights in Africa

Women are central to diversified livelihoods in Africa. They make a significant contribution to food production through farm labor, food processing, and the storage and transportation of farm products (Ilumoka 2012: 423). However, while women's subsistence farming plays an important role in ensuring food security, they have been notable constraints against optimal productivity. One of the impediments to African women's effective engagement in agricultural production is inadequate access to land, which has been attributed to patriarchal land tenure systems in most African states (Razavi 2003: 4). This system evolved from indigenous law and traditional practices. Laws known as customary laws were developed from the various practices and customs of the African people to regulate activities in their respective communities (Ndulo 2011: 88).

The African customary land tenure system is characterized by linage or clan control. The first person to clear the land is believed to have a duty towards using it and passing it down by inheritance to his descendants. The use and ownership of land can be generally obtained through the following sources: inheritance, purchase, or state intervention (Lastarria-Cornhiel and Zoraida 2005). African societies and states usually exclude women from land access and control through these three broad areas. In most cases, documentation is usually required to access land through these means, and women do not usually possess such documents. The land devolves to the son in patrilineal systems and to the sister's son in matrilineal systems (Ensminger 1997: 169). Hence, land rights are controlled by men and women only have access through a male relative, usually a father or husband.

Women do not have direct claim to land, rather their rights are subsumed under their husband's rights (Jacobs 2002: 888). This is the situation in most cases because land rights are granted to the household head. However, in some cases, for example under some land schemes in Honduras, Tanzania, and Zimbabwe, a woman is permitted to hold land where it is evident that she is the household head (Ensminger 1997:169). It goes without saying that, in the traditional system, women are not allowed to hold land as a matter of course; they only do so in exceptional cases. This is due to the erroneous belief that women are generally not permanent members of the family to which they belong. A daughter cease to be a member of her parents' family upon marriage while a wife becomes a member of her husband's family when she marries. However, she might cease to be a member in the case of divorce or the death of the husband. Even in cases where a woman has the financial capacity to purchase land, if she attempts to do so, it would be presumed that she intends to run away from her matrimonial home.

It is implicit from the foregoing that most African land tenure systems are discriminatory. They regard women (wives and daughters) as adjuncts to men, either their father or husbands. Women are excluded from decisions on the allocation and transfer of land in their various communities (Kaarhus et al. 2005: 482). Thus, customary land tenure systems violate fundamental human rights such as the right to dignity and equality, among others. Unequal land rights are one of the factors that promote women's subordination and poverty (Razavi 2003: 4).

Globalization and industrialization have exacerbated this situation, as land resources are now keenly contested. Land acquisition, reforms and resettlement schemes in Africa have reduced women's right to hold land for subsistence farming. Kaarhus et al. put this in context and posit that, "given women's crucial role in food production and provision, any set of strategies for sustainable food security must address their limited access to productive resources" (Kaarhus et al. 2005: 482). Thus, gender equality in property rights as envisaged by various international instruments is essential to ensuring sustainable development in Africa.

Cultural Impediments to Women's Land Rights in Nigeria and South Africa

As noted above, Nigeria and South Africa's constitutions, guarantee the right to equality to every citizen. The constitution is the supreme law of the land. However, in practice, though discriminatory in nature, the lives of the majority of women in most African countries are regulated by customary law. In Nigeria and South Africa, customary law is one of the instruments used to regulate property ownership. The social legitimacy of these traditions is a stumbling block in realizing women's property rights as these traditions regard women as being incapable of exercising control over landed property. In many communities in Nigeria, the longstanding custom that women cannot acquire property like land and fishing areas, among others in their own right persists (Alewo and Olong 2012: 128).

Similarly, in South Africa, despite the constitution's guarantee of gender equality, land reform in many rural areas has not benefitted women due to customary law practices which deny women access to land (Rangan and Gilmartin 2002: 633). In Africa, the bulk of the land, "about 75%, is under customary tenure, administered by unwritten law based on tradition and cultural norms" (Odeny 2013: 8).

In the area of land rights and other areas, customary law does not embrace gender equality. Communal land is allocated by traditional authorities who are usually unelected male community members. Furthermore, the constitution recognizes traditional authorities. In many cases, they are more comfortable allocating land to their male counterparts for commercial farming than to women who mainly need access to land for subsistence farming (Rangan and Gilmartin 2002: 633). The following section discusses some of the cultural practices that inhibit women from exercising their property rights.

Law of Primogeniture

Primogeniture rule is one of the rules of the customary law of succession that states that upon the death of a man, his properties, including land, is transferred to his male children. This practice is well-entrenched in South Africa and Nigeria. Under this system, devolution of property is patrilineal, it follows the blood line and allocates to men permanent membership of the family. The male-child perpetuates the father's dynasty, while women are expected to marry and cease to be members of their father's family. Equally, if a woman marries into a family, she does not bring any property into it and what she acquires in the course of the marriage is due to the conducive environment in the husband's house and as such, belongs to him (Gbadamosi 2007: 285). Consequently, the rule forbids widows from inheriting from their husbands, and daughters from inheriting from their parents.

However, in the Nigerian case of *Mojekwu V Mojekwu*, the property in dispute was owned by one Okechukwu who had married two wives, Janet and Caroline, who were the defendants in the case. The plaintiff, a nephew of their deceased husband, sought a declaration that he was entitled under customary law to the deceased's land since the deceased left no male child. The Court of Appeal ruled that the Oli-Ekpe custom in Ibo land in Nigeria which bars women from inheriting land is repugnant to natural justice, equity and good conscience.

Similarly, in the South African case of *Bhe and Others v Magistrate, Khayelitsha and Others* (2004 2 SA: 544), the court held that excluding women from inheritance on the grounds of gender violates their right to equality and is a form of discrimination: "… it implies that women are not fit or competent to own and administer property. Its effect is also to subject these women to a status of perpetual minority, by placing them automatically under the control of male heirs, simply by virtue of their sex and gender. Their dignity is further affronted by the fact that as women, they are also excluded from interstate succession and denied the right which other members of the population have, to be holders of, and to control property" (Paragraph 92, Bhe case). These rules violate the fundamental rights principles of equality and dignity and are incompatible with the provisions of the constitution, and therefore cannot stand. Primogeniture rule is the genesis of the cultural practice of sex preference.

Patrimony

Land rights play a crucial role in agricultural development and inclusive growth, but in many countries in Africa, women are unable to actively participate in the agriculture and economic endeavours due to gender inequality, which is founded on patriarchal and cultural traditions (Yeboah 2014). Perhaps the most persistent obstacles to improving gender equity in land rights have their roots in patriarchal values and practices (Lastarria-Cornhiel and Zoraida 2005). Preference for the male-child is one of the African cultural practices which jeopardies women's attainment of land rights in Africa. This reinforces patrimony. Patriarchal land ownership systems in many African countries can mean that women are often dependent on men for land use. That is, men, consciously and intuitively, maintain the patrimonial power relations. Lastarria-Cornhiel and Zoraida (2005) maintain that "rights to land - especially women's rights to land - are determined by a complex interaction between the institutions, and underlying power relations, of a society". The authors further put this in a broader perspective thus,

> Political opposition to gender equity is often concealed as protection of cultural values, and interprets attempts to improve women's rights and their status as challenges to the traditional family. The recognition of women's equal rights introduces modifications in existing power relations, leading to further changes in the traditional ways decision are made and undermining stereotypes of a gender-based division of labour (Lastarria-Cornhiel and Zoraida 2005).

As noted earlier, some African cultures do not regard a woman as a permanent member of the family; hence, a male child is always preferred to a female child as such a child is expected to succeed the father and consolidate his dynasty. Most African families enthusiastically celebrate the arrival of a male child, while a girl child does not generate the same level of excitement, especially when she is not the first in the family (Ajayi and Olotuah 2005:60). Given that a female child cannot succeed her father, she cannot inherit property in most African cultures.

While several countries, like Ethiopia and Kenya, have adopted international treaties such as the Convention on the Elimination of Discrimination against Women, and enacted laws to enhance gender parity, land arrangements in most African countries are based on traditions that discriminate against women (Yeboah 2014). In Rwanda, Mali and Ghana, there have been concerted efforts to develop indigenous practices that promote women's involvement in family land management. Basically, there are two modes of land and property inheritance system under the traditional authority: patrilineal systems in which men holds power and inherits property and matrilineal systems that permits women's right to inheritance (Odeny 2013). Male have the right to land, especially through inheritance, while the female group could own or use land only through men under cartain conditions like marriage. In such cases, they can only access land at their husbands' home. Odeny (2013: 8) reaches a conclusion that, "women are treated as people in transit from natal home to join their spouses".

Women as Property or a Chattel

In most African societies, one of the requirements of a valid customary marriage is the payment of a dowry, otherwise called 'bride-price'. In ancient times, the dowry consisted of the labour services rendered by a man to the parent of the woman he sought to marry. This made man to see a woman as a prized commodity. However, modernization has changed this cultural practice and labour services have become monetized. The notion that payment of the bride-price connotes buying the bride is mistaken. It has been argued that the bride-price is a form of compensation to the bride's parents for what they have spent on her. This gives the impression that parents are selling their daughters for a price (Steyn and Rip 1968: 507–508). The bride-price has a grave effect on the fundamental human rights of women as the husband who pays a bride price regards his wife as a commodity that he bought. Consequently, she is a part of his property. This may be responsible for their relegation to the background in societal decision making process. This pint was reiterated by Alewo and Olong (2012). The authors hold that women are mostly omitted from making decisions and contributing to the public decision-making process as recorded in ancient Ibo and Hausa societies of Nigeria. Since they are not equal to men in making decision, then, decisions will not mostly be in their favour.

In declaring his assets, a Nigerian senator listed his two wives as part of his portfolio (Abati 2016). Similarly, in the case of *Omo Ogunkoya v Omo Ogunkoya* (Unreported case Appeal No CA/L/46/88) the Nigerian Court of Appeal opined that: "the wives left are regarded as chattels that are inherited by other members of the family ... of the deceased under certain conditions." Payment of a bride-price entrenches male domination and exploitation and reinforces the domination of women by the men-folk. In another case in Nigeria, *Suberu V Summonu* (1947 2 F.S.C:31), it was stated that "... it is a well settled rule of native law and custom of the Yoruba people that a wife could not inherit her husband's property since she herself is like a chattel to be inherited by the relative of her husband". Such rulings further validate the reality of gender inequality in respect of property rights in Africa.

In most traditional African communities, the primary duty of a woman is child bearing and rearing. Women are not expected to engage in any serious work for their sustenance. They rely solely on their husbands for survival. However, in some cases women support their husbands by growing food crops. Since women are regarded as adjunct to their husbands, they are not expected to lay claim to the farm produce. It is believed that the land, the produce and the woman are the husband's property. Hence, a woman is not expected to inherit her husband's property since she is part of the property that would be inherited. Upon the demise of the husband, the woman is often ejected from the husband's property.

In many parts of Africa, religion has greatly influenced the cultures to a point where there is a convergence of culture and religion. This is more prevalent in an Islamic society like northern Nigeria, where religious-cum cultural practises often undermine women's land rights in the affected societies (Wanyeki 2003). The Islamic principle that constrains women to their homes is often misinterpreted as a valid reason to disable women from land inheritance. Other African societies also believe that the role of the women is that of "house-wives" and "house-keepers". Buttressing this point, Lastarria-Cornhiel and Zoraida (2005) notes that "women are often thought of as housewives; and their agricultural work in the field, harvesting, transporting, storing and processing is considered an extension of their home duties and tasks, not productive work". In northern Nigeria, which is predominantly founded on Islamic belief system through the concept of purdah, women are forbidden from ploughing or sowing in public spheres (Wanyeki 2003). Despite legal framework and activism to abolish gendered relations, there are factors militating against its actualization. Drawing from South Africa, Lastarria-Cornhiel and Zoraida identify one of the factors as the "social costs women bear if they go against cultural norms - from social ridicule to the prospect of losing what social benefits women in patriarchal communities enjoy" (Lastarria-Cornhiel and Zoraida 2005).

Widowhood Practices

Widowhood practices are another cultural practice that constrains women's property rights. Women are not allowed to inherit their husbands' property as their access to land is based on marriage. In most cases a woman loses access to land on the death of the husband, while in some cases she is expected to remain on the land until she remarries or dies. In this situation, she may have access to the land but she is not regarded as the owner (Iruonagbe 2010: 2604). The husband's property devolves to the children, particularly male children. Under native law and custom, devolution of property follows the blood lineage. Since a widow is not of the blood ancestry, she has no share in the property of her deceased husband.

In the case of *Sogunro-Davies v Sogunro-Davies,* the court held that "intestacy under the native law and custom, the devolution of property follows the blood. Therefore, a wife or widow not being of the blood has no claim to any cause" (1929 2 NLR: 80). Most traditional African cultures do not recognize the concept of co-ownership of property. There is a general belief that substantial family property such as land cannot be owned by women (Iruonagbe 2010: 2604). It is implicit from the above that widowhood practices do not reflect the principle of equal ownership of property acquired during marriage.

Conclusion

Although the chapter has identified the germane roles of women in the agricultural development project, highlighted how women have struggled to attain gender parity with men and presented clear arguments to show how cultural practises has hindered women from achieving appreciable land rights; however, the chapter does not hold that sustainable development is guaranteed once women attain land rights. The chapter does not also claim that the issue of the impoverishment of Africans, especially the women-folk, is non-existence with the actualization of women's land rights. The chapter calls attention to those cultural impediments to women's land rights and how such further widens the gender gap between the two sexes. The eradication of gender restrictions to land use and ownership will definitely contribute to Africa's overall development and improvement in livelihood. For instance, the South African 2011 Census, showed that the female population exceed that of men (Brand South Africa 2012); thus, denying a majority South Africans a basic means of production is antithetical to development.

Clearly, some customary laws and practices are at odds with modern realities. Since laws are made for a changing and dynamic society, those laws should also undergo changes to conform to prevailing socio-economic realities. The global population keep rising, and number of farmers depleting due to urbanization and other factors, thus, restricting agriculture to the male population through the denial of women's land rights constitute a sure path to food crisis in Africa. Understanding societal dynamism resulted in the formulations of new laws by government and international bodies, adherence to such regulations are required. This is not a call for the abolition of all traditional and customary practices, but a call for adherence to constitutionalism and development of cultural principles in Africa, South Africa and Nigeria in particular. The two countries have the responsibilities to localise any international treaties they adopted. Conformity of practices could be achieved by modifying those that undermine women's property rights and conform to the demands of development. Where modification of traditions and cultures are complex and unachievable, such practices should be abolished.

Wanyeki (2003) sees the promulgation of new laws and its implementation as a potent approach to achieving women's access and control of land; however, its implementation and legitimacy has become a great challenge. Lastarria-Cornhiel and Zoraida (2005) rightly notes that "even when a gender-parity law is passed, the implementation is most times hampered by customs or traditions". This is one of the bane of the women property right conundrum. Wanyeki (2003) explains the reason for this gap in implementation. According to her, the issue of land is constructed differently by the government and the community. The state conceives land as a highly valued economic resource that should be subjected to market logics like individual land ownership, but the community believes that land is a collective resource, which has great emotional and cultural connotations. Therefore, legal and associate institutions responsible for the implementation of the various laws must be established to ensure that these laws make the necessary difference in the lives of the people for whom they are promulgated. As reinforced by Ashton (2012), establishing institutions is not enough; those institutions should be driven towards effectiveness. There is also a need to change laws that are discriminatory and adopt new laws that recognize equality in land and property rights. This could be achieved by increasing women's participation in legislative processes and other layers of authority.

Civic and human rights education is also essential for the realization of women's land rights. Women that are knowledgeable on fundamental human rights and gender issues have the capacity to utilize the existing legislative and judicial framework to challenge discriminatory cultural practices that violate their land and property rights. At different times, women in both South Africa and Nigeria have challenged the denial of their rights in court. Customary law is subject to the constitution; hence, any laws that are inconsistent with the constitution are declared null and void. However, it is not enough to make a court ruling in favour of the women, enforcement of such rulings should be guaranteed by the state.

Furthermore, stakeholders in the gender activism should engage with the state and traditional authorities towards addressing women land rights and also ensuring that the customary law is reformed and developed to conform to the modern demands of socio-economic realities. As noted by Yeboah (2014), "strengthening women's land rights is a shared responsibility. There is a need to create an enabling environment for land governance mechanisms which support women's land rights, and governments have a role in eliminating discriminatory legislation". For instance, if the legislature fails to outlaw customary laws that discriminate against women, the onus is on the courts to ensure that the laws are interpreted in consonance with fundamental human rights.

References

Abati R (2016) The Misogynist in the Nigerian Senate. http//:wwwreubenabati.com.ng/2016-03-20-The-misogynists-in-the-Nigerian-Senate-By-Reuben-Abati.html

ACHPR (2013) 262: Resolution on women's right to land and productive resources. In: African commission on human and people's rights. http//:www.achpr.org/sessions/54th/resolutions/262/

Ajayi MA, Olotuah AO (2005) Violation of women's property rights within the family. Agenda: Empowering Women Gend Equit 66:58–63

Alewo AJ, Olong MA (2012) Cultural practices and traditional beliefs as impediments to the enjoyment of women's rights in Nigeria. Int Law Res 1(1):134–143

Anseeuw W, Alden C (2011) From freedom charter to cautious land reform - the politics of land in South Africa. Discussion Paper No. 201/1. University of Pretoria, Pretoria

Ashton G (2012) Land reform in South Africa: an unfulfilled Obligation. The South African Civil Society Information Service. http://sacsis.org.za/site/article/1475

Brand South Africa (2012) South Africa's population. https://brandsouthafrica.com/people-culture/people/population

Cousins B, Walker C (2015) Land divided land restored: land reform in South Africa for the 21st century. JACANA Media, Johannesburg

de Satgé R (2013) Synthesis report: land divided: land and South African Society in 2013. In: Comparative perspective. http://www.landdivided2013.org.za/sites/default/files/Synthesis%20Report%20-%20Land%20Divided.pdf

Department of Land Affairs (1997) White paper on South Africa land policy. Department of Land Affairs, Pretoria. http://www.gov.za/files/whitepaperlandreform.pdf

Ensminger J (1997) Changing property rights: reconciling formal and informal rights to land in Africa. In: Drobak JN, Nye JVC (eds) The frontiers of the new institutional economics. Academic Press, San Diego, pp 165–196

Gbadamosi AO (2007) Reproductive health and rights: African perspectives and legal issues in Nigeria, network for justice and democracy. https://books.google.co.za/books/about/Reproductive_Health_and_Rights.html?id=oXy8tgAACAAJ&redir_esc=y

Hall R (2004) A political economy of land reform in South Africa. Rev Afr Polit Econ 31(100):213–227

Ilumoka A (2012) Globalisation and the re-establishment of women's land rights in Nigeria: the role of legal history. Chicago Kent Law Rev 87(2):423–437

Iruonagbe C (2010) Women's land rights and the challenge of patriarchy: lessons from Ozalla community, Edo state, Nigeria. Gend Behav 8(1):2603–2617

Jacobs S (2002) Land reform: still a goal worth pursuing for rural women? J Int Dev 14:887–898

Kaarhus R, Benjaminsen T, Hellum A, Ikdahl I (2005) Women's land rights in Tanzania and South Africa: a human rights based perspective on formalisation. Forum Dev Stud 32(2):443–482

Kariuki S (2009) Agrarian reform, rural development and governance in Africa: a case of eastern and southern Africa. In: Policy Brief, vol 59. Centre for Policy Studies, Rosebank

Lahiff E (n.d.) Redistributive land reform and poverty reduction in South Africa. http://www.plaas.org.za/sites/default/files/publications-pdf/South Africa Lahiff.pd

Lastarria-Cornhiel S, Zoraida G (2005) Gender and land rights: findings and lessons from country studies. Food and Agricultural Organization (FAO). http://www.fao.org/docrep/008/a0297e/a0297e08.htm

Ndulo M (2011) African customary law, customs and women's rights. Indiana J Glob Leg Stud 18(1):86–120

Odeny M (2013) Improving access to land and strengthening women's land rights in Africa. Paper prepared for presentation at the "Annual World Bank conference on land and poverty". The World Bank-Washington DC, April 8–11, 2013. http://web.law.columbia.edu/sites/default/files/microsites/gender-sexuality/odeny_improving_access_to_land_in_africa.pdf

Rangan H, Gilmartin M (2002) Gender, traditional authority, and the politics of rural reform in South Africa. Dev Chang 33(4):633–658

Razavi S (2003) Introduction: agrarian change, gender and land rights. J Agrar Chang 3(1&2):2–32

Steyn AF, Rip CM (1968) The changing urban bantu family. J Marriage Fam 30(3):507–508

Udoekanem B, Adoga DO, Onwumere VO (2014) Land ownership in Nigeria: historical development, current issues and future expectations. J Environ Earth Sci 4(21):182–188

UNDP (2015) The millennium development goals report 2015 http://www.undp.org/content/undp/en/home/librarypage/mdg/the-millennium-development-goals-report-2015.html

Walker C, Dubb A (2013) The distribution of land in South Africa: an overview. Institute for Poverty, Land and Agrarian Studies, PLAAS. Fact Check No. 1, http://www.plaas.org.za/plaas-publication/FC01

Wanyeki LM (ed) (2003) Women and land in Africa-culture, religion and realizing women's rights. Zed Books, London

Yeboah E (2014) Women's land rights and Africa's development conundrum – which way forward? IEED, International Institute for Environment and Development. http://www.iied.org/womens-land-rights-africas-development-conundrum-which-way-forward

Chapter 9
The Chasm Between Sexes in Accessing Land and Its Produce: The Case of Rural Women in Zimbabwe

Listen Yingi

Introduction

It is erroneous to assume a direct correlation between land reform and the liberation of women. Land reform does not automatically guarantee improvement in women land rights. That is, land reform does not necessarily lead to democratic outcomes for women or the elimination of rampant inequalities between the sexes. Instead of curtailing the inequality and inequity between sexes, land reform can reproduce or reinforce existing discriminatory practices and institutions which work to further suppress, repress and oppress women in this twenty-first century. The conflict cum inequalities between men and women in accessing land and its produce has drawn much attention in many countries and various communities; however, there is no consensus towards its resolution. At the global level, debates regarding gender equality have gained much attention; conventions have been formed in order to bring about fair and equitable access to resources starting with the need for cultural, political, and economic reforms which discriminate against women from birth and other social groups around the globe. Presently, the keenly contested issue is the gender struggles over the access to land and its produce thereof. Ngadaye (2015) contents that despite the attempts by international institutions, like the International Monetary Fund (IMF) and the World Bank, and other political elites in the global South to suppress land reform policies, there have been growing social movements pushing for land reform in the past two to three decades. Neo-liberal free trade policies have

L. Yingi (✉)
Department of Sociology, University of Limpopo, Polokwane, South Africa

© Springer International Publishing AG, part of Springer Nature 2019
A. O. Akinola, H. Wissink (eds.), *Trajectory of Land Reform in Post-Colonial African States*, Advances in African Economic, Social and Political Development, https://doi.org/10.1007/978-3-319-78701-5_9

exposed small farmers to devastating global competition (especially from giant mechanised industrial farms in the global North), leaving hundreds of millions dispossessed, and forced into the reserve army of impoverished unemployed or underemployed living in urban slums (Agarwal and Sunita 1992). From Brazil and Mexico to the Philippines and Zimbabwe, social movements advocating for a more just and fair distribution of wealth – particularly land – continue to confront the devastating consequences of neoliberalism. Despite the struggle for equality, in most cases, women are still denied land rights, and could only enjoy access through their men.

The struggle for women to get recognition in social, economic and political arenas is as ancient as Biblical times where the daughters of Zaroephahad had to fight to get inheritance from their father's land (Numbers 36). This is a clear indication that culture in most cases encourages the suppression of women and denies them opportunities in life, especially in the rural periphery of developing countries. The biggest predicament women in rural areas are facing in trying to increase agricultural productivity and their income is the lack of land tenure security Social protest has led even elite institutions such as the World Bank to acknowledge the issue of land reform. The World Bank's Report 2008 contents that, 'Agriculture for Development', at least rhetorically put agriculture and the productivity of small farmers at the heart of a global agenda to reduce poverty (Hall 2014; Gaidzanwa 1999).

Asante (2014) posits that land is a 'shrine' to many African societies. The ownership of land comes with respect and prestige. Accessing land and its produce between men and women is easier said than done. Accessing land is one of the hotly contested issues in many circles the world over. Many governments have undergone the programme of land reform but the issue of access and equality between men and women has remained unattended. In many societies, women are treated as appendages in respect to accessing land, and their access is mediated by men. This has led to the formation of sundry women organisations like Women of Zimbabwe Arise (WOZA), Sisters in Islam (SIS), and The Convention on the Elimination of All Forms of Discrimination Against Women (CEDAW) in order to challenge the ancient dominant patriarchy.

Problem Statement

There is need for a renewed focus on land as a crucial resource in rural livelihoods and the appropriate institutions that can contribute to a more equitable access to land through land reform. To buttress the point, women's relative lack of control over land is a reflection of unequal rights and opportunities between males and females generally. Many societies have enacted laws that embody the principle of equal rights for land ownership between women and men. Land reform is believed to have benefitted the males far more than the other sex. One of the most common forms of gender inequality in the developing world is men's disproportionate control of land and real property (Robinson and Alston 2005). In regions where women farm independently of men and produce a majority of food crops, women's claim to land is typically indirect or insecure. In many societies of developing economies, when a husband dies or disappears, wives often lose their access to land or are forced to engage in costly and often unsuccessfully legal battles to retain their rights to it (land). Women collectively represent an enormous productive potential and often invest their resources in ways that result in better economic and social outcomes than men do, but the predicament which they face is the control of the produce of their own toil (Beckmann 1992).

Research Objectives: The objectives of the study are to:

i. Explore the chasm/inequality between sexes in accessing land and its produce and,
ii. Identify the challenges women face in accessing resources in society;
iii. Suggest practical recommendations to policy makers and community leaders on possible ways to improve women participation in communities based on research findings

Research Questions: The chapter is guided by the following research questions:

1. Do men and women have the same opportunity in accessing land and its produce in Zimbabwe?
2. Are there any government policies that protect women from being marginalized in accessing land?

Research Methodology

This study is explorative and descriptive in nature and uses a qualitative research design to investigate the inequality between male and female in accessing land and its produce in Zimbabwe. Participants were both and men and women, who were purposefully selected based on their experiences regarding the land distribution. Purposive sampling was used to ensure that appropriate individuals were selected to provide rich study data (Babbie and Mouton 2001). The participants were selected with the help of community leaders who acted as gatekeepers to access the women under study. Focus group discussions (FGDs) and field notes were used to collect data. The data collected during the FGDs was supported by field notes, and some interviews which were used as part of the data analysis.

Data Analysis

Thematic analysis was used to analyse the data. The data from the audiotapes were transcribed verbatim and coded into themes, sub themes and patterns. Key issues around the gender disparities regarding land ownership were explored in detail. The research findings were considered in dialogue with literature and current research in order to offer critique, possible applications, and further directions of research and to enhance rigor of the study.

Trustworthiness of the Study

The trustworthiness of the study refers to the criteria used to judge the quality of a qualitative study. The data was evaluated by an external reviewer who concurred with researchers` analysis and interpretation. The external reviewer was an experienced qualitative researcher. The focus group interviews and field notes data were gathered from rural women in Dungwe Village in Mwenezi, Zimbabwe over a period of four weeks in order to enhance the credibility of the study. Focus group interviews were conducted until no new or relevant data emerged. In total, five focus groups were conducted at the end of the study.

Thematic analysis was used to analyse the data. The data from the audiotapes were transcribed verbatim and coded into themes, sub themes and patterns. The research findings were considered in dialogue with literature and current research in order to offer critique, possible applications, and further directions of research and to enhance rigour of the study.

Utility of Land Resource

Women's lack of a secure claim to land has undesirable consequences for development and human well-being as well as for women's own empowerment (Yingi 2013). Land remains one of the most valuable resources in both urban and rural economies. In rural areas such as Mwenezi in Zimbabwe, land is the primary vehicle for generating a livelihood and is a key element to household wealth. Indeed, in some areas of the world, whether rural households have a title to land is a fundamental determinant of whether they are poor or rich (Sachikonye and Makumbe 2000). Because land remains an important economic resource, disparities in land rights affect equality, growth and development thereby brewing conflict between races (inter-conflict) and between genders (intra-conflict).

Women's organizations like Women of Zimbabwe Arise is call on all states to take all appropriate measures to eliminate discrimination against women in rural areas by ensuring to these the right to equal treatment in land and agrarian reform as well as in land resettlement schemes. The fact that we cannot talk of poverty alleviation without mentioning land reform in most developing economies is gaining much support. Sachikonye and Makumbe (2000) argue that land reform is the bone and marrow for development and the 'eradication' of rural poverty. Many people are poor principally because they do not have access to productive land. In the Philippines which have one of the longest running and best known land reform programmes, it was a process that has always been stipulated by grassroots reaction.

Gender Politics and Access to Land

The historical domain of women has been rapidly intensified, commercialized, and in many cases, appropriated by men for their own benefit. Gender politics play a significant role in accessing and the controlling of land in many societies, which means that there is a group of people who have limited access to land while others have much land at their disposal. In other words, some groups are denied access and control of land completely especially women. Zimbabwean women encounter significant discrimination in the matter of ownership rights. Access to land is essential for women; their survival often depends on growing subsistence crops. Yet women are rarely land owners. If land belongs to a village, customary law applies and land ownership is reserved for heads of households – in most cases men (Marongwe 2003).

The *eggs of poverty are promising to hatch* successfully given the fact that the young girls are married at a tender age and the levels of infection by the HIV/AIDS virus is high. This kind of situation welcomes women in a vicious circle of poverty. Land reform can be used as a vehicle for rural development, but the intended beneficiaries are the distant third at the same time are being infected and affected by HIV/AIDS. The issue of race and class are very crucial to the discussion of land reform, but the most immediate issue that needs to be treated as an emergency is the increased inequality between the powerful men and the discriminated weaker women (World Bank 2008).

According to Gowland (2002), in most societies, women are expected to perform so many roles under conditions of increasing poverty and constraint. With fewer resources at their disposal, women are expected to do more. Nieuwenhuijze (1982) is supported by Gowland (2002) who posits that many women embrace their care-giving roles; they are increasingly being expected to perform these roles under conditions of ever increasing poverty and constraint. Where they were once able to divide their time between wide ranges of tasks, they now have to make impossible choices between, spending necessary time and money on agriculture to produce food for the family or looking after a bedridden husband, in most cases, the husband will eventually die. It is of paramount importance to note that many of these women will take on additional caring work, even beyond what they are expected to perform despite the little resources at their disposal especially the uneducated.

Women in Agriculture

Gender analysis focuses on understanding the relationship between men and women, gender household relations, empowerment, access and control, and participation in decision-making at all levels. Gender relations are socially constructed power relations between women and men in society which work mostly against women, and the intensity increases from developed to third world economies. They determine the benefits that women and men can derive from natural resources. Masiiwa (2004) asserts that generally, most authors underscore the need to mainstream gender in the land reform process. The government's lack of sensitivity to the need to allocate land to women as individuals is on its own undermining the cause of women. It is advanced that right from the pre-colonial, colonial to post-colonial periods; women have been marginalized in terms of access to and ownership of land in Zimbabwe (Alice 1992). They argue that various policies in many countries especially developing economies fall short of mainstreaming gender. For instance, there is a glaring absence of the mention and use of terms like equity and justice as instruments that would be used to bring about social justice between men and women.

There is a strong relationship between gender, livelihood and poverty. The subordinate role of women in sundry societies plays a critical role in determining peoples' ability to cope. Haque and Montesi (1997) are of the view that the majority of the poor worldwide are women because of the existing gender inequalities. In the context of Southern Africa, the dependency on natural resources by women for their livelihood has come about due to the limited opportunity that exists for them to forge a decent livelihood. The lack of concrete data to enable gender and climate change policy making and planning in Southern Africa, particularly as regards differentiated impacts of climate change in the region.

There is a need to focus on the rural women as a social group, especially the uneducated and illiterate, as the majority fall consistently among those most vulnerable and deprived. In all categories of rural poor lacking access to land and its resources- landless indigenous groups, sharecroppers – women are often doubly penalized, first for belonging to these categories, and secondly because of their gender. It is suggested that since the 1970s the number of women living below the poverty line has increased by fifty percent (50%) in comparison with thirty percent (30%) for their male counterparts (FAO 1996). To buttress the above point, World Bank (2008) noted that despite this high level of poverty and socio-political marginalization of women, and despite the overwhelming contribution of women to agriculture and their responsibility for the household (and often national) food security, the majority of the poor rural women tend to have access to only marginal and least productive land, and are the last to benefit from any legal land titles and services provided by land reform programmes.

Marongwe (2003) maintains that most women from Swaziland and Zimbabwe have taken over the roles formerly carried out by men in addition to those for which they are traditionally responsible. They do most of the work while men make most of the decisions, even while away for wage employment. Most Sub-Saharan women can expect to live until 34 years- the lowest life expectancy in the world, due to poverty (worsened by limited access to productive resources), HIV/AIDS, difficult child birth and discrimination in all aspects of life (World Bank 1997; World Bank 2008).

In Congo, Namibia, and Zimbabwe, the number of women headed households has increased dramatically. Given the views above, increasing access to social and economic resources to women is of significant importance. Although ninety-eight percent (98%) of women are engaged in full time farming activities, with thirty-five percent (35%) of smallholdings run by women, and according to Hill (2003) only five percent (5%) of Zimbabwean women own land in their own names. Only one member of a household can be appointed as the official beneficiary of land reform, who in most cases is a man, women are losing access through marriage institutions as to be discussed. Moyo (1995) argues that despite women's active contribution-in countries like Zimbabwe, South Africa, and Namibia twenty to twenty-five percent (20–25%) of women are involved in farming activities – women are still culturally and officially seen as non- active economically.

Customary land use practices can determine women's access to land in terms of land use rights or ownership. In Mauritania, under customary law black African women do not have land property rights. In Namibia, rural women continue to gain access to land through men, and in Zimbabwe, women have no direct access to primary land use rights in the communal areas. While women do have legal rights of access in the freehold land sectors, they generally lack the economic resources to acquire such land. In the Sudan, the majority of subsistence farmers operate under customary tenure in which women are accorded usufruct rights to land. Gaidzanwa (1999) asserts that there is a strong belief throughout Africa (Sub-Saharan) that men should have total authority in the home, and many men feel it is acceptable to physically abuse women. One recent report based on fieldwork in late 2002 indicates that the women have not received their fair share of land in the fast track land reform programme. Cultural tradition that understands land as a key ele-ment of hegemonic masculinity and patriarchy is still rampant and continues to terrorize women.

Agarwal et al. (1987) posits that many societies have enacted laws that embody the principle of equal rights to land ownership between men and women, but the problem remains with the implementation of such laws. The customs that surround women parity with men are very forbidding, for example, custom and religion which regards women as far much less important; their duty is to bear children and look after men. Such cultural practices are very dehumanizing. Given the fact that women do not even have control over the toil of their own hands, they do not own themselves, they are owned by men. In other words, land reform is believed to have benefitted men far more than the other sex. This kind of practice means that poverty is much associated with women and their close dependents.

Ownership and command over productive resources is very crucial in making choices regarding livelihoods. However, the skewed access to resources is disadvan-taging women than men. Most societies today are championing and blowing the trumpet loud that women need not have total control over property because they are property too. Even the land that is under the jurisdiction of the state, the institutions that govern that land is populated by men; which gives unquestionable authority to the traditional chiefs which drifts women to be the second class citizens or the dis-tant third individuals responsible for bearing children, caring for the sick, and look-ing after men. The bad situation of women is normally worsened by the frequent droughts in Zimbabwe where food shortages is the order of the day, and this means that coping with a drought is not easy (Kinsey and Burger 1998).

Results and Discussions

Access to Land Based on Gender

FAO (1996) believes that women have a very small percentage of land ownership in most countries and in this case in Zimbabwe. The reasons attributed to this vast inequality were the government and Tribal Authorities' policies of giving first prefer- ence to men at the unexplained expense of women. Most women benefited through their husbands, that is, those who were married. The unmarried or widowed and sepa- rated women struggled to get access to land in their own names, hence, a very small percentage of about ten percent (10%). Ninety percent (90%) of the land is owned by men in the two villages of Dungwe and Chikomati in Mwenezi, Zimbabwe. This is so because men get support from both cultural practices of TAs and the policies of the government which promote equality on paper but practice pure patriarchy.

Sachikonye (2003) asserts that some of the women indicated that they had to access land through the names of their elder male sons. They indicated that the wid- owed had to bring the death certificate of their husbands in order to be recognized. The view that women got their fair share in the whole process of land reform pro- gramme does have a lot of loopholes because from the empirical findings at a local scale, only ten percent (10%) of the women got land in their names, but surprisingly Sachikonye (2003) talking about a fair share of twenty percent (20%) as compared to eighty percent (80%) that of men.

Results

Demographic Information

Few women in Dungwe village own land directly in their own names while the majority were men. Most of the men who own land were absentee land owners. They leave their wives and children on the land while they move to towns or other countries for wage employment, while the men who live on their farms but they are not always available as compared to women. Despite the fact that men have a bigger percentage of land ownership, most of the land is used by women, but the proceeds were not all that much to say that they can alleviate poverty with a significant per- centage because of recurring droughts and poor financial base since the farmers cannot use their land as collateral for borrowing from banks (Table 9.1).

Gender Disparities in Security of Tenure

Meer (1997) and Agarwal (1992) asserts that the problems associated with women's access to land can be broadly divided into structural restrictions linked to the orga- nization of society which have bias towards men since colonial times. The social

Table 9.1 Demographic variables

Variable		Frequency	Percentages (%)
Gender	Male	20	80
	Female	5	20
Age (years)	15–25	4	16
	26–35	4	16
	36–45	6	24
	46 years and above	11	44
Marital status	Unmarried	10	40
	Married	3	12
	Separated	10	40
	Widowed	2	8
Village	Dungwe		18
	Chikomati		72
Tenure (Years)	Less than 1 year	–	–
	1–5 years	–	–
	6–10 years	–	–
	11–15 years	–	–
	16 years and above	25	100

and legal obstacles affecting women in particular, has added to the exclusion and oppression of women. The national land reform programme has formally identified many of the social problems associated with land access, including those facing women today. Land reform has accommodated the customary approach to land which prevents married women from gaining access to land in their own right. Relations between land and tradition are also profoundly concerned with the construction and reconstruction of masculinity. According to Scoones (2010), many people who got land in Zimbabwe were but more than ninety percent (90%) of those ordinary people were men and politically connected.

There is a fierce conflict between men and women of which one of the main causes of gender inequality in the developing world is men's disproportionate control of land and real property. In some regions, women farm independently of men and produce a majority of food crops but women's claim to land is typically indirect or insecure. In some regions, when a husband dies or disappear, wives often lose their access to land or are forced to engage in costly and often unsuccessful legal battles to retain their rights to it. Agarwal (1997) and Kabeer (1994) posits that most society's women collectively represent an enormous productive potential and often invest their resources in ways that result in better economic and social outcomes than men do.

Alice (1992) asserts that given the fact that resources are few women's lack of secure claim to land has undesirable consequences for development and human well-being as well as for the empowerment of women. Land remains a shrine and one of the most valuable resources in both urban and rural economies. In rural areas such as Mwenezi, land is the primary vehicle for generating a livelihood and is a key element to household wealth. Given the location of the district, that is, in the rural periphery, it is far removed from other economic activities such that the villagers spend more than ninety percent (90%) of their time working on the land, of which more than ninety percent (90%) are women while men are in leisure activities or migrant labourers (Mukhopadhyay 1998).

International conventions are laying the foundations to achieve equality in accessing land resources. For Convention on the Elimination of All Forms of Discrimination (CEDAW) (1996), Women Of Zimbabwe Arise (WOZA) and Sisters In Islam (SIS) are pushing the international and national communities for gender equality in land use and ownership. Women are vehemently resisting to merely act as wives, sisters, daughters or widows or any relationship mediated with men. FAO (2009) asserts that positive measures to give priority to women are also essential, as women constitute the majority of the rural poor (Agarwal 1994, Pardoe 2006; Roe 1993).

Employment and Participation of Women in Economic Life

Women employed in the subsistence sector are regarded as not economically active. This blindness is in addition to ignoring unpaid domestic labour especially in third world economies (Agarwal 1994). The official figures severely underestimate the number of African working women, given the fact that since 1970, women in subsistence agriculture have not been included in workforce figures. In most African countries, women are most likely to be employed in temporary, casual or part-time positions. Such jobs are almost invariably less well paid, less secure and enjoy fewer benefits but they can invest more than men do (Scoones 2010). Most feminist authors assert that patriarchal persecution is less in developed countries than in developing economies especially in the African patriarchy. This means that women enjoy less the fruits of their labour despite their hardworking (Table 9.2).

Women in Positions of Authority

In Dungwe and Chikomati, women are given empty positions that is to say, mostly women are given positions but they are not given the necessary power to execute the duties. The women are given high positions but the authority is withheld by men and patriarchal governments. This is a strong call to governments to reform their policies. Winnie Madikizela-Mandela pointed out that, "The African National Congress (ANC)

Table 9.2 Summary of the themes and sub-themes

Themes	Sub-themes
Employment and participation of women in economic life	Women in positions of authority
The influence of Tribal Authorities in accessing land	

led government needs to take stock of its own widespread failure to implement its own policies especially those that have an impact on women". She continued to say that the biggest problem women face is abject poverty precipitated by inequality to resources. Poverty has been feminized and women have to deal with all mushrooming problems of society despite their limited access to the needs to solve those predicaments. The Zimbabwean government must know that the women have continued inequality cannot be addressed by annual women's day rallies that are aimed at simply 'celebrating women' (City Press 08 August 2010, World Bank 2002).

In most societies the authority of women is a slice from patriarchal authority. This means that their sphere of influence is regulated by men. Winnie Madikizela-Mandela refuted the opinion that Noluthando Mayende Sibiya –the woman at the helm of the Ministry for Women, Children and people with disabilities- is a lame duck. *"How can she be a lame duck when we do not know to what extent she has been empowered? If she has the powers and was not using them, then she would be a lame duck. But I do not think she has the budget or the power to call on relevant ministries, to me she is not empowered at all"*. It is time for the ANC to go back to the drawing board and to assess how it will realistically implement policies. According to her, it is not the quantity of women in government that will deliver women's empowerment; it is the quality of women in power that matters.

The Influence of Tribal Authorities in Accessing Land

In most African economies, policies that seek to empower women and bring equality to access resources greatly needed for human survival had been drafted but the stumbling block remains with the implementation of such policies. The policies are on paper not in practice especially in the African continent where the chronic practices of patriarchy are rampant. In Zimbabwe, the passing of the Traditional Leaders Act in 1998 was to give the Chiefs all the veto powers in the control of land and the rights to its use. In 2000, the Zimbabwean government introduced the 'Traditional Leaders Act number (42:5) in 1998 which gave the patriarchal traditional leaders unquestionable authority in dealing with land issues. The ownership and command over the productive resources is very crucial in making choices regarding livelihoods (Sokwanele 2012). However, the skewed access to resources of paramount importance is disadvantaging women than men. Most societies today are championing and blowing the trumpets loud that women need not have total control over property because they are property too. The land that is under the control of the state, the institutions that govern that land are populated by men, which gives unquestionable authority to the traditional chiefs and the headsmen- women are drifted away to be the second class citizens mostly responsible for bearing children and caring for the sick. Since these areas are managed by traditional authorities, they are most unlikely to entertain women's interests if they contradict traditional practices. Lipton (1993) assert that land reform has begun though in a controversial state but stopping it is not an option and this view is supported by recent studies by Hall (2014) who post that land reform is so urgent in many countries and delaying it can lead to political turmoil. Nel (2015) argues that many political parties are using land as a campaigning tool given the fact that it land is an unresolved impasse.

Given the fact that the oppression of women through patriarchy is here to stay, women have responded to the erosion of their rights in ways that appear paradoxical, some undergoing Christian conversion while others use husband taming herbs (Mupfuhwira- Shona; Korobela – seSwati; and Seratiso-seSotho) and other women fall in love with those in authority, and some opt for poisoning their husbands or those in authority in order to acquire land. These responses simultaneously contest the prevailing norms and values and beliefs under the umbrella of patriarchy. The increasing scarcity of natural resources of land and water is having a severe impact on individuals and households whose rights to these resources are being eroded; this view applies most to people who are said to be weaker members of the society which is mostly composed by women and children (Gaidzanwa 1999, Women of Zimbabwe Arise 2000).

The belief that women should share these resources on an equal footing with men is gaining widespread international acceptance, but despite the existence of the civil code, Africans prefer customary practices; especially regarding family law and property law. An ordinary citizen, especially women who happens to follow cultural practices which them in their way to acquiring economic resources for the betterment of their lives (Ngadaye 2015).

Conclusion

Land control issues overlap significantly with gender inequalities. As in the case of Zimbabwe, a promise of land reform in the past explains the current social, political, and economic dilemmas. This is the case in most developing countries, for example, South Africa, Namibia, and Swaziland. Even when women have access to land, their security of tenure is often precarious concurrently unsecured. Under customary law, men and women usually have clearly defined rights to land, trees and water as well as usufruct rights bestowed on them by the community elders but the problem which comes with these laws is that they are discriminatory in the sense that men are preferred more than women (Runnel 1977; Olivier 2015).

As long as the poor are denied a political voice, chronic vulnerabilities such as insecure land rights will remain, and this trend affects women more than any other group. Many societies have been the architects of their own misfortunes through mismanagement of resources and also gender discrimination. It is no surprise, therefore that empowerment of women through the promotion of gender equality and eliminating gender disparities in primary and secondary education is a key to poverty reduction; a message forcefully conveyed in the World Development Report (2000/2001). There is need to reform the cultural laws which act against women in many societies. The government needs to work with tribal authorities in order to curtail gender inequalities as far as resource access is spelt.

References

Agarwal B (1992) Gender Relations and Food Security: Coping with Seasonality, Drought and Famine in South Asia. In: Unequal Burden: Economic Crisis, Persistent Poverty and Women's Work. Cambridge University Press, Cambridge

Agarwal B (1994) A field of one's own: gender and land rights in South Asia. Cambridge University Press, Cambridge

Agarwal B (1997) Environmental action, gender equity and women's participation. Cambridge University Press, Cambridge

Agarwal A, Sunita N (1992) Toward a green world. Centre for Science Development and Change, New Delhi

Agarwal A, D'Monte D et al (eds) (1987) The fight for survival: peoples action for the environment. Centre for Science and Environment, New Delhi

Alice K (1992). Struggling over scarce resources. Women and maintenance in Southern Africa. Regional report: women and law in Southern Africa research Trust. University of Zimbabwe, Harare

Asante MK (2014) Facing south to Africa: toward an Afrocentric critical orientation. Lexington Books, United Kingdom

Babbie E, Mouton J (2001) The practice of Social Science Research. Cape Town: Oxford

Beckmann B (1992) Rights of women to the natural resources, land and water. Women and Development. Ministry of Foreign Affairs, and Development Cooperation, Information Department, The Hague

CEDAW (1996) Considerations of reports submitted by States under article 18 of the Convention on the elimination of all forms of discrimination against women. City Press 08 August 2010

FAO (1996) World food summit and the signing of 'the Rome declaration'. Corporate Communications

FAO (2009) The world summit on food security. FAO, Rome

Gaidzanwa R (1999) Women and the access to land. University of Zimbabwe, Harare

Gowland R (2002) The struggle for land, the struggle for independence. Sydney district Secretary Communist Party of Australia

Hall R (2014) Land reform and its aftermath in South Africa. J Agrar Chang 14(1):121–137

Haque T, Montesi L (1997) Tenurial reforms and agricultural development in Viet Nam. Land Reform, Land Settlement and Cooperatives

Hill G (2003) The battle of Zimbabwe. Zebra Press, Cape Town

Kabeer N (1994) Reversed realities: Gender hierarchies in development thought. Verso, London

Kinsey B, Burger K (1998) Coping with drought in Zimbabwe: survey evidence on responses of rural households to risk. World Dev 26:89–110

Lipton M (1993) Land reform as commenced business: the evidence against stopping. World Dev 21:641–657

Marongwe N (2003) Farm occupations and occupiers in the new politics of land in Hammar, Raftopous B and Jensen S (eds), Zimbabwe's Unfinished Business. Weaver Press, Harare

Masiiwa M (2004) Post-independence land reform in Zimbabwe. Controversies and impact on the economy. Friedrich Stiftung, Harare

Meer S (1997) Gender and land rights: the struggle over resources in post-apartheid South Africa. South Africa

Moyo S (1995) The land question in Zimbabwe. Sapes Books, Harare

Mukhopadhyay M (1998) Legally dispossessed: gender, identity and the process of law. Calcutta. Street

Nel Y (2015) Land grabs to take off in South Africa. The Observer, Polokwane

Ngadaye A (2015) The multiple roles of women in Africa. African Women, Transformation and Development, IFAA, UK

Nieuwenhuijze OV (1982) Underdevelopment: basic needs unmet. Problems and prospects of the Sociology of development. Caracass Chronicles

Olivier H (2015) Land size and production. A response to the State of the Nation Address (SONA) February 2015

Pardoe C (2006) Becoming Australian. Before farming and claiming, Corral

Robinson M, Alston P (2005) Human rights and development towards mutual reinforcement. Oxford University Press, Oxford

Roe EM (1993) Public service: rural development and careers in public management: a case study of expatriate advising in African land reform. World Dev 21:3

Runnel D (1977) Fighting for equality. The dream that will come true. Elsivier. Sage

Sachikonye R, Makumbe J (2000) Reclaiming the land: land reform and agricultural development. Sapes Books, Harare

Scoones I (2010) Zimbabwe's land reform. Myths and Realities Cape Town, James Currey The Zimbabwean Newspaper, 4 November

Sokwanele. (2012) Why the land reform issue continues to define Zimbabwe's past and future. www.Sokwanele.com/node/2366

Women of Zimbabwe Arise (2000) Fighting for human rights. Human Rights Watch Zimbabwe, Harare

World Bank (1997) India: achievements and challenges in reducing poverty. World Bank, Washington, DC

World Bank (2002) World development indicators. Washington, DC. Online

World Bank (2008) Land policy and land reform in sub-saharan Africa: consensus, confusion and controversy. World Bank, Washington DC

Yingi L (2013) An investigation of land reform and poverty alleviation in Zimbabwe. The case of Chikomati and Dungwe Villages in Mwenezi District. University of Limpopo. South Africa

Chapter 10
Land Conflicts in Southern Ghana: A Reflection of Multiple Ownerships of Land and Usufruct Rights to Land Use

Collins Adu-Bempah Brobbey

Introduction

Ghanaians embraced the 1992 constitutional regime with great enthusiasm and optimism. This is exemplified by the relatively successful six consecutive general elections conducted including peaceful transition since the early 1990s. This is unprecedented event in the annals of the Ghanaian body polity (Abdulai and Crawford 2009). There was widespread optimism among the population that liberal democracy is not only a change agent that has guaranteed individuals' rights and freedoms but also a new political order ensures economic growth and development. Liberalism has given impetus to the establishment of strong institutions and improved economy, which generated an upsurge in the rural-urban migration coupled with dramatic increase in the population of urban centres like Accra have led to a high demand for land use and ownership, especially for both residential and industrial use. This high demand for land use has in turn heightened the land commodification, monetization and commercialisation[1] phenomenon Accra and its environs.

Series of literatures attest to the fact that the high value placed on land as a commodity accounts for land conflicts in land administration issues in southern Ghana (Kom 2003; Quantson 2003; Attuquayefio 2009; Awortwei-Mensah 2001). However, this study claims that there is a disconnection between land commodification,

---

[1] In the context of this study, 'commodification of land' means land has become a commodity for sale or land has become more or less a useful commodity with an exchangeable value. 'Monetization of land' delineates a parcel of land that is presented in terms of its monetary value, while 'commercialization of land' is an expression of sales and purchasing of any given parcel of land. In other words, land has assumed a high purchasable and/or saleable rate often in large quantities for commercial purposes.

C. A. -B. Brobbey (✉)
Department of Social Studies, Ghana Institute of Journalism,
University of Ghana, Accra, Ghana

© Springer International Publishing AG, part of Springer Nature 2019   139
A. O. Akinola, H. Wissink (eds.), *Trajectory of Land Reform in Post-Colonial African States*, Advances in African Economic, Social and Political Development, https://doi.org/10.1007/978-3-319-78701-5_10

monetization and commercialization and the implication for multiple ownerships of land as well as usufruct rights to land use. And that the opportunity to make money off the sale or lease of land facilitated a number of conflicts between families, communities, and individuals particularly, on the usufruct rights to land use issues (Awortwei-Mensah 2001).

Land conflicts had hitherto, been exacerbated by the complicated dynamics of land administration motivated by the manipulation of colonial land reforms (Amanor 1999; Azu 2011), and lack of usufruct rights to land use in southern Ghana (Attuquayefio 2009). This study hypothesizes that multiple land ownerships, though, far from exclusion, is a function of land conflicts in southern Ghana. The phenomenon of multiple ownerships of land and the challenge of usufruct rights to land use in Ghana is explainable in terms of pervasive land commodification, monetization and commercialization that has characterized land administration in Ghana. The critical questions this study raises include what accounts for the multiple ownerships of land and the challenge of usufruct rights to land use in Ghana? Why has the land policy in Ghana failed to address these ominous challenges? How could the usufruct rights to land use.be made enforceable to minimize land conflicts related to land acquisition and ownership in sub-Saharan Africa in General and southern Ghana in particular?

Methodology

This study utilized correlational and explanatory paradigms; hence the use of both quantitative and qualitative research approaches. The purposive sampling technique was used as the most suitable technique to select the participants who understand the social dimensions of the problem understudy as well as providing the most vital responses to the unstructured research questions (Kumar 2013; Norman and Lincoln 2013). Creswell (2012) sees it, as the act of obtaining 'an insider's exclusive perspective' on a phenomenon. Besides, in the survey, 600 set of questionnaire was administered to some selected policy experts and stakeholders in land administration, while unstructured interview was conducted among purposively selected major actors in the land scheme.

Historical Background to Land Conflicts in Southern Ghana

This section attempts at situating land conflicts in southern Ghana in context. It provides background to land conflicts in Accra, southern Ghana with specific reference to Accra, a suburb of Greater Accra Region and its environs and second, it expatiates land conflicts by demonstrating the changing trends in land disputes as envisaged in many parts of the country. The chapter reinforces the theoretical reflections that argue that violent conflicts are neither new in, nor restricted to, sub-Saharan Africa, but a global phenomenon (Amanor 1999; Darkwa 2012).

Since the end of the Cold War, violent intra-state and inter-ethnic conflicts associated with land disputes have occurred in swift succession in sub-Saharan Africa in general and Ghana in particular, with disastrous impacts on every aspect of life on the sub region (Amanor 1999; Attuquayefio 2009; Darkwa 2012). These conflicts have been characterized, among other things, by the dramatically high ratio of civilian casualties, widespread population displacement, destruction of human capital and assets through the deliberate use of major and minor militant agencies such as child soldiers and land guards and cadres correspondingly, among other militants. The resolution of these conflicts have been protracted and less decisive, resulting in long periods of "no war, no peace" (Darkwa 2012).

In Ghana, land conflicts dates back to the colonial era (Amanor 1999; Pogucki 1955). In British West Africa, there were strong interference with the indigenous native property rights and land tenure system by the colonial power (Darkwa 2012). There seemed to be no justification whatsoever for the break-up of land tenure, or for the alienation of native land arrangement. Meanwhile, traditionally, land in sub-Saharan Ghana was communally owned and commonly used (Amanor 1999; Darkwa 2012). The pre-colonial Ghana, an ownership and an entitlement popularly known as land tenure system has been the practice largely by most Ghanaian indigenous population. Land tenure system, a process of land proprietorship usually vested the usufruct rights to land use largely in the hands of the chiefs[2] with the intention to reserve/preserve the land for present and future uses as well as to protect the interest of the indigenes regarding the usufruct rights to land use (Amanor 1999).

However, the land reforms introduced by the British colonial administration in the Gold Coast, in the late 1890s and the early 1900s, simultaneously facilitated the pervasive commodification, monetization and commercialization of land. Accordingly, land which was communally owned and commonly used became a commodity for sale by the traditional chiefs. This land monetization economy/regime has not only replaced individual's rights to use the land by long term holdings such as leasehold, but also led to over-commercialization of land and its attendant multiple ownerships of land and 'landguardism' (Pogucki 1955). As a result of pervasive monetization of land in most parts of the country, the issue of usufruct rights to land use in Ghana has seriously been undermined.

This chapter identifies three major ways by which the usufruct rights to land use has undergone alterations. These include; ownership, acquisition and distribution/application. Ghana has experienced high volumes of rural-urban migration, a surge in the urban population, and a high demand for land for both residential and industrial development. The high demand for land has enhanced the commercialization of lands, especially in Accra and its environs. The high value placed on land does not only have severe implications for land ownership, acquisition, and transfers but also offer the opportunity to make money off the sale or lease of lands and hence facilitated a number of ownership conflicts between families, communities, and individuals. These conflicts were often exacerbated by the convoluted dynamics of land management that had been occasioned by the distortions of colonial rule and

---

[2] Often describe as the custodians or trustees of the land within a given community.

the consequent plural legal systems that emerged (Darkwa 2012). Broader understanding of ownership and the rights and duties of lessors became much more prominent with the increase in land commodification following the return to constitutional rule in 1992. The challenge was compounded with the ineffective land administrative procedures (Amanor 1999).

The rapidization of industrialization and the expansion of housing amenities has put a pressure on the need for land in the country. Indeed, Pogucki (1955) notes in 1955 that demand of land was exceeding supply and causing an increase in food prices because of the "retreat of cultivated areas as a result of the extension of town limits" brought about by the increase in population. He discusses issues of ownership and the rights and obligations imposed by customary law on those in charge of indigenous land administration and conflicts. His work provides useful insights into the traditional structures for land management in the pre-independence period (Pogucki 1955: 10–11).

Although Pogucki (1955) raises the definitional challenge of ownership in traditional land administration, his discussion is limited to the range of rights that a political head may exercise for a group on whose behalf he administers land. Although the dispute over the rights to exercise certain measures of authority contributes to the insecurity confronting landowners in Ghana today, Pogucki's study does not delve into the issues of multiple sales and criminality confronting contemporary land management. This chapter tries to interrogate this important land question.

Meanwhile, Gough and Yankson (2000) believe that the challenges have come as a result of rapid increases in urban populations given impetus to overcrowding conditions in many cities in Ghana. They maintain that the overcrowding conditions in Accra have resulted in high costs of rent and subsequent commercialization of lands. According to them, the peri-urban areas which previously only had indigenous settlements and were used for subsistence farming have been converted into residential areas (Gough and Yankson 2000: 2.489). This has led to an increase in the price of land and facilitated perceptions of alienation and inequality among the poor indigenous people and especially among the youth. This perception often pits the youth in some communities against traditional rulers who are not 'allodial' title holders- (do not have the power to sell the lands) accusing them e of selling community lands for their personal gains. Furthermore, their work reveals some challenges that have arisen between the youth and some chiefs over perceptions of land alienation, it did not provide explanation of the rational for the multiple sales of land and also the extent to which sale of community land could undermine the usufruct rights to land use.

Similarly, Amanor (1999) explains that the unattractive nature of agriculture to youth in the modern era and as a result of its meagre pay offs, combined with high levels of unemployment in rural communities, facilitates rural-urban migration, which undoubtedly increases the urban population and hence pressure on land. Although his work focuses on agribusiness, he provides useful insight into the effects of land expropriation for the production of produce for the international market on the people living in those communities. Woodman (1996) in his work *"Customary Land Law in the Ghanaian Courts"* also offers an exposition on the customary law provisions for modes of creation and transfer of land, and the persons who may hold interests in land. His work explains a number of concepts and entities in land administration including the parameters of the authority given by various groups in the traditional system (communities, families, clans, etc.) to persons charged with the administration of lands other than their personal properties.

Woodman postulates that persons entrusted with the management of lands on behalf of groups cannot make unilateral decisions concerning the appropriation of the land without consulting the principal members of the group. He however, lamented on the conflicts between some of the customary law provisions and the provisions of the modern state system. His work uncovers the neatly laid out *de jure* provisions for the management of land in Ghana and the tensions present in the *de facto* application of the laws.

Although there are efforts at reforming land management in Ghana, "usufruct rights to land use-" land policy intended to protect land ownership, land application and distribution as well as land use have been scantly addressed empirically. In other words, land policy that guarantees legitimate rights to land ownership and usage, landed property in exchange for remuneration in cash or in kind, is generally lacking in Ghana and particularly in Accra where cases of multiple sales of lands and long legal processes or arbitration over land conflicts abound. Accordingly, the perceived corruption and bias; as well as weak law enforcement have more or less facilitated the activities of gangs in the land industry (Darkwa 2012). A respondent confirmed that

> Notwithstanding, the situation has further given impetus to land guards often presenting themselves as private security operatives who operate outside the framework by utilizing threat of violence (guide against or prevent encroachers and kill to protect the property) in the provision of the so-called security for land and landed properties.

Admittedly, the activities of these land guards are illegal and a contravention of the existing laws on the provision of private security services.[3] As already stated, the use of land guards for protecting and securing rights to ownership of land as well as application/ distribution and uses of land engender land-related conflicts. As reinforced by a respondent,

> Notably, this land conflict does not only affect the enjoyment of property rights (**thus, undermines the usufruct rights to land use**), but also disadvantages those without the resources to employ land guards as they often lose their lands to those with the capability or capacity to pay for such services.

The land guards have become a lord of their own in some parts of Ghana.

Realities of Land Conflict in Ghana

Land conflicts in southern Ghana delineates a phenomenon involving violent disputes often ensue between individuals within a community, families, local authorities including for instance, chiefs, organizations as well as government over a parcel

---

[3] An interview with a victim who has lost his land in disputes because he could not afford to pay extra money to the other land disputants.

or parcels of land (Darkwa 2012). According to Darkwa, and attested by a respondent, land-related disputes ranges from land-grab, especially in situations where one of the disputants is more powerful and able to subdue others, by using either legal or illegal, legitimate or illegitimate means to seize the land. This is achievable through the use of protective mechanism. This could through the services of land guards to intimidate or cause physical harm to the real or perceived land claimants and/or by resorting to the use of traditional, spiritual or consultation of deities popularly known as "JUJU"[4] to deter others from encroaching on the land or kill the so-called trespassers.

Interestingly, political, social and economic liberalization have simultaneously engendered high volumes of population mobility particularly, rural-urban migration and provoked high demand for land for both residential and industrial uses. Accordingly, the upsurge in the urban population coupled with high demands for land for both residential as well as industrial development has further ignited the passion for land commodification, monetization and commercialisation in southern Ghana. Literature indeed, attest to the fact that the high value placed on land as a commodity is a recipe for pervasive land commodification, monetization and commercialization and which turns to undermine the usufruct rights to land use (Amanor 1999; Darkwa 2012; Gough and Yankson 2000). Thus, the issue of traditional or customary appropriation- land ownership, acquisition and transfers is not only dwindling but also eventually eclipsed by the former.

Traditionally, land tenure system which has been the practice largely by most Ghanaian indigenes in many parts of the country is not only intended to reserve/preserve the land for present and future uses but also to protect the interest of the indigenes regarding the usufruct rights to land use. However, the land reforms introduced by the British colonial masters led to land commodification, monetization and over commercialization of the land resource in Ghana. Land which was communally owned and commonly used became a commodity for sale by the chiefs. This land monetization economy/regime has not only replaced individual's rights to use the land by long term holdings such as leasehold, but also led to over-commercialization of land and its attendant landguardism.[5]

Forms of Land Conflicts

Generally, land conflict in Ghana is associated with the question of ownership. However, the case of southern Ghana varies and reflects multiple dimensions. Forms of land conflicts include, land grabbing, land commodification, monetization and commercialization with its attendant multiple ownerships of land, landguardism, land distribution as well as uses of land. The most common forms of land grabbing

---

[4] JUJU refers to black magic or occultism.

[5] These are private armed groups trained to protect land or confiscate land for anyone that can pay for their services

involved snatching or confiscating land either by the most powerful in society- notably the rich and wealthy individuals or by the chief or the state (government) for a particular interest.

The upsurge in the urban population, like Accra, coupled with a high demand for land for both residential and industrial development often motivates land grabbing. Land conflicts have been exacerbated by the lack of appropriate land documentation and over-centralized land administration that had been occasioned by the distortions of colonial land reforms. Land tenure system in this country is not only intended to reserve/preserve the land for present and future uses but also to protect the interest of the indigenes regarding the usufruct rights to land use.

However, change in the land tenure system by the British colonial administrations is partly responsible for the pervasive land conflicts in southern Ghana. It is important to note that the high demand for land has resulted in land becoming a commodity (anything that is useful and has exchangeable value) for sale. Also, the high value placed on land (in monetary terms) turns to appreciate the value of land over time, Similarly, the increasing sales and purchase of land (as land become highly commercialized) like any other commodity in Ghana, particularly Accra, has changed the value of land from an invaluable possession to quantifiable commodity. Thus, indiscriminate sales of land have not only given impetus to widespread multiple land ownerships phenomenon but also aggravated the already existing challenge of usufruct rights to land use in Ghana.

Land as a Commodity

This section establishes a linkage between pervasive land commodification, monetization and commercialization and multiple ownerships of land and the persistent disputes over the usufruct rights to land use in Accra.

Background of Respondents

The respondent comprises of 600 respondents for the survey and few selected interviewees. The sample of 600 respondents selected from the masses (primary, secondary and tertiary land dealers); the sex distribution of the respondents was as follows. 57.5% of the respondents were male whereas female respondents constituted 40.5%. Some 2.0% of the respondents failed to indicate sex status. This means that the sex distribution was fairly balanced. There was also a regional balance as Table 10.1 indicates.

For ease of accessibility, Ghana was zoned into three Belts namely; Northern Belt, Middle Belt and Southern Belt and Tamale, Kumasi and Accra were selected to represent the northern (urban), middle (urban) and southern (urban) belts respectively whilst Tolon, Ejura Sekyedumasi and Ablekuma were selected to represent

Table 10.1 What is your region of origin?

		Frequency	Percent	Valid percent	Cumulative Percent
Valid	Non- response	6	1.0	1.0	1.0
	Southern –Accra (Urban) Ablekuma (peri-urban)	402	67.0	67.0	68.0
	Northern –Tamale(Urban) Tolon (peri-urban)	36	6.0	6.0	74.0
	Middle –Kumasi (Urban) Ejura Sekyedumasi (peri-urban)	156	26.0	26.0	100.0
	Total	600	100.0	100.0	

Source: Survey Questionnaire

Table 10.2 Respondents' age group

		Frequency	Percent	Valid Percent	Cumulative Percent
Valid	Non-response	9	1.5	4.0	4.0
	18–25	63	10.5	10.5	14.5
	26–35	159	26.5	26.5	41.0
	36–45	174	29.0	29.0	70.0
	46–55	69	11.5	11.5	81.5
	56–65	99	16.5	16.5	98.0
	66 and above	27	3.5	2.0	100.0
	Total	600	100.0	100.0	

Source: Survey Questionnaire

northern (peri-urban), middle (peri-urban) and southern (peri-urban) respectively. Incidentally, the survey conducted in Accra understandably had a majority of 67.0% of the respondents while Kumasi and Tamale had the minority of 26.0% and 6.0% respectively, only about 1.0% did not indicate their region of origin. The age distribution was also somewhat balanced with respondents coming from all the age groups as Table 10.2 below shows, even though majority of the respondents came from the 36–45 (29.0%) and 46–55 (26.5%) age groups, however, only a few respondents 4.0% failed to mention a particular age group within which they belong.

With regards to the selected constituency, 100.0% each of the respondents were residents of Tamale central and Tolon, Kumasi Bantema and Ejura Sekyedumasi, Accra, Ablekuma, Kasoa, Ashiaman and Tema correspondently. Indeed, this indicates that all the three belts i.e., Northern, Middle and Southern belts were duly covered in the survey as shown in Table 10.3.

With regard to employment status, 71.0% of the respondents indicated they are employed, 27% of them stated they are unemployed whilst only a small minority of 1.0% did not respond to the question 'employment status' Regarding monthly incomes in Ghana, 36.0% of the 71.0% of the respondents with employable status indicated they earn a monthly income of about GHS 3700. 00 and above. Also, 14.0% of the respondents indicated they earn between GHS3, 500.00 and GHS3700.00, 8.0% of those employed earn between GHS2, 300.00 and GHS3500.00,

Table 10.3 Constituency and area of residence

		Frequency	Percent	Valid Percent	Cumulative Percent
Valid	Northern Belt Tamale Central	100	50.0	50.0	50.0
	Tolon	100	50.0	50.0	100.0
	Total	200	100.0	100.0	100.0
	MiddleBelt/Kumasi Bantema	100	50.0	50.0	100.0
	Ejura Sekyedumasi	100	50.0	50.0	100.0
	Total	200	100.0	100.0	
	Southern Belt Ablekuma/ Accra	50	25.0	25.0	25.0
	Kasoa	50	25.0	25.0	50.0
	Ashiaman	50	25.0	25.0	75.0
	Tema	50	25.0	25.0	100.0
	Total	200	100.0	100.0	

Source: Survey Questionnaire

while 4.0% earn between GHS2, 100.00 and GHS2300.00 per month. Moreover, 3.0% earn between GHS2000 and GHS2100.00 per month, while 5.0% earn between GHS1000.00 and GHS2000.00 monthly. Furthermore, about 2.0% earn between GHS500.00 and GHS900.00, 11.0% earn between GHS400.00 and GHS500.00 per month, and 17.0% receive between GHS300.00 and GHS400.00 monthly.

Again, at least, all the respondents have a basic elementary education. About 59.5% of the respondents were married couples, 33.5% were singles and 5.5% were widowed whilst only about 1.5% was divorced. In the case of respondents' knowledge about disputes over sales of lands (conflicts), an overwhelming majority 73.5% responded "Yes" to the question, "Are you aware of the prevailing conflicts over sales of lands (conflicts)? However, 22.5% answered "No" whilst a tiny minority 4.0% failed to respond. In all, 67.0% of the respondents indicated that they have involved in multiple sales of land saga before, 23.0% indicated they lost their land through land grabbing – confiscated by District Chief Executive (DCE), 6.0% indicated clashed through Assemblymen, 2.0% indicated land guards while 2.0% indicated they lost land through chiefs' as a result of land appreciation in prices.

Analysis and Discussions

The data analysis revealed a number of interesting findings about commodification, monetization and commercialization and their linkage to the challenges of the usufruct rights to land use in Ghana in general and Accra in particular. This section addresses each in turn.

As already stated, the study began the data analysis by ascertaining the level of Ghanaians' knowledge about commodification, monetization and commercialization and their linkage to challenges of the usufruct rights to land use. Table 10.4 confirms that 100.0% of Ghanaians attest to the fact they understand commodification of land,

Table 10.4 Understanding of the use of land's terms

		Frequency	Percent	Valid Percent	Cumulative Percent
Valid	Commodification of land - means land has become a commodity for sale or land has become a useful commodity with exchangeable value.	600	100.0	100.0	100.0
	Monetization of land - means land is commoditized or land has been given monetary value or expressed in terms of money	600	100.0	100.0	100.0
	Commercialization of land -means – land is bought and sold in in a large quantities or commercial quantities	600	100.0	100.0	100.0
	Total	600	100.0	100.0	

Source: Survey Questionnaire

monetization of land and commercialization of land however, in the case of how each of these phenomena undermine the usufruct rights to land use they offered different perspectives.

According to a respondent,

> Southern Ghana has over the years, experienced high volumes of rural-urban migration. And that a surge in the urban population coalesced with a high demand for land for both residential as well as industrial development spurred commercialization of lands with its attendant conflicts, especially in Accra and its surrounding environs.

Another respondent affirmed that,

> The high value placed on land had implications for the former politics surrounding land ownership, acquisition, and transfers. And that the opportunity to make money off the sale or lease of lands facilitated a number of conflicts between families, communities, and individuals on ownership issues.

Speaking in similar vein, one of the respondents commented thus,

> These conflicts were worsened by the intricate dynamics of land administration that had been characterized by the alterations of colonial rule and the consequent plural legal systems that emerged." To him "Questions surrounding the definition of ownership and the rights and duties of land owners became much more prominent with the increase in land commodification following the return to constitutional rule in 1992.

Meanwhile, the challenges confronting the land sector are not necessarily a new phenomenon. The findings collaborated with Pogucki's hich suggests that "the rising land values in Accra were a result of "rapid residential development and congestion in the commercial and industrial areas" (Pogucki 1955: 10–11). In 1955, demand exceeded supply and caused an increase in food prices because of the "retreat of cultivated areas as a result of the extension of town limits", which was brought about by the increase in population (Pogucki 1955, 10–11). He discusses the issue of ownership and the rights and obligations imposed by customary law on those in charge of traditional land administration. His work therefore provides useful insights into the traditional structures for land management in the pre-colonial period.

However, Pogucki position contradicts the position of this chapter. He raises the challenges associated with ownership in traditional land administration, though his discussion is limited to the range of rights that a political head may exercise for a group on whose behalf he administers land. Thus, although the dispute over the rights to exercise certain measures of authority contributes to the insecurity confronting landowners in Ghana today, it does not delve into the issues of multiple sale and criminality confronting contemporary land management.

Major Drivers of Land Conflicts

This study reveals a number of drivers of land conflicts. The land-guards has been identified as one of the key actors involved in the land conflict. For instance, a respondent indicated that "a group of irate youth suspected to be landguards attacked and vandalized property at the Opeikuma Chief's palace in a dispute over land" (Personal communication, Accra). Narrating his ordeal, the respondent further said,

> A member of the royal family who was at the palace when the incident occurred said the land guards attacked and shot people on sight over ownership of stool lands which are in disputes…the land guards, mostly well-built young men, are armed with guns and cutlasses and move in groups ready to deal with anyone who attempts to disobey or challenge them over the ownership of the land in question.

Despite a plethora of work on the problem associated with land management in Ghana, this study did not only come across any work that addresses the phenomenon of "landguardism" and its effects on the security of Ghana but also the issue of how multiple sales of land undermines the usufruct rights to land use did not come out forcefully. Although there were efforts at reforming land management in Ghana, "landguardism," the phenomenon of employing constituted groups of mainly young persons who engage in the use of illegitimate force to protect land and landed property in exchange for remuneration in cash or in kind, has been on the rise in Accra. Furthermore, a respondent said,

> This is arguably due to the challenge of multiple sales of lands; long legal processes for the resolution of land conflicts by the courts; lack of faith in the police and court systems as a result of perceived corruption and bias; and weak law enforcement, which facilitates the activities of gangs in the land industry…Although land guards seek to present themselves as private security operatives, they operate outside the framework for the provision of private security services and utilize violence and/or the threat of violence in the provision of security for land and landed properties. Their activities are illegal and a contravention of the existing laws on the provision of private security services. Therefore, the use of land guards for the resolution of land conflicts affects the enjoyment of property rights, as those without the resources to employ land guards often lose their lands to those capable to pay for such services.

Aside the activities of the land-guard, there are other factors responsible for land conflict in Ghana. Indeed, Gough and Yankson (2000) admit that the primary challenges underlying the management of land markets in developing countries are the complex relationships between people and land, the different tenure systems that existed among the various societies within states, the exertion of state control over lands in the post-independence period, and the plural legal system which pitches Western legal provisions against the customary laws of the diverse societies.

Meanwhile, a respondent revealed an interesting reason for land conflict thus, "the rural-urban drift and its associated challenges of over-population or rapid increases in urban populations has resulted in overcrowding conditions in southern Ghana, and hence the pressure on land acquisition, residential accommodation as well as high cost of house rent."

Lack of Effective Land Management

Gough and Yankson (2000) assert that the overcrowding conditions in Accra have not only resulted in high costs of house-rent but also indiscriminate selling of land in the city. A respondent confirmed that "this perception often drives the youth in some communities against traditional rulers who they accuse of selling community lands for their personal gains." In a sharp contrast, a respondent explained that,

> Some chiefs may exercise political and administrative authority over a parcel of land which they do not have the power to sell the lands." As a result, while the lands may be sold, the bulk of the revenue accruing from such sales may not get into the community where the land is cited.

Another respondent revealed that,

> Some of the contradictions that have arisen between the youth and some traditional leadership over the issues of land has been the alienation, quest for transparency, corruption, and inequity. Also, the discord could have been as a result of the youth's lack of knowledge regarding the actual ownership of the land as well as the indiscriminating sales of land without proper documentation.

And those practices often facilitate multiple sale of land. Confirming this assertion, another responded said,

> Had I known, I would have put some stones and sand to secure the land. When I was told by the Landlord to do something on the land I purchase from him else it might be taken away from me, I considered it a joke and now the land have been taken over by a so-called rich man in the area who threatens to deal with anyone who trespass on the land.

Land ownership in the community have therefore come under the authority of the might and most powerful and not based on communal property rights or individuals' ownership.

Usufruct Rights to Land Use

In his work *Customary Land Law in the Ghanaian Courts,* Woodman (1996) provides an exposition on the customary law provisions for modes of creation and transfer of land, and the persons who may hold interests in land. His work provides definitions for a number of concepts and entities in land administration. He also provides the parameters of the authority given by various groups in the traditional system (communities, families, clans, etc.) to persons charged with the administration of lands other than their personal properties. His work suggests that persons entrusted with the management of lands on behalf of groups cannot make unilateral decisions concerning the appropriation of the land without consulting the principal members of the group. Woodman touches on the conflict between some of the customary law provisions and the provisions of the modern state system. Woodman's work reveals the neatly laid out *de jure* provisions for the management of land in Ghana and the tensions present in the *de facto* application of the laws. Similarly, a respondent noted that,

> The challenge of multiple ownerships of land and the usufruct rights to land use has not been adequately addressed empirically, and that the introduction of monetized economy created wealth for a group of people, given them power to question the authority of the chiefs over land ownership (as being the custodian of land) and usage. And hence, the chiefs lost their legitimate custodianship and thus weakened their rights to control their subject in land matters.

Besides, the difficulty in upholding land rights, an interviewee said "also, their loyalty and allegiance from the subjects seriously undermined and eventually eroded. A respondent believed that,

> The individual member's rights to use part of the communal land were closely related to his obligation to perform certain services to the stool. Thus, it must be noted that as the rights of the subjects to use the land was replaced by long term holdings such as leaseholds, the subjects' attachments and obligations to perform certain services to the chief also reduced considerably.

Generally, the results of the field study revealed that the increasing demand for land had far exceeded supply leading to land conflict, sale a parcel of land to multiple persons and extreme high prices for land. These occurrences had led to what Darkwa (2012) calls 'landguardism' in southern Ghana. This new land regime seriously undermines not only the management of land administration but also distort the usufruct rights to land use.

Policy Option: *Establishment of Land Bank and Lank Banking Strategy*
In an attempt at finding lasting solution to the problematic nature of land conflicts in southern Ghana and particularly, in Accra and its immediately environs, this study proposes a construction of what this study calls the 'Land Bank' and 'Land Banking' strategy, which is displayed below. "Land Bank"[6], otherwise called 'Land Bank Secretariat', would focus on the registration, collection of Indentures/certificates and Building Permits. The 'Land Bank secretariat would consult with a land banking institution, which would be involved in the land development financing to transact business regarding the purchasing, sales, registration and development of lands within a given area.

---

[6] Land bank delineates a situation where all lands in a given geographic area which have been well-demarcated, is brought under a common jurisdiction.

The land banking system would function inter-alia as an institution to register all lands- government, stool, community, family and even individual lands and to ensure that land that are acquired, bought, sold, leased, of granted as consignments are duly registered with the Land Banking establishment. Indeed, the establishment of such the institutions would require a Legal instrument through the Act of parliament. This will not only help to provide a firm or legal basis but also ensure the enforcement of its operational principles.

The Land Bank process would involve linking the land bank secretariat to the other key departments within the land administration which include: land commission (in-charge of land document authentication, search and approval of genuineness of land ownership); Land Achieves (sourcing and storage of vital land documents); Geo-engineering Survey Department (in-charge of surveying, cadastral plotting, appropriate demarcation); Town and Country Planning Department (issuance of directives regarding types and structure of building permissible and investigating and approving building plans); Civil engineering – Draftsmanship (for site plans and building plans and other building documents); land Administration (for lodging of building documents and liaise with Achieves); and finally, the Metropolitan/Municipal/District/Unit committee (in-charge of building permit approval and issuance) (See Fig. 10.1 above).

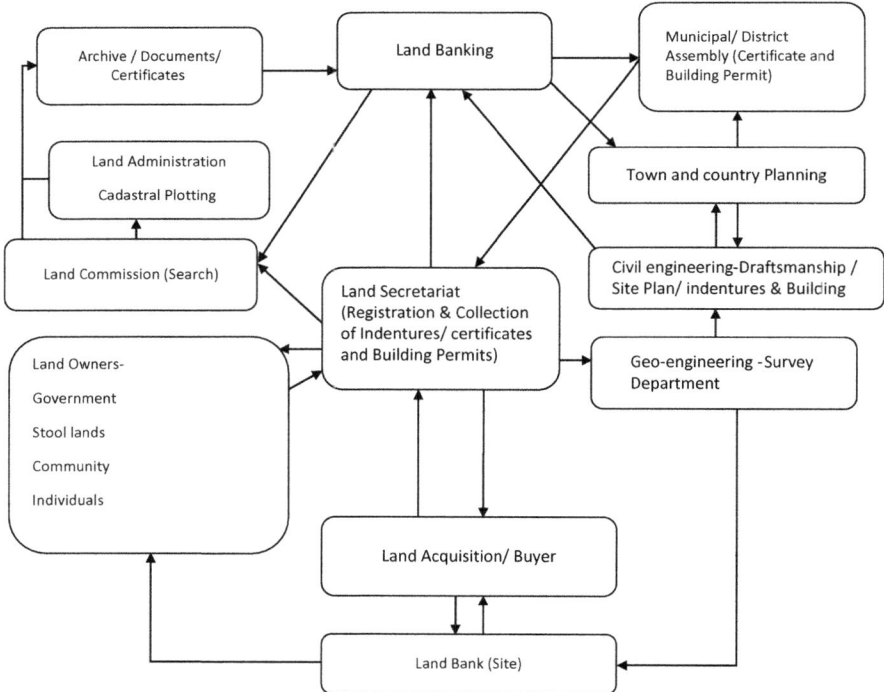

Source: *Author's Construction*

Fig. 10.1 A flow chart of 'land bank'/'land banking' strategy (Source: *Author's Construction*)

Expectedly and as demonstrated in Fig. 10.1, any potential buyer/purchaser/seller of any form of land would not meet the land owner or seller directly. Therefore, the issue of landguardism, multiple sales of land as well as land grabbing issue would be non-existence.

Conclusions

This study concludes that pervasive commodification, monetization and commercialization of land is a function of land conflicts in Southern Ghana. The prevailing land question in Sub-Sahara Africa is largely tied to the Gold Coast land question. The proper implementation of the recommendations in this chapter and its success lays the background to resolving other cases of land conflict in Sub-Sahara Africa. It is thus important to proffer solution to the protracted land conflict towards ensuring peaceful settlement of land conflict. This would ensure the security of freehold lands or leasehold properties against continual or persistent conflicts.

Indeed, it's difficult to understand the nature of the problem better than keen observers of the land projects in the country. Land conflicts affect vitally every Ghanaians. The effect of land conflict in Ghana can only be understood by Ghanaians. Governance and control of land in sub-Saharan Africa in general but Ghana in particular is therefore expected to decouple European legacy which is characterized by proprietary rights which is in dissonance with the indigenous land tenure system. To be able to see through these pervasive land conflicts, Ghanaians should adopt the indigenous strategy devoid of any colonial mentality. And hence this study offers a 'Lank Bank and 'Land Banking strategy' as an option to resolving the detrimental land policy that has bequeathed to Ghanaians by the colonial masters.

The stakeholders in land administration should be cognisance of the fact that land conflicts affect the people in a way that is not conventionally revealed in the public sphere; hence, it is instructive to explore the utility of public enlightenment and mass education to expose the citizens to their land rights and availability of land-related conflict resolution mechanisms. In conclusion, the establishment of 'Land Bank' and associated institutions remain a potent land policy option for land administrators in their quest to curtail land conflicts in Southern Ghana.

References

Abdulai and Crawford (2009), 'Political Will in Combating Corruption in Development and Transition Economies: A Comparative Study of Singapore, Hong Kong and Ghana' International Journal of Financial Crime. pp234–258

Amanor KS (1999) Global restructuring and land rights in Ghana: forest food chains, timber and rural livelihoods. Nordiska Afrikainstitutet, Uppsala

Attuquayefio P (2009) Understanding the work of land guards. Daily Graphic, 25 March

Awortwei-Mensah P (2001) Crowd besieges court. 27th February 2001. Available at: http://www.ghanaweb.com/GhanaHomePage/NewsArchive/artikel.php?ID=13815

Azu V (2011) Land guards terrorize businessman. The Daily Graphic, 01 August. Available at: http://www.modernghana.com/news/342898/1/land-guards-terrorize-businessman.html

Creswell JW (2012) Research design: qualitative, quantitative, and mixed methods approaches, 3rd edn. Sage Publications, Inc, Los Angeles

Darkwa L (2012) Understanding the work of land guards. Daily Graphic, 26 August

Ghana: Act No. 29 of 1960, Criminal Offences Act [Ghana], 12 January 1960, Amendment (2012) Available at: http://www.refworld.org/docid/44bf823a4.html. Accessed 2 Feb 2017

Gough KV, Yankson PWK (2000) Land markets in African cities: the case of peri-urban Accra, Ghana. Urban Stud 37(13):248–265

Kom ED (2003) Security of title to land in Ghana. In: Land as a resource for development. Ghana Universities Press, Accra, pp 14–27. (Proceedings of the Ghana Academy of Arts and Sciences, v. 36)

Kumar R (2013) Research methodology. A step by step guide for beginners. Sage, Thousand Oaks

Norman KD, Lincoln YS (2013) Handbook of qualitative research. Sage Publications, Inc., Thousand Oaks

Pogucki RJH (1955) Gold coast and land tenure: land tenure in Ga customary law. Gold Cost Lands Department, Accra

Quantson KB (2003) Ghana, national security: the dilemma. Dansoman. Accra, Napasvil Ventures

Woodman GR (1996) Customary land law in the Ghanaian courts. Ghana Universities Press, Accra

Chapter 11
Land Tenure and Family Conflict in Rwanda: Case of Musanze District

Joseph R. Rukema and Sultan Khan

Introduction

Colonialism in Africa shaped the way in which indigenous communities acquired and utilised land. It impacted negatively on traditional structures that prescribed land ownership and its use. At the end of colonialism, new contestations arose to meet the needs of land users and claimants. Central to this is the return to customary prescriptions for achieving land security against rising levels of scarcity prompted by urbanization and commercial agriculture. In Africa, many states like South Africa, Nigeria, Zimbabwe and Rwanda have experienced growing conflicts with respect to land ownership and access. Rwanda, being besieged by the most horrific genocide in the history of humankind has not been spared of violent land conflicts especially from those that have suffered land displacement. As part of its reconstruction, land tenure in Rwanda is now perceived to be an important mechanism towards peace building and social stability. According to Rurangwa (2002), half of all disputes in Rwanda are over land particularly over inheritance involving families living in the rural parts of the country. This threatened social cohesion, stability and lasting peace. It is in this context that this chapter explores the extent of family conflict over land ownership, the causes of family conflicts over land tenure and the nature of community and prevailing government mechanisms for settling family disputes over land with specific attention to the Musanze District. The chapter draws from qualitative data arising from focus group studies with forty respondents', twenty (20) males and twenty (20) females, and in-depth interviews with community leaders and local government officials on the nature and extent of family disputes over land.

J. R. Rukema (✉) · S. Khan
University of KwaZulu-Natal, Durban, South Africa
e-mail: Josephr1@ukzn.ac.za

© Springer International Publishing AG, part of Springer Nature 2019
A. O. Akinola, H. Wissink (eds.), *Trajectory of Land Reform in Post-Colonial African States*, Advances in African Economic, Social and Political Development, https://doi.org/10.1007/978-3-319-78701-5_11

In Rwanda, family land related conflicts are prevalent. This threatens social cohesion and sustainable peace, especially in rural areas where the inhabitants rely mainly on land-related activities and where land is a source of livelihood. Family arrangements in Rwanda is dominated by polygamy, and this remains the major cause of family land conflict and a challenge to property inheritance. In addition, the culture that discriminates women against land inheritance, as against the Rwandan Law that guarantee women access to the land, is another complication and a factor responsible for protracted conflict in the country. Moreover, there is lack of public awareness on the existing law on land redistribution and the level of literacy in rural areas hamper the process of land distribution among members of the family and creates misunderstanding which result in conflict and in some instances violence and murder.

The study draws attention to different local structures and government institutions established for reconciling land disputes between and among families; however, the activities of these institutions remain ineffective. Many internal contradictions explain the failure to combat the emerging land conflict in the country. According to Rurangwa (2005), male dominance at grassroots levels and the prevalence of illiteracy within the community, hamper the dispute settlement process. Inability to reach an amiable resolution within the community prompted some of the complainants to refer their cases to the courts of law for resolution. This exposes the fact that the government established structures and local mediators have failed to resolve family land conflicts in the country.

The chapter is divided into four sections. The first is the introductory section, followed by the background to the study, which historicizes the land conflict and draws attention to African pre-colonial traditional land patterns. Furthermore, the section highlights the roles of community leaders in land conflicts and assesses the influence of colonialism in the Rwandan land pattern. The third section, results of the study, presents the findings of the field-study. This is followed by the conclusion.

Background to the Study

The colonial legacy of land tenure systems has influenced conflict dynamics over land rights, ownership and control in most parts of Africa in general, and Rwanda in particular. The Food and Agriculture Organization of the United Nations (FAO) regards land tenure as,

> the relationship, whether legally or customarily defined, among people, as individuals or groups with respect to land, adding that it (land tenure) define how access is granted to rights to use, control, and transfer land, as well as associated responsibilities and restraints (FAO 2015).

In pre-colonial Africa, land tenure systems were largely governed by ancestral occupation, customary or traditional norms, based on oral communication or consent, without any form of written agreements or contract in respect to ownership and control of land (Cotula et al. 2004). The management of this land tenure system, and adjudication of disputes arising thereof, was the responsibility of African traditional leaders in the form of village heads, headmen, chiefs, and traditional leaders or council of elders (Cotula et al. 2004; Place and Hazell 1993).

Besides the customary and traditional land tenure systems, different parts of African societies had their own indigenous systems which was in operation in the pre-colonial dispensation. According to White (cited in Kajabo 2002), pre-colonial Africa land tenure systems was based on the following: the acquisition of land rights by residence whereby individuals clear unoccupied virgin land or inherited it from their forefathers as was the case in Zambia; and acquisition of land rights under matrilineal transfers. Furthermore, it comprises the acquisition of land rights through Kings or Aristocrats who exercised power over all land in centralized Kingdoms such as that of the Barotseland in Zambia and Mossi Empire in Burkina Faso. The acquisition of land rights in feudal systems remained with landlords and tenants/serfs in Kingdoms such as the case of Bunyoro Kingdom in Uganda and the Mailo community in Buganda (Kajabo 2002:2–4).

The advent of colonialism in Africa in the nineteenth century manifested with many structural and institutional changes to the African socio-economic and political organizations. As widely reported, colonialism in Africa was institutionalized and effected through military conquests. It resulted in distortion of traditional authority, and the exploitation of Africa's natural resources, including land grab and invasion of large tracts of productive land from indigenous Africans, which was reallocated for the few colonial settlers (Barrows and Roth 1990; Place and Hazell 1993; Boone 2007). In Africa pre-colonial and post-colonial epochs, land remains an important resource, a valuable property and an essential factor of economic production, means of livelihood, source of food security and instrument of poverty reduction (Cotula et al. 2004:1).

The first implication of colonial land invasions and land dispossessions was the abolition of the indigenous land tenure system by the colonial administrations, who eventually legitimatized land ownership and conferred land rights to the new 'white' landowners (Mamdani 1996). Thus, colonialism brought new dimensions to the mode of land ownership, land rights, land title and land management, which was a departure from the African traditional or customary land tenure systems (ECA 2009). These imposed or 'imported' land tenure systems were differently applied across Africa by colonial governments depending on their respective policies or pattern of administration (Amin 1972). Colonial settlers were mainly granted leasehold tenure or freehold tenure on land that became crown or state land that was largely earmarked for large-scale commercial agriculture, whilst also maintaining the customary or traditional land tenure systems especially for peasants living in the communal or rural areas (Kajabo 2002).

The colonial land tenure systems in Africa, which were later inherited by independent African governments was categorized by the Economic Commission for Africa (2009:4–5) as freehold. This implies "absolute right to control and manage" land, and leasehold in which land belongs "to one entity and is leased to another for a fixed period of time", statutory allocations whereby land allocation is based on statutory provisions; and customary systems in which land tenure rights are "controlled and allocated" are based on traditional practice.

In Rwanda, the land tenure system in the pre-colonial period was characterized by the collective ownership of land that reflected complementarities between agriculture and livestock. Peasant class mostly practiced agriculture. The land rights were enjoyed under the supreme protection of the King known in *Kinyarwanda* as "*Umwami*", which means the guarantor of the well-being of the whole population. Further, the local institutions had authority over land use, its management and allocated land to their subjects according to use. On the other hand, subjects who acquired land from the King had to express appreciation, known as "*guhakwa*," by offering free labor to the Kingdom for community welfare. This system promoted economic production and was a factor of stabilization and harmony in production as well as in terms of social relationships.

Regarding family properties, members of families were grouped in lineages. These were in turn grouped in clans. Each clan had a chief and clans were spread all over the national territory based on different proportions according to regions. Land ownership relationships were thus based on free land use and on the complementarity of the modes of production (Takeuchi and Marara 2009). The land tenure system was under the authority of the king. In Rwandan community, there are different type of traditional land tenure system. The first land tenure system was known as "*Ubukonde*" or clan rights, held by the chief of the clan, who was the first land-clearer. The chief could own vast tracts of land on which he would resettle several families, known as "*Abagererwa*". The latter enjoyed land rights, subject to certain customary conditions (Rurangwa 2005). There was also a system of land tenure called "*igikingi*". This land tenure system pertained to the right of grazing land allotted to those families that specialized in livestock agriculture, granted by the King or one of his chiefs known as "*Umutware w'umukenke*". Up till the advent of colonialism, '*igikingi*' was the most common land tenure system, especially in the central and southern parts of the country (Rurangwa 2005). Lastly, there was another land tenure system known as "*inkungu*" which referred to vacant land whereby the custom enables and authorizes the local political authority, on his own or on behalf of others, to own abandoned land.

With the socio-political and administrative structures becoming stronger and better organised, land resources became more important. The need for good management of these resources was symbolised by the presence of a chief in charge of the land, "*Umutware w'ubutaka*", and a chief in charge of livestock, "*Umutware w'umukenke*", both considered to be at the same level as the chief of the army, "*Umutware w'ingabo*" (Rurangwa 2005). Under this arrangement, land rights were valued and transferred from one generation to another based on the traditional custom. These rights were enjoyed under the highest primacy of the King who was considered the guarantor of the wellbeing of the whole citizen.

In 1899, Rwanda became a German colony. After the defeat of Germany during World War 1 in 1919, Rwanda became a mandate territory of the League of Nations under the administration of Belgium. Belgium's colonial administration later introduced written "codes and laws of Rwanda" to guarantee land tenure security for settlers and other foreigners wishing to invest in land in Rwanda (Takeuchi and Marara 2009). In 1920, a decree on land tenure law use was introduced with two main features: only the colonial public officer could guarantee the right to use the land taken from indigenous Rwandans, and land use should be accompanied by a title deed (Takeuchi and Marara 2009).

In post-colonial Rwanda, there was a shift in land tenure policy. The right to acquire a portion of land was governed by custom, which managed almost all the rural land and promoted the excessive parceling out of plots through the successive 'father-to-son' inheritance system (Rurangwa 2005). Undeniably, land rights were respected and passed on from generation to generation according to Rwandan tradition and custom (Takeuchi and Marara 2009). Land tenure policy did not cater for women and they remained excluded from inheriting land due to customary laws.

The post-genocide Rwandan state, acting in alignment with good governance, made land reform and redistribution its priority. In 1999, Rwanda embarked on a land reform exercise for land redistribution and management. As noted by Binda and Kairaba (2012), the country adopted policy, legal and regulatory frameworks to guide the process such as the National Land Policy (2004), the Organic Land Law (2005) and the Land Tenure Regularization Process (2009). Such laws and administrative policies determine the modalities of allocating, acquisition, transfer, use and management of land in Rwanda. The administration and implementation of the land policy and regulatory frameworks was undertaken by the Office of the Registrar, National Land Centre (NLC), District Land Bureaus (DLBs), the National and District Land Commissions (NDLCs), and Sectors and Cells Land Committees (Rwanda Land Administration System Procedures 2012).

Regarding family possession of land, Rwandan legislature adopted law regarding matrimonial regimes, liberalities and successions. The new legislation provides that all legitimate children of the deceased parent (*de cujus*), in accordance with civil laws, inherit in equal parts without any discrimination between male and female children (Art.50 of the law n° 22/99 of 12/11/1999 of the Rwandan Constitution). The government's adopted land tenure policy on land registration provided some gender equality best practices, including the increased awareness of women on their land ownership rights. Despite government's attempt to re-distribute land equally, disputes and conflicts emerged and continue to hamper the process and effectiveness of land redistribution in Rwanda.

Since the reforms and policy initiatives adopted post-independence in Rwanda to redistribute land, there is still an imbalance in land ownership between rural and urban areas. A total of 70 percent of the country's agricultural land is still managed by 24 percent of households comprising wealthy elites (Rurangwa 2013). In essence, many landless citizens are ultimately poor and marginalised. This persisting imbalance, coupled with increasing population, history of land expropriation and land conflict has "put pressure on the customary land tenure system" (Rurangwa 2013:3).

Results of the Study

This section presents a robust analysis of the field-study employed in the study. It starts by presenting the characteristics of the respondents followed by the interpretations of the results in respect to the objectives of the study.

Characteristics of Respondents

Respondents were asked to provide details on their age, gender and education level. The respondents comprised members of Cyuve, Kimonyi and Musanze communities which are part of Musanze. The profile of respondents is presented in Table 11.1.

The sample was dominated by respondents between the age category of 31–40 years (32.5%), followed by those in the category of 51 years and above which represented 27.5% of all respondents. This was followed by those between the age categories of 41–50 years, which represented 22.5% of respondents, and lastly, those of the age between 21 and 30 years, which represented 17.5% of all respondents.

An equal distribution (50%) of male and female respondents made up the sample. The equal representation of respondents allowed for the capture of both men and women voices on issues related to land re-allocation, which is the most contested subject in Rwanda.

Educational level of the respondents was considered in the analysis on the grounds that it would provide a level of understanding in respect of laws and policies governing land re-distribution in Rwanda. With regard to the level of education, 50% of participants had primary schooling, 37.5% were illiterate, and 10% had high school education, while 2.5% attended the university.

Causes of Family Conflicts Associated with Land

The research findings examined the main causes of family disputes related to land. The people interviewed were classified into two categories: questionnaire addressed to community leaders and questions to members of the community. The focal point was to identify the main causes of family conflict associated with land ownership.

Table 11.1 Profile of Respondents

Characteristic	Variable	Frequency	Percentage
Age	Between 21–30 years	7	17.5%
	Between 31–40 years	13	32.5%
	Between 41–50 years	9	22.5%
	51 years old and above	11	27.5%
Gender	Male	20	50%
	Female	20	50%
	Total	40	100%
Educational level	Illiterate	15	37.5%
	Primary school	20	50%
	Secondary school	4	10%
	University	1	2.5%
	Total	40	100%

Source; field data, September 2014

During the interviews, participants stated that despite the fact that polygamous marriages was illegal in Rwanda, the prevalence of polygamy was plentiful. There are still cases in which some men are found to have two or even three wives, without legally marrying any one of them. In this case, polygamy impedes land registration and constitutes one of the causes of family disputes in Musanze District. Often, there are cases whereby more than one woman and their children claim rights over a land that belongs to one man. All women claimed to have equal access (possession) to the land in question in the interest of their children. Indeed, family disputes related to land originated in the problematical issue of polygamy due to conflicts over inheritance, ascending partition, grabbing and unlawful transfer of land without free consent of all the family members.

While conducting this research, 50% of women and 30% of men agreed that family land conflicts are prevalent in polygamous families and conflicts emerge during land registration and acquisition. The statement reads:

> Yes, in families where one man has more wives, there are always problems when their children have to access the land. There is misunderstanding of who are the legitimate children and who are not and this lead to serious conflict. Sometimes people kill each other because of the land. Children of the same man can turn against the other from different mother. In some case even children from same both parents conflict over the land (Participant one, 2014).

However, some respondents, in the men category, opposed the idea that land disputes are the result of polygamy, but they pointed out that land is generally scarce. They argued that: "When a man has more than one woman, he tries to divide his plot of land and gives each woman her share" (Participant two, 2014). Some men claimed the main cause of family disputes, nevertheless, relate to landownership originating from inheritance claims, boundary encroachment and poverty. An old male respondent claimed that "polygamy is not the major cause of family disputes, in the past we used to marry more than one woman, but there were no family conflicts because every woman had his plot of land" (Participant three, 2015).

Indeed, it was revealed that the issue of polygamy overwhelmingly dominated most of the family disputes related to land. Polygamy is the source of inheritance or succession problems between heirs or successors (children). Polygamous wives that are jealous, tends to provoke family dismemberment and aggravates land disputes within the family.

High Demographic Density and Land Disputes

There is a relationship between high population density and the impact on land usage and demand. Survey results show that the total population of Musanze District between the years 2010–2011 comprised 416,000 inhabitants. This represented 21% of the total population of Northern Province and constituted 3.9% of the total population of Rwanda. Females comprised 54.1% of the population of Musanze District, while the youth population (with 40-years benchmark) was 84% of the total age population. The majority of the respondent, especially community leaders, argued that the higher demographic density provoked negative effects, produced negative social attitudes and undesirable behaviors.

A community leader argued that high population pressure affects the size of cultivable land, which explains the decrease in the volume of arable land in the area. He argued "the government is trying to take special measures for reinforcing the limits of higher demographic density, because this provokes the augmentation of poverty and social conflict especially family conflicts related to land (Respondent one, 2014). It is worth noting that Rwanda is highly populated and this resulted into government taking measure to create communal villages called "imidugudu". These regroup thousands of household in a small piece of land.

In fact, as other research argue that the overpopulation of the country (Rwanda), apart from exerting extreme pressure on the already fragile and unfertile soils, has also brought about excessive parceling out of land by successive father-to-son inheritance under customary law (Ministry of Lands, Environment, Forests, Water and Mines 2004) which result into family conflict where a father had more wives and members of the family had different positions on how the land could be distributed among family members.

It was also found that the higher demographic is another challenge that causes land disputes because the majority of Musanze residents are employed in the agricultural sector. One would have expected higher agricultural productivity, but the reverse is the case. Higher demographic rate, which increases competition for arable land in Musanze District, results in land degradation and eventual deterioration or total loss of the productive capacity of the soils for present and future use. Increases in an area's population density and size may temporarily cause frustration and hostility among residents, especially when there is a dwindling farm productivity.

Unawareness of Land Regulation and Policies

During the data collection, it was found that in Musanze District, people have mixed responses. Some indicated that they were ignorant of the land law and land policies. It was found that the lack of awareness was common, whenever the government adopted land law and policy without adequate mass consultation and mobilization in support of the land reforms. For instance, respondents' had many issues with the complexities involved in paying land lease fees. During land registration, there was no information about land taxation. Local authorities (community leaders) in research areas (Cyuve, Kimonyi sectors in Musanze district) acknowledged that people overwhelmingly received the land registration process positively, but the majority of the respondents had different position to what was claimed by local authority leaders. The participation of landlords in providing information related to their land was motivated by the advantages that local authorities and land officers derived by advertising them (bank loan access, land related dispute avoidance, etc.)

The above claim was confirmed by the survey whereby 68% of the respondents affirmed that they went to register their land to reconcile land related disputes, and

25% that did register their land had easy access to bank loans. However, a handful of respondents mainly in the rural areas registered their land to comply with the local authority's order. Another respondent claimed that,

> during land registration, the land officers didn't give us all necessary information regarding land taxation, we knew that fact after registration at the moment of collecting title deeds certificates of our land, to this, many people don't know more about land law" (Respondent four, 2014).

However, this narrative carries one single message that the fees for land lease was kept secret (either willingly or not) by land officials up to the end of the land registration process. The reason why officials decided to keep this a secret was to ensure the obligation for landowners to pay land lease fees. Nevertheless many make assumptions that the reason behind this could have been to encourage people to tell the truth about the size and use of their land because if they knew that the lease fee could be proportional to the land's size and location, some landowners would be tempted to provide false information (Focus Group Discussion, 2014).

Many of the respondents claimed that land officials and land authorities did not make much efforts to inform the people about these fees Hence, even if people are conversant with the law, they need a comprehensive understanding of its interpretations and their obligations in respect to the laws Whilst there would be a need for the community to be educated on land law and policies, the primary issue to be addressed would be to ensure that the people within the community have the intellectual capacity or ability to understand and interpret land laws and policies.

Conflicting Legal Texts

Even though traditional land relations and laws was based on the African custom that discriminate woman vis-à-vis the right to acquire title deed to land; the research however notes some gaps in the current legal framework under which the land tenure system operates. This is despite the inviolability of the constitutional provisions for private property rights, whether personal or collective property rights. As provided by the constitution, the right to property may not be interfered with except in public interest, in circumstances and procedures determined by Law and subject to fair and prior compensation (Art. 29 of the Constitution of the Republic of Rwanda as amended to date).

It was discovered, in the course of the field-research, that the constitution generated some contradictions in respect of land rights. For instance, in the event that a surviving spouse remarried, the Council of Succession can, in the interest of the children, allow him or her to remain the usufructuary of the same patrimony (Art.75 para 2 of law N° 22/99 of 12/11/1999). This violates inalienable rights, and the council of succession can be an obstacle to the well-being of the surviving spouse and the product of the marriage. Normally, in case of death of one of the spouses, the surviving spouse ensures the administration of the entire patrimony while assuming the duties of raising the children and offering assistance to the needy parents of the *de cujus* deceased.

In the event of third party intervention (especially the family council members) in such land matters, the family loses the right to private property owned by all the family members due to the intervention of third parties regarded as family council members. Occurrences like this increases the number of family conflict cases related to land ownership. Most of the time, it is the widow that experiences this kind of problem. Another challenge in the land project relates to the complexity of laws in connection with families whose couples are not legally married. These families are affected by the dearth of legislation that specifically deals with the right of family property. Most people in rural areas are not legally married and this presents a challenge when it comes to land inheritance.

Adherence to Cultural Practices that Discriminate Women

The study reveals persistent adherence to traditional practices that discriminates women from land ownership. Some respondents (35% of men, mostly old) supports the claim that land ownership is the prerogative of men, and land rights are inherited from father to son. However, 99.3% of women respondents rejected this assertion. Clearly, gender inequality constitutes a major source of land conflict in Rwanda. Women are unable to claim their rights to land in those communities, which still preserve their cultural beliefs, and practices that see men as the custodian of land. Despite the laws that guarantee both male and female child access to inherit land, the research notes that girls are excluded from inheriting family land. Some of the parents still believe in the customary principles which prevent woman from land ownership. The majority of respondents interviewed such as District Coordinator, Deputy Land Registrar in charge of Northern Province, Court Registrars and presidents of mediation committee (*Abunzi*), stated that adherence to traditions and culture that reinforces gender inequality are the major sources of gender violence in the rural community.

Furthermore, more than 89% of respondents, including leaders, reiterates the fact that parents actually discriminate against their children in order of ascending partition. Normally, the ascending partition is an act accomplished by parents while they are still alive, by which they share their patrimony between their children or their descendants who acquire, each for the portion devolved to him or her, full ownership.

Concluding Remarks

This chapter examines the causes of family conflicts over land tenure as well as the extent of family conflict over land ownership in Rwanda. It also assesses the effectiveness of community and government mechanisms for settling family disputes over land in the Musanze District of Rwanda. The chapter draws from qualitative data arising from focus group studies with twenty males and twenty females, and in depth interviews with community leaders and local government officials on the causes, nature and extent of family disputes over land.

The findings from the study demonstrated that family land related conflicts are prevalent and seem to be a threat to social cohesion and lasting peace especially in the rural area whose main activity is on land. The study also revealed that the major cause of family land conflict is polygamy which complicates the inheritance of children from different mothers. In addition to causes of conflicts is the culture that discriminate women against inheriting land despite the current Rwandan Law that guarantee women access to the land. Moreover, there is a lack of awareness on the existing law on land redistribution and the level of literacy in rural areas hamper the process of land distribution among members of the family and create misunderstanding, which mostly leads to conflicts and in some instances to violence and murder.

The study has also found that there are two complementary structures - traditional and governmental – involved in the settlement of land disputes between individuals and among families; however, these remain ineffective. Male dominance at grassroots levels and illiteracy levels among the community hamper the dispute settlement process and complainants have to refer their cases to the courts of law for resolution. Despite government and traditionally established structures of mediators to deal with land claims and disputes, the prevalence of family land conflicts remained unabated in Rwanda. This in most of cases result into members of the same family killing each other or resulting in family conflicts.

References

Amin S (1972) Neocolonialism in West Africa. Penguin Books, Hammondsworth

Barrows R, Roth M (1990) Land tenure and Investment in African Agriculture: theory and evidence. J Mod Afr Stud 28:265–297

Binda EM, Daale J, Kairaba (2012) The impact of land lease fee on land owners: Rwanda case study report

Boone C (2015) Land tenure regimes adn state structure in rural Afica. Implications for the forms of resistance to large scale land acquisitions by outsiders. Journal of Contemporary African Studies 33(2):171–190

Cotula L, Toulmin C, Hesse C (2004) Land tenure and administration in Africa: lessons of experience and emerging issues. International Institute for Environment and Development, London

Economic Commission for Africa (2009) Land tenure systems and their impacts on food security and sustainable development in Africa. ECA/SDD/05/09. ECA Publications, Addis Ababa. http://www.uncsd2012.org/content/documents/land_tenure_systems%20and%20their%20 impacts%20on%20Food%20Security%20and%20Sustainable%20Development%20in%20 Africa.pdf

Food and Agricultural Organization of the United Nations (2015) Land tenure and rural development. http://www.fao.org/docrep/005/y4307e/y4307e05.htm

Kajabo GM (2002) Land use and land tenure in Africa: towards an evolutionary conceptual framework. University of Zambia, Lusaka

Land Tenure Regularization (2009) Land tenure regularization in Rwanda. Good practices in land reform - Case study. African Development Bank Group, Abidjan

Mamdani M (1996) Citizen and subject, contemporary Africa and the legacy of late colonialism. Princeton University Press, Princeton

National Land Policy (2004, February) Ministry of Lands, Environment, Forests, Water and Mines. Republic of Rwanda. http://www.minirena.gov.rw/fileadmin/Media_Center/Documents/RNRA_LMD/Land_Policy.pdf

Place F, Hazell P (1993) Productivity effects of indigenous land tenure Systems in sub-Saharan Africa. Am J Agric Econ 75(1):10–19

Organic Land Law (2005) Determining the modalities of protection, conservation and promotion of the environment in Rwanda No.04 of 08 April 2005, Official Gazette of the Republic of Rwanda

Rurangwa E (2013) Land tenure reform. The case study of Rwanda. International Gorilla Conservation Program. Rwanda. Paper presented at the conference on 'land divided: land and South African Society in 2013, in comparative perspective. University of Cape Town, 24–27 March 2013. http://www.landdivided2013.org.za/sites/default/files/rurangwa%20Land%20Tenure%20Reform_Rwanda%20Case.pdf

Rurangwa E (2005) Land administration developments in Rwanda, in International Federation of Surveyors (eds), Proceedings. Secure land tenure: New legal frameworks and tools. Totdrukwerk bv Apeldoorn

Rwanda Land Administration System Procedures (2012) Land administration manual 1. Government of Rwanda, Ministry of Natural Resources and Rwanda Natural Resources Authority

Takeuchi S, Marara J (2009) Conflict and land tenure in Rwanda, JICA-RI Working Paper Series. JICA Research Institute, Tokyo. https://jica-ri.jica.go.jp/publication/assets/JICA-RI_WP_No.1_2010.pdf

Chapter 12
Land Reform in Africa: Towards Resource Utilization and Sustainability

Adeoye O. Akinola and Wissink Henry

Introduction

Africa is not lacking in the required land mass and arable land for enhanced food security, land-related productivity and sustainable development. However, the continent has been on the brink of socio-political instability and economic malaise due to the under-utilization of land and lack of implementation of effective policies in the land sector of most African countries. The result was the evident land hunger, land related resource conflicts, communal clashes occasioned by competition for land use, food insecurity, illegal occupation, land capture or land-grab and many other associated land related concerns. For a continent renowned for his agricultural productivity and mineral resources, the issue of land utility and sustainable policy on land have definitely attracted big interests from state and non-state actors involved in Africa's quest for resource utilization and sustainable development (Hall and Kepe 2017). The quest to reform the land sector led to the implementation of diverse kinds of land arrangements in the continent. For instance, in Ethiopia and Mozambique, land belongs to the state; while in Nigeria and South Africa, both the state and its population (through different means) have a shared land ownership and use.

A. O. Akinola (✉)
Public Administration, University of Zululand, KwaDlangezwa 3836, South Africa
e-mail: AkinolaA@unizulu.ac.za

W. Henry
University of KwaZulu-Natal, Durban, South Africa
e-mail: Wissinkh@ukzn.ac.za

© Springer International Publishing AG, part of Springer Nature 2019
A. O. Akinola, H. Wissink (eds.), *Trajectory of Land Reform in Post-Colonial African States*, Advances in African Economic, Social and Political Development, https://doi.org/10.1007/978-3-319-78701-5_12

Despite the recurrent policy initiatives by African states to reform the land sector, there are evidence of protracted land conflicts, policy gaps and complex land arrangements in the region. It is thus imperative to re-examine the current trends and realities of land reform in Africa. The continent has witnessed different kinds of policy enactments, improvement in the legal frameworks guiding land tenure and concerted efforts to addressing the land utilization questions. Across Africa, the larger parts of the population lacks access to land as reflected in land agitations, family conflict over land, land occupation and invasion, land-related communal conflicts, and farm conflicts between farm workers and farm owners. Moyo (2003: 2) maintains that "variegated struggles at varying scales and localities over escalating unequal access to and control of land represent Africa's real land question". In Nigeria, land based conflict resulted in the destructions of many communities as a result of competition over land ownership; Southern Ghana presented another case of land conflict; the case of South African racially-inclined conflict over land is well-known; while in Rwanda, families took up arms to exert authority over parcels of land. These exposed the absence of effective policies to deal with land-related concerns in Africa. Furthermore, under-utilization of land, due to many contradictions in the land arrangement and recurrent land reform schemes, has generated serious concerns for stakeholders in the African development project.

Therefore, this chapter captures the policy implications of land reform in Africa and engages the conventional scholarship on the motivations and trajectories of land policies in the immediate post-colonial Africa. Some of the current discourses have failed to capture the developmental realities of the modern socio-political and economic order. Also, many of the hitherto agrarian economies, like that of South Africa, that rely on land as the most important factor of production has become industrial; hence, diversification of African economies, in a way, and particularly, the rural-urban surge has diminished the importance of land to human survival. Furthermore, there are other identifiable complexities in the land reform project, especially those in the former settler societies of southern Africa, due to the contradictions between 'return our land' demands by previously disadvantaged communities, negotiated constitutional democracy and demands for sustainable economic development.

It was soon discovered that most of the lands taken from the 'white' and redistributed to the 'black', to redress the historical injustices and combat poverty, has generated diverse results and developmental contradictions that undermine the land productivities. Many own land or have had land restituted to them, but remain poor. Therefore, land is no more the most instructive property for improved livelihood. Many post-colonial states concentrated on nationalization of land, redistribution of land to correct the racially-skewed land arrangements, thereby abandoning gender parity in respect of upholding women land rights. Although, the authors recognize the threat that unresolved land tenure system portrays for Africa, the chapter proposes a dispensation to promote equitable land arrangement that promotes gender equality, land productivity, food security and both human and national sustainable development.

Land and the Imperativeness of Policy Shift

Many factors reinforced the need for land reform in Africa. Across Africa, land reforms have engendered different forms of contradictions. For instance, in South Africa, "land reform is in flux– and, arguably, in crisis. We argue here that the widespread criticism of its slow pace fails to capture the extent of this crisis" (Hall and Kepe 2017: 1). Therefore, there have been calls to revisit and effect changes in the land reform projects of African states because of the shortcomings of the prevailing land policies in the continent. The AUC-ECA-AfDB Consortium tries to capture the motivations for a change in land policies in the continent. According to the report,

> Contemporary processes of social organization and mobilization including those derived from class, gender, region, culture, ethnicity, nationality and generational cleavages now predominate in shaping access to, control and utilization of land, resulting in a complex basis of claims and conflicts over land resources (AUC-ECA-AfDB Consortium 2010: 3).

Land has occupied a strategic importance in the African developmental initiatives, and this is enhanced by the revelation that about 60% of the population draws its livelihood and earnings mainly from agricultural production, and related activities (AUC-ECA-AfDB Consortium (2010: 7). Accordingly, the contribution of agriculture and livestock farming to African economies have dwindled in the past decades, primarily due to the discovery of natural resources on previously productive agricultural land, divestment in agriculture and development of industrial economies in many countries; however, the vibrancy of the farming sector could "be considerably enhanced through radical restructuring of a number of constraints" (AUC-ECA-AfDB Consortium 2010:7).

The first should be the transformation of African states land tenure patterns. Land tenure captures "the set of rules that determines how land is used, possessed, leveraged, sold, or in other ways disposed of within societies. These rules may be established by the state or by custom, and rights may accrue to individuals, families, communities, or organizations" (Garvelink 2012). Although government policy usually emphasizes the need for tenure security, and aims to achieve this through the provision of long-term leases, Hall and Kepe (2017: 4) found an awkward land tenure systems and an arrangement whereby beneficiaries often do not have leases in any of their cases of study. Generally, strengthening the property rights of the rural poor leads to increased investment and contributes to economic growth and more equitable development (Garvelink 2012).

The imperative and urgency to accelerate land deeds in countries like South Africa remains a necessity, especially due to the inability of the land beneficiaries to seek capital from financial institutions whose conditions for loans is contingent upon the availability of land titles and deeds. Although, the South African land reform process apportions land rights to communities and recognises the Community Property Association (CPA), recurring conflicts among members have raised concerns over the appropriateness and the sustainability of this policy approach. As reinforced by Adams et al. (1999: 24), rights are best vested in the land users, who have a clear interest in utilising resources for their own benefit, rather than in institutions (such as civic organisations, traditional or tribal authorities), which have often been hijacked by elites for personal gain. In pre-colonial Africa, land was accessible for all those who have are in need of land for any productive engagements, and such land were mostly freely allocated, except in few cases where stipends were paid to family or communal authorities. The modernization of land tenure has however changed land relations in Africa.

Land in post-colonial Africa have been integrated into the monetized global capital, where land is regarded as economic capital and a commodity subjected to market forces. This conception is informed by the utmost universal liberalist approach to land tenure system: an approach imposed on Africa by western neo-liberal actors. As asserted by Moyo,

> The growth of resource conflicts in Africa increasingly reflect contradictions steeped in both colonial and post-colonial land policies and the significance that land concentration takes in contemporary struggles over 'development' and accumulation under global capitalism, as well as struggles for democratization. These contradictions question the capacity of neo-liberal market and political regimes to deliver land and economic reforms which can address both inequity and poverty (Moyo 2003: 1).

In another publication, Moyo further reinforced his earlier perspectives on the land-globalization nexus, and explained that,

> The land question in Africa is a by-product of globalized-control of land, natural resources and minerals in general, reflecting incomplete decolonisation processes in ex-settler colonies along with the penchant for foreign 'investment' in a neo-liberal policy framework that marginalises the rural and urban poor. Global finance capital is increasingly entangled in conflicts over land, as the exploitation of oil, minerals and natural resources expands into new African enclaves that highlight the external dimension of distorted development (Moyo 2007: 1).

European colonial powers assumed control over land through all kinds of "agreements", treaties, conquests and appropriation in Africa. Specifically, a report reveals that "direct control of land and engagement in agriculture was prominent in Southern Africa (i.e. South Africa, Zimbabwe, Namibia) and in North Africa (Egypt, Algeria and Libya), Kenya in East Africa, Ivory Coast in West Africa, and to a lesser extent in the DRC and Cameroon in Central Africa" (AUC-ECA-AfDB Consortium 2010: 6).

During this period, African indigenous land governance system was diluted and replaced by the prevailing state-centric land management system that disposed of the community and traditional authorities as the sole custodians of land in the continent. In Ethiopia, the integration of land resource into the capitalist system was reflected in the sugar industrial economy, while the South African 'willing buyer, willing seller' approach to land reform marked the conversion of land to a commodity within the Rainbow Nation paradigm. The question remains - how sustainable is the willing buyer-willing seller in a countries experiencing increasing and consistent inflation? More so, land is not just a resource, it is not just an economic commodity, it is a social resource that binds societies to universal heritage and also acts as instruments of social stability and security. It is also a source of livelihood for rural dwellers who rely on agriculture and engage in diverse land-related activities.

Land Resource: Utilization and Policy Sustainability

The land utilization question continues to dominate discourse on land reform in the globe. In the case of Africa, there have been an outcry to the under-utilization of the land mass of land in the continent. As strong as the reality seems, some scholars downplayed this concern, Osieny (2015), however appropriately reiterated the argument that about 75% of underutilized land in the world is in Africa and that any piece of land which is not used for commercial food production is near idle and as such unutilized. He contended with this assertion and declared that "land in Africa is not idle nor is it unutilized" (Osieny 2015). He further maintains that,

> Africa has been and still remains an epitome of subsistence agriculture, where the populations till land to produce food for family consumption. This is the model that has sustained rural populations for decades. That Africa's model of food production wasn't mechanized doesn't translate to its agricultural land not being utilized. They simply utilize it differently (Osieny 2015).

As much as Osieny's response to the land utilization question seems plausible, across Africa, from Nigeria to South Africa, hectares of uncultivated lands, especially in the rural and semi-rural areas, are evident. Rural-urban migration due to the attractiveness of city life and industrialization, jettisoning of farming by the younger generations, absence of farming support for rural dwellers and contradictions and failure of land reforms in the continent has led to drastic decline in land utilization in the agricultural sectors. In some African countries like Nigeria and South Africa, with decent industrial growth, there are declining numbers of younger people in the villages, and there are fewer subsistence farmers residing in many villages. Some have become farm labourers in big commercial farms in the rural areas or urban-suburbs while others have all migrated to the cities in search of jobs in growing industrial economies within cities. These are individuals that should have benefitted from land reform efforts and positioned themselves as emerging small-scale farmers.

Generally, and in Africa in particular, population has been the major driver of agricultural expansion. Even though the positive correlation between population growth and cropland is expected due to increasing demand for food, it is also true that people tend to settle in areas suitable for agriculture (SD21 2012). In South Africa, the regions with cultivated land or rainforest (KwaZulu-Natal) attracts high population than those of the desert like the Northern Cape which records scanty population. According to the 2011 Census in South Africa, the Northern Cape has an area of 372889.36 km² and a population of 1,145,861 (3.07 per km²), while KwaZulu-Natal Province has an area of 94361.32 km² and a population of 10,267,300 (108.81 per km²).

One of the most decisive policy gaps in the land reform project is the misappropriated use of arable land for non-agricultural purposes. Across Africa, cultivated land are used for other endeavours like mining, industrial construction, erection of malls, while farmers are longing to have such arable land for agricultural use. This constitute arable land waste and misplaced priority in terms of land allocation and use. The government needs to apply understanding of the topographic nature of the land distributed and the potential use of such lands. The fierce competition for access to land for industrial use in densely populated areas like in the Lagos State of Nigeria, Nairobi in Kenya, Gauteng or KwaZulu-Natal Provinces in South Africa, represent policy-gaps amidst large parcels of fallow land in other regions of the respective countries. For example, policy could be enacted to encourage the creation of industrial villages, cities or zones in Northern Cape of South Africa or northern part of Nigeria where the prospects for land cultivations is very low due to the 'rocky' (in the case of Northern Cape) or dusty (in the case of northern Nigeria) nature of the land.

Under-utilization leads to food insecurity in the continent. Despite the Economist Intelligence Unit's 2017 Global Food Security Index that ranked South Africa as the most food secure country in Africa and occupied the position of 44th out of 133 countries worldwide, the country is experiencing food security at the household level (Sihlobo and Boshoff 2017). According to the report, South Africa's relatively high evaluation has been made possible by robust agricultural output over the past years as one of the few net exporters of agricultural products in the continent.

It must be noted that South Africa continues to experience rise in food prices, while the majority of the population groans under the weight of lack and food shortages. Reportedly, about 13.8-million South Africans currently live under the food poverty line (Sihlobo and Boshoff 2017). Food exportation does not necessarily reflect food security for the country involved, just as national wealth does not automatically correspond to improvement in the livelihood of the mass of the population. In the early 2000, the Nigerian government, embarked on aggressive food (cassava) exportation at the detriment of the masses who experience shortages and dramatic rise in the cost of cassava. Financial and other technical support were afforded small-scale farmers to push-up the production of cassava. However, the policy was unsustainable and eventually crashed.

Many countries in Africa, which prided itself in substantial agricultural produce for internal consumption and export have been hit with dwindling agricultural outputs and eventual food shortages. For instance, apart from the fact that the Lever Brothers of Unilever founded its first oil palm plantation in the country, and by 1958, became the first palm-oil exporter in the world, Congo was among the largest exporters of perennial crops in the world. Nigeria overtook Congo in the export of palm-oil in the 1960s; however, both countries are presently experiencing shortages in agricultural outputs, which could be explained by distorted land-related policies and the policy 'confusion' between the large-scale and small-scale approach to the farming system. The Nigerian government opted to boost commercial farming through the 1978 land reform. However, the 1978 land policy in did not significantly increase agricultural produce. Rather, by 1983, the country was on the brink of serious food shortages and a dire economic crisis.

The critical question is: How do we address the question of national food security in the midst of the large-scale versus small-scale farming debate? Can we continue to favour the redistribution of land to small-scale farmers as the panacea for national or continental food security? As much as land inequality constitutes impediments to social stability and emancipation of the rural population, stakeholders in the land reform agenda should also be mindful of implementation policies that will enhance agricultural productivity, sustainable food production and national food security. Therefore, there is a need to rethink the over-concentration of land to few commercial farmers, especially in cases of under-utilization of substantial part of the land within their reach, and also be cognizance of the danger inherent in mindless allocation of cultivable land for small-scale farmers, majority of who do not have the necessary institutional support, farming skills and capital required for optimum farm productivity. Depending on the realities in different countries, the government should strike a balance between these two options.

There is renewed interests in smallholder agriculture as an engine for poverty reduction and rural development, thereby refocusing on land tenure and tenure security within the broader debate of land reform (Garvelink 2012). Tenure security provides incentives for long-term land investments in the agricultural and other sectors (SD21 2012: 15). For instance, investors will be wary of engaging in tree-planting in a land arrangement without tenure security and land property rights. Although, as reported by (SD21 2012: 15), investors might take the risk of utilizing land for long-term farming like tree-planting to 'force' the government to extend land ownership to such investors. Generally, lack of finance and absence of institutional support for farmers, especially small-scale entrants into the farming business, have also become impediments to land utilization.

According to Osieny (2015), the factors responsible for land under-utilization in Africa are, "climatic conditions, poor land tenure systems in some countries, conflicts that discourage stable settlement needed for agricultural development, as well as policy weaknesses like low agricultural financing that negatively impact on sustainable agricultural development".

Based on findings, SD21 (2012: 10) reiterates the fact that "access to road, electricity and communication infrastructure is strongly correlated with agricultural total factor productivity". Absence of basic amenities impedes the motivations for farming and those who embark on farming in those areas encountered great challenges that stunted land and agricultural productivity. An example is the Khomani San of the Southern Kalahari, South Africa (Francis et al. 2016). Allocation of land to small-scale farmers and new beneficiaries in the rural areas lacked most of the farm infrastructure like water, electricity, access roads, while many lack good schools and markets for the rural inhabitants and the farmers respectively. The result was that "land transfers end in failure with new owners walking away from their investments after struggling to turn a profit" (Garvelink 2012).

Therefore, it becomes very important for government to provide the basic infrastructure to the rural areas, especially areas with the propensity for small-scale and big commercial farming. This will open-up the areas for agricultural markets, leading to agro-allied industrialization and the gradual migration of people from the already saturated cities into the rural areas. It is important to create "access to markets and information helps land users to make informed decisions. Farmers with access to market information will respond to market signals and could respond favorably when they have better access to market and information" (SD21 2012: 11). It is almost impossible to attain the goal of agrarian reform and increase agricultural production when necessary infrastructure and institutional support for new and small-scale farmers are lacking. As emphasized by Kepe and Cousins:

> Although necessary, land reform will only be effective if embedded within a broader programme to restructure the agrarian economy. Amongst other things, this must ensure access to inputs, equipment, draught power, and marketing outlets. Infrastructure for transport and communications, and support services such as extension, training and marketing advice, are also essential (Kepe and Cousins 2003: 2).

No doubt, land reform needs to address land distortion and dispossession during colonialism and minority rules; however, this should be divorced from emotional or political considerations. Rather, land reform should effectively deal with land inequality towards achieving agrarian transformation and rural development.

Furthermore, gender construction in terms of land allocation and ownership also deepens land fallowness. Since women constitute the majority of economically active group in rural areas, measures to strengthen women's access to land are crucial for economic development and realization of their fundamental human rights (Adams et al. 1999). In Cameroun, women have significantly contributed to agricultural production than their men counterparts. Despite the enactment of gender neutral legislations and extension of land rights to the women group in many African countries like Kenya, Nigeria, South Africa and Zimbabwe, such laws are only effective in the urban centers, while denial of women's land rights still exists in many rural parts of African countries. Traditional norms which reinforces patrimony, as obtainable in Africa's pre-colonial era, are still in operation in many South Africa's rural areas. It therefore becomes important for these governments and civil society organizations to embark on sensitization exercises in the rural areas and also devise ways of monitoring adherence to gender equality in terms of land access, use and ownership. As found by many studies, whoever owns land, amasses both power and control. Land is a valuable socio-economic resource, both in agrarian, mineral resource and industrial economies; thus, he that owns land controls the society. Therefore, denial of women of land rights represents denials of their decision-making power within the society. Land reform is thus not only wealth redistribution, but the redistribution of power. Hall and Kepe (2017: 4) raised a queried, "without redistribution of power and wealth to those who are the ostensible beneficiaries, is it even land reform?" (Hall and Kepe 2017).

In countries like Zimbabwe and South Africa, land is still owned and controlled by few elites and powerful politicians. The hijacking of the land reform project by the political and social elites was predominant in many parts of Africa. For instance, the case of Zimbabwe was a point of note. The neo-land capture in the country led to the popularity of the slogan, 'land to the people and not to the politicians'. Postcolonial Africa has witnessed neo-land capture by emerging African elites to the detriment of the landless and vulnerable group who continue to pitch their tent with the land-hunger train. States in developing countries continue to propagate the interests of the few elites over that of the masses. This replicates the monopolization of land previously perpetrated by the colonial powers and minority regimes. Existing land policies have not significantly redistributed lands to the landless (both in the rural and urban areas) who requires land for agricultural purposes and other productive endeavours. Therefore, it will be flawed to allow the state to have free reign in the land reform exercise. Civil society organizations, think-tank, academics, and traditional authorities should be engaged and encouraged to get more involved in the designs of land arrangements in the continent. Policies should be well monitored to create land access and productive cultivation of land.

African states should explore the utility of skills transfer from one state to another. For instance, African countries that are burdened by difficulties in securing land tenure like South Africa should learn from few that made progress and designed recourse to the pre-colonial land arrangements in Africa, and that paid less attention to land registration. Uganda and Tanzania have put intense efforts at decentralizing their land tenure administrations and creating regional and community land management administrations that address the diverse pressures of land hunger at every layer of the society (Garvelink 2012). Instead of the utter jettisoning of traditional land tenure by the modern state and its replacement by the state's centric land arrangement in Africa, it is more beneficial to integrate the indigenous tenure systems with a modern and democratic systems of land administration, which will capture the reality of land use and ownership. As noted by the Rights and Resource Initiative,

> In Tanzania, Uganda, and Zambia, the high percentage of community-based tenure recognition reflects the fact that national laws automatically recognize all customary community lands without requiring communities to register their lands. This automatic recognition reduces procedural requirements that can be burdensome and deter communities from formalizing their land rights (Rights and Resource Initiative 2015 2).

Even countries that tend to merge the two approaches to land governance (traditional and liberal) were unsuccessful in its implementation. African governments keep violating the customary land rights of the indigenous population at will. Uganda presents a clear example. Although the Constitution and Land Act of 1998 recognize customary law in respect to land rights, but the state have consistently failed to uphold the rights (Rights and Resource Initiative 2015: 3).

One of the most decisive policy gaps in the land reform project is the misplaced used of arable land for non-agricultural purposes. Across Africa, cultivated land are used for other endeavours like industrial construction, erection of malls, while farmers are longing to have such arable land for agricultural use. This constitute arable land waste and misplaced priority in terms of land allocation and use. The government needs to apply understanding of the topographic nature of the land distributed and the potential use of such lands. The fierce competition for access to land for industrial use in densely populated areas like Lagos State of Nigeria, Nairobi in Kenya, Gauteng or KwaZulu-Natal Provinces in South Africa, represent policy-gap amidst large parcels of fallow land in other regions of the respective countries. For example, policy could be enacted to encourage the creation of industrial villages, cities or zones in Northern Cape of South Africa or northern part of Nigeria where the prospects for land cultivations is very low due to the 'rocky' (in the case of Northern Cape) or dusty (in the case of northern Nigeria) nature of the land.

The Need for Contextual Case Studies Resulting from Policy Analysis and Implementation

Generally, the need for theory in any of the fields of public affairs or administration remains to be an important focus. Land restitution and reform is one of those functional areas, which requires smart and contextual based policy analysis and implementation. In as much it is also desirable to theorise in a general sense, or provide normative theory regarding the African context and the generic solutions that we may be able to apply to certain problematic contexts, it is also appropriate to consider the importance of performing descriptive and case-by-case analyses in order to learn from successes or failures of policies. From a policy point of view it is critical that the specific problematic situations, defined by its own set of variables and contexts be brought to the decision-makers attention in the form of rational and realistic policy analysis. This provides the basis for good governance (Cloete et al. 2018). Associated with good policy analysis, it is important that case studies are written to describe and narrate some of the generic and unique settings of certain land reform and restitution issues. These cases are valuable learning tools for students, academics and building capacity of practitioners alike. Added to such case studies, should be guides or even follow up narratives describing the efforts to implement and evaluate the outcomes and impacts of policy solutions derived from the initial policy analyses.

It would be the intentions of the authors to follow up this text with such a case book on specific policy issues and contexts in Africa, in order to provide this learning contribution. This may very well be a task to be supported by the African Union and its Specialized Technical Committee (STC) on Agriculture, Rural Development, Water and Environment which recently opened on the 5th October 2017 at the AUC Headquarters (AUC 2017), as well as the AUC-ECA-AfDB Consortium (2010).

Conclusion

Land has continued to constitute impediments to socio-political stability and drivers of structural violence in many African states, and despite the concurrent reform of the land tenure of various states in the continent, the land question remains unresolved. From the North to the South, East to the West, land (both arable or nonarable land) have been subjected to fallowness. The reality of under-utilization of land is not actually the main problematic, the concern lay in inability of state to devise sustainable land policies that enhances optimal land utilization. Thus, the complexity of addressing the land question is not due to the absence of policy enactment in the land sector, but that of identifying the most effective approach to its implementation and having robust understanding of the place of land in the development-security nexus. The attachments of African states to liberal form of land redistribution or land tenure has replaced the more flexible approach to land governance in pre-colonial Africa. Land policy should therefore be a combination of traditional and modern approach to land tenure system.

It is also decisive to review the role of the state in the reform processes. Thus, one may ask: How impartial is Africa's governments in the land reform schemes? Can a capitalist state, especially that which is subjected to the dictate of global capital, be neutral in relation to resource allocation and accumulation? States, especially in developing countries, have been hijacked by the elites, who serves the interest of global capital in furtherance to maintaining the hegemonic hold of the advanced capitalist countries on emerging democracies. This is achieved through the subjection of natural resources to the caprices of the market a market controlled by the 'visible hand' of global capital and entrepreneurs. Therefore, reforming a valuable resource and capital like land by the state under the liberal framework, without a proper policy analysis and assessment of the value and sustainability of such actions, may not reflect the interest of the state and the majority of its citizens. Ultimately, it may simply be seen as reinforcing the accumulative prowess of the elites and their enterprises. The optimism that preceded land reforms in the continent soon faded away, due to the failure of many African states to meet the expectations of its growing population, and the concomitant needs for sustainable development, economic growth, and food security.

References

AUC (2017) Second Ordinary Session of the Specialized Technical Committee on Agriculture rural development, water and environment. https://au.int/en/newsevents/20171002/second-ordinary-session-specialized-technical-committee-agriculture-rural

AUC-ECA-AfDB Consortium (2010) Framework and guidelines on land policy in Africa: land policy in Africa: a framework to strengthen land rights, enhance productivity and secure livelihoods. https://www.uneca.org/sites/default/files/PublicationFiles/fg_on_land_policy_eng.pdf

Adams Martin, Ben Cousins and Siyabulela Manona (1999) Land Tenure and Economic Development in Rural South Africa: Constraints and Opportunities. Working Paper 125, London, Overseas Development Institute.https://www.odi.org/sites/odi.org.uk/files/odi-assets/publications-opinion-files/2760.pdf

Cloete F, De Coning C, Wissink H, Rabie B (2018) Improving public policy for good governance. Van Schaik, Pretoria

Francis S, Francis M, Akinola A (2016) The edge of the periphery: situating the ≠Khomani San of the Southern Kalahari in the political economy of Southern Africa. African Identities, pp. 1–14

Garvelink W (2012) Land tenure, property rights, and rural economic development in Africa. Center for Strategic and International Studies. https://www.csis.org/analysis/land-tenure-property-rights-and-rural-economic-development-africa

Hall R, Kepe T (2017) Elite capture and state neglect: new evidence on South Africa's land reform. Rev Afr Polit Econ. https://doi.org/10.1080/03056244.2017.1288615

Kepe T, Cousins B (2003) Debating land reform and rural development. Policy Brief No: 3, PLAAS. http://www.plaas.org.za/sites/default/files/publications-pdf/PB%2003.pdf

Moyo S (2003) The land question in Africa: research perspectives and questions. Draft paper presented at Codesria conferences on land reform, the agrarian question and nationalism in Gaborone, Botswana (18–19 October 2003) and Dakar, Senegal (8–11 December)

Moyo S (2007) Land in the political economy of African development: alternative strategies for reform. Afr Dev XXXII(4):1–34

Osieny A (2015) 'Land utilization' in Africa: a misunderstood concept? https://www.linkedin.com/pulse/land-utilization-africa-misunderstood-concept-andrew-osiany/

Rights and Resources Initiative (2015) Factsheet: who owns the land in Africa? Formal recognition of community-based land rights in sub-Saharan Africa. http://rightsandresources.org/en/publication/who-owns-the-land-in-africa/#.WifbqDdx200

Sihlobo W, Boshoff T (2017) Policy cannot disrupt food production. Mail & Guardian, 2 December. https://mg.co.za/article/2017-12-01-00-policy-cannot-disrupt-food-production

Sustainable Development in the 21st Century (SD21) (2012) Sustainable land use for the 21st Century. https://sustainabledevelopment.un.org/content/documents/1124landuse.pdf

Printed by Printforce, the Netherlands